CONTENTS

To
Cincinnati Historical Society
Filson Club
Kentucky Historical Society
The Literary Club

—which have tolerated my
papers and talks for more
than 50 years.

NOT UNDER OATH

by ESLIE ASBURY

Typography by
The Thoroughbred Press
Lexington, Ky. 40586

Printing and Binding
C. J. Krehbiel Company
Cincinnati, Ohio 45227

NOT UNDER OATH

INTRODUCTION

Eslie Asbury has asked me to write an introduction to this, his latest book. I really don't know why, unless he is in his dotage. Most men aged 91 would be in their dotages, but not "As". He is in his anecdotage. This book proves it, as I have been lead to believe that it is a collection of sketches of men and events which have impinged on As' life and left their impressions on his memory and perhaps even molded his character. Since As has not let me see the galley proofs of this book, I cannot comment with accuracy on its contents and am limited to some remarks about its author who is easily remarkable. Most of us have grown a bit tired after passing the 60-year milestone but for As the riffling pages of time have not turned into loose leaf but into bound volumes — more and more of them. His enthusiasm remains unabated and his mind stays keenly alert to the humorous in any situation, particularly if the locus of the situation is his beloved state of Kentucky. He is not rusting on his laurels.

Second only to As' fondness for Kentuckiana is his affection for the horse. He has bred and raced horses for the majority of his 91 years and he fancies himself to be a great judge of horseflesh. He is that but he is not infallible. I am told that he once bought a mare which, shortly after the purchase, developed numerous ailments. After treatment, As anxiously asked the vet, "Will I be able to race her?" "Certainly", was the reply, "and you'll be able to beat her, too."

As loves to write and is the oldest member of the Literary Club of Cincinnati, having joined its ranks in 1926. Many of the chapters of this book had their "try-outs" as papers presented to the Literary Club. As has his heroes and they keep bcbbing up in his Literary Club papers. My guess is that they will surface in this book. Anthony Trollope and Charles Wilby were well-loved friends. Charles Wilby? He was a Literary Club member whose output of papers was even more prolific than that of As. If these heroes are somehow missing from this book, be patient, gentle reader, for As will write another book. There is plenty of time left.

To those who are devoted readers of Asbury, this book will only add to their previous pleasure. To those not so fortunate, the discovery of this book will be serendipity, like searching for a needle in a haystack and finding the farmer's daughter.

James L. Elder
Secretary of The Literary Club

FOREWORD

Most of this book consists of unpublished talks and papers written in my early years. The other chapters were created expressly for this volume. The contents are varied. If the book has a central theme, it is the philosophy of a man who has been engaged in different activities at a moderately high level over a long life span. I have had close contact with all kinds of people including those rich in money, those rich in talent, and those rich in both talent and money.

In going over my old papers I made a discovery: I write better in my old age. I credit the improvement to the study of E. B. White's "Elements of Style" and to the help and close friendship of noted authors mentioned in this book. I confess to editing the chapters originally written in my callow youth. I do not underrate my youthful experience. Without it I probably would be unable to write anything in my old age. At age 91, I have omitted references, feeling that my statements are as reliable as any source.

I have been a member of the Cincinnati Historical Society, the Kentucky Historical Society, the Literary Club and the Filson Club for over 50 years. All have published my unscholarly papers, listened to my addresses, and carried reviews of my books. That is why I am giving any profits of this book to these worthy organizations.

I dedicate this book to them.

Eslie Asbury

NOT UNDER OATH

CHAPTER 1

WRITING, SPEAKING AND ANECDOTING

Writing is an art form. Public speaking, story telling and reading papers are performing arts. Everyone who has published a book or who has been involved in the media feels qualified to express his views about writing, speaking and media interviews. Everyone feels competent to tell a story. Having reached the age of permissible indiscretion and possible dotage (age 91), I feel free to express my opinions. I hope I learned something through writing five books and over 300 papers and talks. I did learn by antithesis while listening to bad interviews on T.V. and to butchered stories at the club lunch table. I learned much by reading Anthony Trollope's novels and listening to Winston Churchill, Fred Allen, Bob Burns, Jack Benny, W. C. Fields and 1,000 Literary Club* papers. My guides to writing have been Wm. Strunk's "Little Book" and E. B. White's *Elements of Style.* If Sparky Anderson, not a great player, can be a great manager; if psychiatrists, with unsuccessful lives, can advise patients about their lives, I feel encouraged to discuss writing, interviews and anecdoting.

Few women impose stories on their companions. Women have more social sense than men. Nearly all men try to tell stories. Some are compulsive and constant offenders. Possibly one in two hundred amateurs should be allowed this privilege. Most amateurs

*The Literary Club (Cincinnati) 100 members, meets each week, 137 years old.

ramble, depend on sex and four letter obscenities, and end by hazing the punch line. The master raconteur never inflicts a long story on a group. In fact, he seldom intrudes. He never interrupts a friend's story, however boresome. His infrequent stories are concise and clean, with a short punch line. His humor is tailored to the region, the occasion, and the level of the audience. He never agrees to speak publicly unless he knows the exact words he will use. Winston Churchill, the most effective speaker I ever heard, refused to make impromptu speeches. He endlessly rehearsed each word and each pause.

Talk show hosts seek spontaneity. Many hosts get too much "spontaneity" when they refuse to rehearse with their amateur guests. Some interviewers almost ignore the guest or use him to air their own wit and philosophy. One of the best radio and T.V. series of all time was Groucho Marx's "You Bet Your Life." An employee of the show told me that the visiting couples knew in advance the questions Groucho would ask. They had time to prepare colorful answers. Groucho took it from there. Irma Lazarus, a host of P.B.S., also gives her guests a break.

Amateurs should insist on Groucho's formula even if they risk the withdrawal of the invitation to appear on the show. Only actors and their first cousins, the politicians, should accept totally unrehearsed apearances. I learned this the hard way.

Interviews for publication are different. Even if they refuse to let you check the finished article before it goes to press (as thy usually do), reporters give you more time. They are more sympathetic and they do not hog the stage. Some important, busy people refuse to be interviewed; some also are brusk with I.R.S. investigators. This is a mistake. I talked with E. P. Taylor, the leading industrialist of Canada, about this. He said, "I learned from experience. These people have a job to do. If you don't cooperate, you antagonize them."

An author is on his own. His time is not limited. He can plan and he can revise. There are few Anthony Trollopes. Even experienced authors should write and rewrite. Each time they go over the manuscript they find better arrangements. They eliminate adjectives, modifiers, and redundances. Good writers check for clarity. They remove many "hes" and "shes," using the real name even if this means repetition. They also look for misplaced verbs. For pungence, they favor short sentences. Instead of one long sentence with a but or an and, they use two sentences.

In one respect prose is like poetry. It should have rhythm. The flow of prose should please the ear. While revising, the writer should repeatedly read the manuscript out loud to arrive at better cadence. This practice is especially valuable before making a speech or reading a paper in order to achieve proper pauses and emphasis. Gerrit Sykes said, "Speak or read enthusiastically, confident that you know more about your subject than the audience. Above all, do not drop your voice at the end of sentences." Happy Chandler added, "Show your emotion but keep your voice under control."

All writers are influenced by other authors, but good writers develop their own style. They learn to write simply. When possible they avoid big words. They do not parade erudition nor obscure quotations. A good writer is not afraid to use his own experience and imagination. He has an exclusive secret weapon—Himself!

WRITING AND OLD AGE

Why do so many old people, previously not authors, write memoirs? Some write books hoping to provide money for themselves or their families. Ninety-five percent are written at a loss. Only a few, such as the memoirs of Presidents Grant, Truman and Eisenhower and the ghost-written diatribe of President Iaccoca of the Chrysler Corporation, showed a big profit. Some write to pass the time, and to relieve boredom, the worst hazard of old age. Some write a book to promote a cause. Many high-placed, controversial figures write memoirs to present their side, to improve their image, and to make money. Greed led to President Nixon's downfall. He was saving his tapes for his memoirs. Following poor legal advice, Nixon did not burn the tapes. The tapes burned him.

Like the old doctor in the play *The Man Who Came to Dinner,* many people feel they owe the world the benefit of their experience and wisdom. For them writing a book is an ego trip. Ninety-nine percent of these volumes make no impact. They are valueless as historical, philosophical and literary documents. Busy in their own fields, the majority have neither the time nor the literacy to write. That is why most of the books are ghost written. There are exceptions such as Booker T. Washington's *Up from Slavery* and Benjamin Franklin's autobiography. They were not ghost written. Both are permanent contributions.

Some important literary people refused to write the story of their lives. Somerset Maugham said it was impossible to tell the whole truth. Freud said autobiographers lie and conceal. Dr. W. J. Mayo said, "If I admitted my mistakes, I would give ammunition to my critics. If I recounted my successes, I would be accused of advertising." Some refuse because they are reluctant to expose themselves. They realize that their success was based on luck or dubious practices. Max Hirsch, Ben Jones and Count Frederico Tesio, possibly the greatest horse trainers of all time, refused to be interviewed or write memoirs, not because they thought they had secret forumulas. They were unable to put in words the unerring instincts which guided them in picking yearlings which became champions and the methods they used to prepare a horse for the Derby. I have known famous figures who refused to cooperate even with biographers. This is a mistake. Entirely on his own, the exasperated writer is apt to stress the unfavorable. Prolific authors don't need to write autobiographies.

Everything they write is unconsciously autobiographical in one sense or another.

When my academic friends looked over the material I planned to use in my semi-autobiographical book *Both Sides of the River,* they said I should be more subjective: that I had not included enough about my motives, frustrations and mistakes. I felt like Mark Twain, who said no book could be big enough to contain the myriad of thoughts that swished around in one's brain. I elected to recount the facts and stress the positive rather than the negative.

I have written five books and a large number of articles and speeches. I have had help from authors such as Don Whitehead, Lawrence Thompson and Haden Kirkpatrick and many fine advisers, but I have employed no ghost writers nor researchers. I have written nothing to advance causes nor to enhance my posthumorous image. My books and speeches have been modestly profitable, but I am still an amateur. All the proceeds of these efforts go to educational institutions. If I write for neither fame nor fortune, why do I write? Many people have asked me this question. At first I replied, "For applause." Later the true motive dawned on me.

I write for satisfaction and pleasure. "But," people say, "writing is hard and lonely work. The satisfaction is understandable if the book is a success. Where is the pleasure?" The pleasure comes from the memories evoked, especially in writing memoirs. You revel again in your small triumphs and experiences. You commune again with friends, long since gone, and with people who were landmarks in your life. That is why old people love to reminisce. Memories are greater assets than *more* money in the bank. Memories are treasures which "moth and rust doth not corrupt." Only Alzheimer's disease can steal them. They are stored in the best vault: your memory bank.

Writing also provides a form of competition. For retired people, competitions are limited. Bridge or owning a mare in foal are possible, but golf is no longer a serious game. To the aged, golf is only a form of exercise. Writing can fill the competitive gap. Does the quality of authorship deteriorate in old age? I think not. Many young geniuses had short, productive careers. Some led stormy lives and died early. Edgar Allen Poe is a good example. Most famous authors continued to produce as they got older. Plato, Robert Frost, and P. G. Wodehouse wrote as well in their eighties and nineties as they ever did. The last novels of Anthony Trollope and Henry James were better than their early novels. In looking over my first Literary Club papers, I was appalled. They needed editing, better arrangement, and the elimination of a lot of adjectives. A healthy old writer is in the position of a veteran, major league shortstop. The veteran may have lost a step, but he more than compensates by his knowledge, how to play hitters and where to throw the ball. The mature writer has learned the tricks of the trade. He knows what amuses or interests readers.

I could not have written the books and papers of my old age without the experience of writing in my youth. Except in a rare instance, the ability to write does not come naturally. Even if it is conceded that healthy old people can learn as well as they ever could, they don't learn as fast. They haven't sufficient energy nor desire, to master the basic skills of writing. If you wish to be an author in your old age, you had better start writing when you are young.

Since my retirement from surgery ten years ago I have continued to plant trees, write, and breed thoroughbreds. Horses are great substitute competitors for old people. Along with some essays and speeches, all six of my books have been created in my retired years. However, this volume is different. With editing, half of the chapters consist of papers written during my active years, some dating back as far as sixty years. I may write more papers and speeches, but my friends will be glad to know this is my final book.

CHAPTER 2

JOHN CIARDI

John Ciardi was a friend acquired in my old age. It is a common illusion that close friends are made only in the younger years. In my old age, I have made a number[1] of valued friends. Some are generations younger than I am. At the age of 91 I have lost all of my old friends. I need replacements. You cannot exist without friends. Friends make the nauseous draughts of life more palatable. Older people will make new friends only if they continue to circulate and to engage in challenging activities. If anything, I cherish the friends of my old age even more because they help to relieve boredom, the greatest hazard of age. Some, by favorable reviews, have helped the sale of my books. I am indebted to several professional writers for guidance. Without their advice, my publications would have been even worse.

My most recent but not least cherished friend and adviser was the famous poet John Ciardi. I met John in 1985 at the home

---

[1] Don Whitehead (Pulitzer price), Lawrence Thompson (University of Kentucky), Nelson Dawson (Filson Club), Byron Crawford (Louisville), Fred Russell (Nashville), Bennett Roach (Shelbyville, KY), J. Ed McConnell (Frankfort, KY), Don Edwards (Lexington, KY), Tom Clark (University of Kentucky), Tom Siler (Knoxville), Tennant Bryan (Richmond, VA), Warren Shonert (Falmouth, KY), Jack Hicks (Cincinnati Enquirer), and other great friends acquired in my old age who are Tom Goodloe and B. Ray Thompson (Naples), Bill Marquard (New York), and all members of the Hole-in-the-Wall Golf Club and the Naples Athletic Club, especially those who have invested with me in horses, Charles Depuy, Carol Paterno, Norman Herren, Bob Telford; also my golf buddy, John Knox, and my Berea friends, Addison Brown.

of my young friend David Herriman, a brilliant businessman living in Covington, Kentucky. At that time John was in temporary residence at Northern Kentucky University. We had a long conversation and instant rapport. I was flattered that he bought, and even read, my current books. We exchanged several letters. When I told him I was writing this book (*Not Under Oath*), he gave me valuable advice. Thinking I would attempt more humor he wrote:

"I admire your ambition in starting another book. I find myself worrying about it. It is not that I expect you to run out of time, but is there enough additional Kentucky humor for it? I once had a friend, a great scholar, who spent his life assembling American Humor, state by state. After the book was finished, the binding machine inadvertently omitted the Kentucky part. The New York Times reviewer didn't miss it!"

Think twice, my friend. Clowns always look sad. Beware of humor that it may darken your days. You may be dabbling in profundities beyond the fallen angels!"

Upon reflection, I agreed with John. I didn't expect this book to be immortal, but I remembered that, except for Mark Twain, great authors were not primarily humorists, that great actors prefer Macbeth to Falstaff, and that solemn asses get the monuments. Lincoln used humor merely to gain time before making decisions.

John Ciardi (born in 1916) was at the zenith of a great career when he died a month ago. John had degrees from Tufts and the University of Michigan and honorary degrees from Tufts, Bates, Ursinus, Wayne, Ohio Wesleyan and Washington University. He was professor of English at Rutgers, poetry editor of the *Saturday Review*, and was the recipient of many honors: the Tiejens, Hopwood, and Monroe poetry awards: the Levinson and Blumenthal prizes, some earned while serving in the USAF (1942-45). In the sixties he ran a weekly, nationwide T.V. program (CBS). He had various radio programs.

Ciardi was the author of many poems, especially poems for children and translations of Dante's *Inferno, Purgatorio,* and *Paradiso. Who's Who* devotes 43 lines to him, ending with this bit of Ciardi philosophy:

> Any many who believes he has succeeded has settled for a limited engagement. At anytime in one's life there is only the process of engaging more fully. If there is achievement it is to be put by. Achievement is only what brings into view the next thing to be engaged. Stop that process of engagement and the man is stopped dead. Let him go on breathing: he is dead.

I again agree with John. In my book *Both Sides of the River,* I state: "To remain healthy, a retiree must always have a serious challenge. He must have fear and worry to activate the glands of internal secretion which control the functions of our internal organs."

John and I spent winters in Florida. He wrote: "You chose Naples. Beware! When you walk through Naples, be sure to lift your knees high. The peril is not that the place is built on wall-to-wall money but that the pile is so high a man could disappear into it. I chose the half-gilded slums of Key West. The town slogan reads 'Poor but Venal,' though I expect a steady increase in venality to eliminate the poverty."

I cherished John for his humor and his realism. The great poets I have known, including Ciardi, Robert Frost, Allen Tate, Robert Penn Warren and John Crowe Ransom, (of the "Vanderbilt Five"), had no illusions about the eternal verities, in contrast to many

---

[2] One of the compensations for writing books is meeting other authors. That is how I met Alex Haley, author of *Roots*. Alex, a member of the board of Berea College, was given a copy of my book *Horse Send and Humor in Kentucky*, the profits of which go to Berea. When Alex was in Cincinnati a year ago to make a talk, he invited me to dinner with him and Fulton Oursler, editor of the Readers' Digest. I found Mr. Haley a charming person with a sane outlook on the world. He had no racial hangups.

writers and some academicians who never get over their sophomoric naivete.

Eslie Asbury
Read at the Literary Club
May 5, 1986

CHAPTER 3

E. B. WHITE AND THE NEW YORKER

The Literary Club 1986

E. B. White for over 50 years possibly had greater influence on American writers than any person in history. My excuse for this chapter is that I knew him and had dealings with him about my small article for the *New Yorker* on old hams, much edited by him. I knew White through George Ryall, who wrote the racing column for the *New Yorker* for 55 years, beginning with the first issue. Ryall, an English immigrant, wrote under the assumed name "Audax Minor," copying the assumed name of the famous English turf writer "Audax Major." Ryall deserves a separate chapter. I met him in 1945 at Belmont Park when our Revoked ran a big race in the Hopeful Stakes. We became life-long friends, I visited with him in New York and he with me in Kentucky. Ryall devoted his weekly column almost entirely to the leading races and the top horses rather than to the people who owned them, but over the years he involved Forest Retreat in two columns. His articles were widely read. Each time our names were mentioned we had numerous letters from nonracing friends. Ryall was a private man; he kept to himself at the racetrack and he never went near the offices of the *New Yorker,* sending in his contributions by messenger. When I asked why, he said he disliked several members of the staff. They were too liberal for him, especially Lillian Hellman. Neither he nor I forgave Hellman for her series of articles in the *New Yorker* viciously attacking L. B. Mayer, helping the extreme liberals in their takeover of MGM from Mayer, a right winger and Senator Robert Taft's greatest supporter.

Ryall weighed 100 lbs., but he was a literary heavyweight. With the exception of Joe Estes, Joe Palmer and Abe Hewitt (educated in England), we have had no turf writers who equalled the English turf writers, and this generally has been true in the world of letters. E. B. White did not have to edit Audax Minor's columns.

White also was diminutive in physical stature, but he was a giant in the literary world. For 50 years White was the editor of the *New Yorker* and dominated its contents. Fortunately, Harold Ross recognized his genius. He wished all his writers were E. B. Whites. White never ranted and raved nor bulldozed others. He wielded his power by the example he set and the standards he demanded of the staff and outside contributors. Brendan Gill, in his book *Here at the New Yorker* said White had the affection of his readers and the respect of other authors, the ultimate accolade. He edited everything that went into the magazine, wrote the editorial page ("Talk of the Town"), helped cartoonists with captions and recognized raw talent. Everyone connected with the *New Yorker* was indebted to him. He furthered the careers of many who became famous writers, notably James Thurber, one of the few who criticized White behind his back, illustrating the axiom that no good deed goes unpunished! White ignored Thurber's jealousy and made the maximum use of Thurber's great talents.

Our friend Jim Maxwell, one of the best of all Cincinnati writers, published two series of articles in the *New Yorker* ("There Never was an Arab Like Him," a World War II story; "The Gold Plated Piano," a story of Remus, a famous bootlegger). Jim had the prevailing view among authors. "Because of the prestige," he said,

"I would rather accept $300 from the *New Yorker* than the $1,000 or more offered by other magazines."

During White's regime, the *New Yorker* had an anti-establishment tone. The business tycoon was the butt of the humor in stories and cartoons, especially in the contributions of Peter Arno and Ring Lardner, Jr. White must have gone along with this view, fashionable at the time and historically fashionable among writers and intellectuals, a result of their environment. I don't understand how they know as much as they do, living among themselves in a dream world. With no experience in the practical world, they are only half educated. That is why I like the novels of Louis Bromfield, C. P. Snow and Anthony Trollope. Trollope's works reflected his broad experience gained through his post office position, his fox hunting, and mingling with all sorts of people in the Garrick Club. C. P. Snow held important university and government offices. Only a small minority of *New Yorker* contributors had the breadth of these authors.

White's views of the world were tempered by the many years spent with his wife Katherine on their farm in Maine. Roger Angell, White's stepson, was a realistic writer and reporter for the *New Yorker*. Katherine was the fiction editor, but she also was a power in the affairs of the magazine. In addition to a fine husband and wife relationship, they had a working literary partnership. Katherine preferred to live in New York, but she bowed to Andy's desire for the simple life in Maine. White and I had one thing in common. Both of us had "sissy" first names. I preferred to be called "As." White was born Elwyn Brooks White. All his friends knew he preferred to be called by his nickname Andy, acquired at Cornell. Andrew White was the first president of Cornell. Any student named White was called Andy.

I became acquainted with White long before I met him. Dr. Stanley Dorst, dean of the University of Cincinnati Medical School, gave me a copy of White's book *The Elements of Style,* a republication of Wm. Strunk's *Little Book* plus chapters by White himself. Prof. Strunk was White's revered English teacher at Cornell. This book has been my Bible; I have given 25 copies of it to members of my family and friends. Any writer who reads it will benefit from it. He will write with greater clarity and simplicity and leave out many adjectives.

My summer home at Biddeford Pool in Maine is not too far from White's farm. I was tempted to visit him, but second thoughts intervened. A call by an unimportant acquaintance would have been an imposition on his cherished privacy.

I shall never forget his comment on a common problem of authors. "When I'm confronted with a new writing chore," he said, "I first consume three martinis; after that, I'm on my own."

CHAPTER 4

HENRY WATTERSON

The Literary Club 1932

> "Things have come to a helluva pass
> When a man can't whip his own jackass"

Marse Henry Watterson with this doggerel headed his last political editorial, blasting his party for nominating Cox to run against Harding and illustrating his wit and lifelong, partisan independence. As editor of the *Louisville Courier-Journal* for 50 years, Watterson was the most influential newspaper writer in an era which included giants such as Joe Pulitzer, Horace Greeley, Murat Halstead, and Carl Schurz. I talked with him twice in my teens. His sister, living in Henry County, Kentucky, had lingering tuberculosis. My father was her doctor. When he knew Watterson would be present, he took me with him to meet the great man.

"Son, what do you intend to be," he asked.

"A doctor," I replied.

"Well," he chuckled, "that's better than being a newspaper hack."

Watterson looked like his cousin Mark Twain, a resemblance he cultivated in his dress, moustache, and pungent literary style.

His life touched Cincinnati. For a short time he was editor of the *Evening Times*. His grandmother (sister of the wife of Supreme Court Justice Stanley Matthews) lived in Glendale near Cincinnati; Nixon Denton, writer for the *Times-Star*, and Forest Frank, a reporter and long-time executive secretary of the Charter Party, both got their training in Louisville under Watterson. Watterson's friendship with Murat Halstead and his later encounter with the *Enquirer* are well known.

Henry Watterson was born in Washington, D.C., in 1840. His father was a congressman from Tennessee, and much of Henry's childhood was spent in this state at the prosperous plantations of both his grandfathers. His formal education ended with high school, which he finished at the age of sixteen at the Episcopal Academy in Philadelphia. The next two years were spent with private tutors, during which he haunted the embryonic Congressional Library, with which he became so well acquainted that he was assigned to explain the layout to a newlyappointed librarian.

At the age of eighteen he got on with Mr. Raymond of the *New York Times* as music critic, a position for which a musical education fitted him; but it was not long before he was back in Washington, where from 1858 to 1861 he was a space writer for the *Daily States* and correspondent to the *Philadelphia Press*. On the *Daily States* he was associated with Mrs. Casneau, assistant editor, who had become famous for writing the treaty ending the Mexican War. He always credited her with teaching him how to write.

During the Civil War Watterson held various commissions, usually staff positions under Forrest or Hood. Always for the Union, he had no choice but to go with his own people, as did many other southerners, unable to escape or prevent the conflict brought on by politicians, hotheads, and propagandists who had never seen a slave.

In 1862 he became editor of a paper in Chattanooga, bought by the state of Tennessee to be the official organ of the state. Watterson named it the *Rebel* and made it the official organ of the Confederacy. This underway, he started on a commission to England to sell a hundred thousand bales of cotton. After many adventures, he had reached the home of his grandmother in Glendale, Ohio, when the war ended. His uncle, Judge Matthews, introduced him to Calvin W. Starbuck, owner of the Cincinnati *Evening Times,* who gave him a job subbing for Alex Starbuck, away fishing in Canada. His job was to report the amusements, but it was not long before he was chief editor, the occupant of that position having fallen off a ferry boat into the Ohio River and drowned. Watterson called the *Times* "a queer old curiosity shop" which he proceeded to turn inside out and rearrange according to his "advanced" journalistic notions. Soon thereafter, the first edition of the new arrangement was gotten out. This threw the spotlight on him. The *Cinncinnati Commercial* lost no time in opening up on the new editor, alluding in a humorous vein to his lurid rebel past.

A few days later Artemus Ward was in town and, as a friend of Watterson, tried to help him by inviting some prominent citizens to a dinner. Among them was young Murat Halstead. Presuming upon this recent acquaintanceship, Watterson sped to the office of the *Commercial* and asked for Mr. Halstead, who received him very blandly. Watterson said, "Mr. Halstead, I am a journeyman laborer in your city — the merest bird of passage, with my watch at the pawnbrokers. As soon as I am able to get out of town, I mean to go — and I came in to ask if you think the personal allusions to me in today's paper are quite fair." Watterson said that Halstead looked at him with that seriocomic stare which so became him, and with heartiness replied: "No, they were darned mean. The mark was so tempting I could not resist, but there shall be no more of them. Come, let us go and have a drink." This was the beginning of a lifelong friendship which did not end until Watterson helped lay Halstead away in Spring Grove Cemetery.

He remained only a few months in Cincinnati, itching to get

back to Nashville to be near his intended wife. An opportunity with the *Nashville Banner* decided him to leave Cincinnati. This paper was owned by the father of his best friend and companion in the war, Albert Roberts. He and Roberts went out and personnally obtained subscribers and inside of a year drove all but one of their competitors out of business. This prosperity enabled him to marry and go abroad on a honeymoon, carrying a letter of introduction to Thomas Huxley from a northern surgeon he had befriended during the war. Huxley invited him to dinner, where he was introduced to gentlemen by the names of Tyndall, Mill, and Spencer. Artemus Ward, in London with his show, took him to the Savage Club, where he met Swinburne, Reade, and Thackeray. This was great luck for a budding literary man but did not overawe him. "Finding them a bit off on the Irish question and certain American affairs," he said, "I set them right with much particularity and not a little satisfaction."

On his return he was invited to Louisville to be the editor of the *Journal* through the recommendation of a Confederate comrade whom he had cared for while ill in camp. George D. Prentice was still the editor of the *Journal,* but he was over seventy years old and wished to get out of the saddle. Mr. Prentice was a celebrated figure and Watterson had a big job ahead of him to fill his shoes.

Journalism in the day of Prentice was a lurid affair, the publications not newspapers but journals; usually political organs, depending for their existence on the circulation and party support. They could fight, offend, and brawl without fear because advertising was not so relatively important. A sample of the kind of story printed in the newspapers in the fifties and sixties is illustrated by one which George D. Prentice published in the *Louisville Journal* concerning a mishap which occurred to his competitor on the *Courier.* The previous day Mr. Prentice and many others, including the other editor, were sitting on a fence watching a political parade. In the midst of the excitement the fence fell down. It so happened that the rival editor's position on the fence was just behind an old-fashioned outhouse, into the business end of which he nearly, if he did not actually, fall. Next morning Mr. Prentice commented in the *Journal* that he was very much surprised to see the *Courier* out today, as on last evening he thought he saw its editor thoroughly *interred.*

W. N. Haldeman was, at the same time, resurrecting the *Courier.* Watterson offered to consolidate on an even basis. This was refused by Haldeman. Whereupon Watterson set to work and ran the subscribers of the *Journal* from 1800 to 10,000 daily, and from 1500 to 50,000 weekly, all in the course of a year. Haldeman then saw the advantages of a union of the two papers. The deal was made and the combination bought out the *Democrat,* the only other remaining publication, giving the new *Courier-Journal* the exclusive field. This lasted two years, when it was found that at least the appearance of competition was indispensable. A Republican organ was organized as a foil and given the Associated Press dispatches. Not until then did the *Courier-Journal* have any financial success.

Watterson was the editor of the *Courier-Journal* for fifty years (1868-1919). During this time he had free rein. His partner, Mr. Haldeman, concerned himself only with the publishing end. His success lay not only in his ability and personality, but in his early background. He lived until the age of eighteen in the old Willard Hotel in Washington, where he was in contact with the statesmen of that day. Thus, from the first, he had an inside knowledge about political schemes. His extensive reading in the Congressional Library has already been noted. It was a time of great stress and of powerful party leaders. Vivid impressions were made on the young mind, later intensified by his own participation in the Civil War and his short but varied newspaper experience before, in 1868, settling down to the *Courier-Journal.* This literary craftsmanship, his knowledge of American history and politics, his early environment, combined with his colorful personality, made him a feared and influential editorial writer for a period of over fifty years. From the first he had one policy: to strike at only those issues which could be settled, and to continue striking until they were settled. He advised everyone to keep to the middle of the road, but when he got on his editorial "high-horse" he attempted to ride down everything on the road. He would keep after one issue until the battle was lost or won. Old readers of the *Courier-Journal* can recollect almost every one of his editorial subjects, for the most part concerned with national or international issues. The oratory and political writings of his time, particularly in his home state, were flamboyant but at times mellifluous. While Watterson showed these characteristics, his editorials had the merit of literary quality and real thought, with so much humor and color that they were always interesting and widely quoted.

Watterson rarely took up cudgels on minor issues. If no large battle appeared, the editorial columns were filled with literary offerings and jocose comments on the affairs of the day. Many readers turned to the editorial page first. On picking up the paper my father often remarked, "Let's see what Marse Henry has to say this morning." Some of the issues for which he fought lasted throughout his lifetime. One was a tariff question. Never advocating free trade, but "tariff for revenue only," he agreed with Calhoun that protectionism was sectional discrimination. The following is a quotation from an editorial on the tariff. "Spain has made a great deal of history. The front betwixt Gibralter and the Isle of San Fernando — Tangier on one side and the Straits of Tarifa on the other — has had its share."

"Before lawyers had learned to frame pillaging statutes, the gentle pirates of Tarifa laid broad and deep the foundations for the protective system in the United States."

All may not agree with him on the tariff, but what about the following prophecy in an editorial when prohibition was proposed: "I might as well rail at God for bringing sin, disease and death into the world as to seek to encompass them by sumptuary legislation. Men may be made hypocrites by law, but never saints."

"Repressive laws culminate in reactions. Radical puritanism in England was succeeded by the debaucheries of the Restoration, and prohibition in the United States will not diminish drunkeness, but will bring in its train scandals and evils as hurtful as drink has brought to that limited section of the community given to the excessive use of intoxicants; contempt for law, evasions of law, and adulteration; the corruption alike of the officials and the drink; lawful and needful revenues extinguished in favor of lawless indulgences, the fanatical preacher and the grafting politician uniting to work the spy system each for his own end, but against the mass of society."

This was written at the time of the passage of the Eighteenth Amendment, and William Howard Taft used almost the same words in giving his dissenting opinion on the Volstead Act before the Supreme Court.

Due to his fiery nature and some of his habits, it is probable that Watterson was much misunderstood. The natural effusiveness of the southerner has often been mistaken for insincerity and shallowness. Of his personal habits much has been said. It is certain that he could drink his associates under the table, although his favorite beverage was beer. Conviviality was a family trait. His father cut quite a figure in Washington. Once he and a friend were coming home late at night, well dined. The friend fell into a canal. After several efforts to extricate him, the elder Watterson said, "Joe, I can't get you out, but I can get in with you," which he did. When rescued, they seemed much pleased with themselves.

It was said that Watterson delivered some of his finest lectures when so drunk that he had to be helped to the platform. The truth is that most of these stories were exaggerated. He lived in fairly good health to the age of eighty-two. Such an age is compatible with moderate drinking, but as he once remarked, "Sufficient whiskey has never been made to account for all I am supposed to have consumed."

I can imagine no greater pleasure than a Sunday afternoon call at Mansfield, Watterson's home outside of Louisville. His friends came to chat, but chiefly to listen to stories told in his inimitable style. A few people knew him in this way, hundreds heard him at political conventions, but it was as a lecturer that he came in contact with thousands of people. He was always in demand for Decoration Day ceremonies, North and South alike. His favorite topics were his talks on "Lincoln," "The Money Devil," and a host of others which he published in a book called the *Compromise of Life*.

Watterson was more a lecturer than a debater, although, as debating was the order of the day, he occasionally took part. He once was invited to debate in Philadelphia with McKinley on a subject which read: "Which political party offers the workingman the best solution of the tariff problems?" He was very busy, but he did not like to pass up the stipend. He was about to refuse when he remembered an old lecture called "Money and Morals," which he resurrected, added a preface and an end, and thus armed went to Philadelphia. Never a word about the tariff. Instead, he began, "In that chapter of the history of Ireland reserved for snakes, the historian informs us that there are no snakes in Ireland. I am afraid that on the present occasion I shall have to emulate this flight of the Celtic imagination. I find myself billed to speak from a Democratic standpoint as to which party offers the most benefit to the workingman. If I am to discharge this duty, I must begin by repudiating the text in toto, because the Democratic party recognizes no political agency for one class. The bulwark of its faith is laid in the declaration: Freedom for all, special privileges to none."

"Who among us has the single right to claim the divine title of workingman? We are all workingmen; the plodding scholar in the library, no less than the poor collier in the mine."

McKinley, who was to have the rejoinder the next night, expected to fire back at him on the tariff, but had no ammunition. They were great friends and on meeting soon afterwards enjoyed a good laugh over the affair.

At the 1884 convention in Chicago, Watterson found his platform opposed by General Ben Butler, who remarked, "If you adopt this platform of my friend Watterson, God may help you, but I can't." This gave Watterson an opening. Coming next on the program he said, "During the last few days, I have learned to love General Butler, but I must declare that in an option between him and the Almighty, I have a prejudice in favor of God."

His party activities reached the highest point in 1876. In espousing Tilden's nomination, he envisioned the man to relieve the South of its burdens and to bury the bloody flag. Some of his most influential editorials were written in this period, largely directed against sectionalism and greenbackism. One of these editorials was aimed at the *Cincinnati Enquirer* for its support of Governor Allen, a greenbacker. At the convention in St. Louis it soon appeared that the South was strong for Tilden, but Tammany, with "Sunset" Cox as its leader, opposed Tilden because of his reform acivities, notably the exposure of the Tweed Ring. At the last minute, Watterson, as buffer between the northern and southern elements, was chosen temporary chairman. He was unprepared for the keynote speech and knew nothing of parliamentary procedure. Working almost all night, the speech was written and the first sentences memorized. Colonel Johnston, concealing the manuscript in his hat, lined the words out to him during the cheering. This was detected by an opposing member who yelled out, "See that fat man behind him! He's telling him every word he says." During the rest of the convention rulings were made with entire ignorance of Robert's rules of order but carried due to the force with which the gavel was pounded and the resonant voices of the chairman.

In the ensuing campaign Watterson's battle for Tilden consisted of attacks on Grant's administration and the defalcation of his Secretary of War General Belknap and his attempt to line up the northern and southern people behind sound money and nonsectionalism. Again the spectre of Civil War came with the disputed succession. Watterson to the last never revealed certain matters touching this election. He always claimed that a fatal telegram sent to the *New York Times* about midnight by the treasurer of the Democratic National Organization (Barnum of Massachusetts) asking about the returns from Florida, Mississippi, and Oregon, was the cause of the dispute. The papers had already conceded the election to Tilden in an earlier edition. The editors of the *Times* reasoned that if Barnum was uncertain, why not everybody, so the later edition announced the probable election of Hayes. At the request of Tilden, Watterson accepted an unexpired term in Congress in 1877 to represent him in the controversy. He sent screaming editorials to the *Courier-Journal* calling for 10,000 unarmed Kentuckians, and at least a hundred thousand from the other states, to be present in Washington on the day the commission was to meet. He even intimated that stronger measures would be justified if the succession was seized by force. When time came for certification of the Louisiana vote, Watterson and others went to New Orleans, finding many prominent Republicans such as Judge Matthews and Garfield already on the ground. In his memoirs he relates that a state senator approached him with an offer to bring in a Democratic verdict for $250,000. Watterson replied, "Senator, your terms are as cheap as dirt. I don't happen to have the amount about me at the moment." He always claimed that money could have swung the issue but that neither Hayes nor Tilden would hear to bribing. The strong Republican group in Washington ran the affair with promises of patronage as the medium of trade.

Watterson never got over his disappointment when Tilden was counted out and, when his health failed him, he could not run again. In all fairness, it must be said that many upstanding

Republicans were a party to this injustice because they sincerely felt that anything was justified at that time to keep out the Democrats.

It is probably true that Hayes did more for the South than Tilden could have done. His removal of the troops together with some appointments did much to allay the bitterness.

In 1880, although disappointed in not obtaining the renomination of Tilden, Watterson supported Hancock against Garfield, with the slogan, "Turn the rascals out." Many other famous phrases which wielded national power were coined during the campaign of Cleveland because it was at this period that Watterson was most in the public eye. One of these was in justification of Tilden's refusal to run again in 1884. If elected he said we might "follow the glory of triumph to an open grave." The reason for the popularity of these party slogans was that he wrote the Democratic platform in 1876, 1884 and 1888. The "star-eyed goddess of Tariff reform" was linked with "tariff for revenue only" and "Democracy unterrified and undefiled" in the 1884 fight for Cleveland. In the 1888 campaign, he divided his time between supporting Cleveland and fighting the latter's stand on civil service reform. It was during this pre-election fight that he wrote the editorial directed against James Russell Lowell's stand for Blaine. Lowell is not remembered as a politician, although he did write the *Bigelow Papers*. He bolted the Republican ticket, voting for Cleveland in 1884, but in 1888 bolted back to the support of Blaine. In an editorial Watterson quoted from the *Bigelow Papers*, in which Lowell states that "a batch o'bread that haint riz once, aint goin to rise again," to prove the futility of running Blaine the second time.

Cleveland and Watterson were friendly during his first administration, but they later fell out because Cleveland did not like the tariff and civil service ideas which Watterson placed in the platform of 1888 and 1892 over Cleveland's protests. After considerable correspondence, Watterson and Cleveland became lifelong enemies. This was a sad end to the intimate friendship of the first term. Then Watterson was at home at the White House when in Washington.

It was well known that President Cleveland liked to play poker. There was a group of senators known as the "road gang" who usually made up the game. Whenever Watterson was in Washington he was invited. At one of these sessions were Don Cameron, Cleveland, Watterson, and John G. Carlisle of Covington, Kentucky. The limit was five dollars, and the game, draw poker. Carlisle knew very little about cards and could least afford to lose of any present. Finally, Watterson picked up a pat flush and Cleveland a pat full house. Cameron opened the pot, Watterson raised and they back raised each other several times. During this time, Carlisle saw every raise. On the draw, Carlisle asked for four cards. Watterson opened the betting, Cleveland raised, and Carlisle backraised. After several rounds of raising, Cleveland took pity on Carlisle and called. At the showdown, Carlisle had four kings. "Take the money, John. If I'm ever President again, you shall be Secretary of the Treasury. But don't make that four card draw too often." When Cleveland was elected in 1892, he appointed Carlisle secretary of the treasury.

Cleveland had a bill come up for his signature calling for improvements on the Licking River. He fumed about this until someone suggested that Carlisle ought to know about it. Carlisle was sent for. Cleveland said, "John, they tell me the Licking River is down your way. What do you think we ought to do with it?" Carlisle replied, "Pave it."

Watterson often said that the Democrat party (Democrat party is proper; both parties claim to be "democratic") ceased with Cleveland, and blamed Cleveland for splitting the party, allowing Bryan and free silver to prevail. At the time of Bryan's nomination Watterson was in Europe. He telegraphed Haldeman as follows: "No compromise with dishonor." The *Courier-Journal* opposed Bryan bitterly, lost half of its circulation, and, for the first time, Kentucky went Republican in a national election.

Even after the free silver craze subsided, Watterson never became reconciled to Bryan, although in 1907 he was lukewarm toward him. In an editorial he once said, "Mr. Bryan was a young man of notable gifts of speech and boundless self-assertion. When he found himself well in the saddle, he rode furiously and ruled despotically. A party leader more short-sighted could hardly be imagined. None of his judgments came true. But for the Taft-Roosevelt fight, the Republicans might have held sway indefinitely."

Watterson, by the way, predicted the Taft-Roosevelt split as early as 1909 in an editorial which at once became the subject of a good-humored controversy with the *New York World*. A portion of this editorial fight is interesting, not only because of its foresight; it is characteristic of Watterson's best jocose style.

(World)

"We should hardly have expected that Henry Watterson would take 'the return from Elba' seriously, yet he is convinced that there is a strong movement on foot to bring about the renomination of President Roosevelt, and believes that 'the result will be a division between the Taft and Roosevelt men, which may split the Republican party.' At present, there is no more danger of a Republican split over Taft and Roosevelt than of the Colonel's voting the straight Republican ticket in 1912."

(Watterson)

"This is a surface view. It does not consider human nature. There is a good heal of human nature in politics. Mr. Roosevelt has been suspected of it."

Watterson never succumbed to office seeking. For thirty years he was accused of contriving something for himself, but early he saw the only man whom he regarded as near the ideal in public life, elected but counted out, his character blackened, his health impaired. Early in life, he became disgusted with what he saw of cheap politics around Washington. He once remarked that he had personally known every President from Jackson to Harding and would not have been any one of them.

Watterson was always too independent, belonged to the wrong party, and came from the wrong part of the country to be personally successful in politics. The wonder is that he was able to write the platform of his party for five straight conventions in which he closed the debate, moved the previous questions, and each time was sustained.

His leanings were toward the artistic. The only friends for whom he had thorough admiration were actors such as Joe Jefferson and writers such as Mark Twain (a first cousin), Herbert Spencer, and Thackeray, upholding the latter in editorials against Dickens in that famous literary war. He knew nothing of the business side of his paper, causing Mr. Haldeman many grey hairs. Whenever short of money, he had a habit of helping himself from the safe. Balanced accounts were impossible. The exasperated treasurer finally requested that he leave a record of the amount taken. A few days later the clerk found the safe empty except for a note saying, "I have taken it all, Henry."

One of the most productive periods of his career was the Wilsonian era and the World War. The echo of the first gun of the war had hardly died in 1914, when the editorial "To Hell with the Hozenzollerns and the Hapsburgs" appeared, much to the delight of Lord Northcliffe. There was never any question in his mind as to what our attitude should be, crying for war from the first. At the age of seventy-eight, during 1917, he wrote two editorials, "The Compensations of War" and "Vae Victis," for which he received the Pulitzer Prize. Later in the same year, another editorial with the caption, "No peace with Potsdam," created another slogan and enabled him to flay the German-Americans who had fought him bitterly before our entrance into the war.

In 1918, when he retired as editor of the *Courier-Journal*, Judge

Bingham, who had bought his stock, insisted on his retention as Editor Emeritus. A special edition of the paper commemorating Watterson's 78th birthday was published, containing letters from public men of all nations. Soon afterward, came his final retirement, due to differences of opinion with Judge Bingham on the League of Nations. He bowed out with no illusions. His last editorial, entitled "Fame," ended with this verse:

"A mound of earth a little higher graded,
Perhaps, upon a stone a chiseled name;
A dab of printer's ink soon blurred and faded,
And then oblivion, that — that is fame."
— Henry Watterson

CHAPTER 5

FRANCES TROLLOPE

The Literary Club 1985

Frances Trollope wrote the *Domestic Manners of the Americans* after a disastrous trip to the United States. She made the trip to find a career for her ailing son Henry, and to get away from her incompetent husband Tom Trollope, Sr. Mr. Trollope, an intellectual Micawber educated at New College, Oxford, England, inherited a comfortable 1000 pounds a year and started his law practice with bright prospects, but his disputatousness and his cocksure stances in his liberal social dissents cost him the friendship of his colleagues and most of his law practice. Had he lived in the era of the Roosevelts, Rockefellers, and Kennedys, he would have realized that he was not guilty enough, rich enough, nor opportunistic enough to justify idealistic or demagogic opposition to the existing status quo. His lack of common sense also led him to acquire a farm, 12 miles from London, to which he moved his family and thereby lost much of his capital.

In the midst of this ruinous farm experiment, his vivacious wife Frances, who always seemed to have the current parlor revolutionaries around her, came under the influence of wealthy Frances Wright (a ward of General Lafayette), who, like Amelia Bloomer, was one of the loud, ludicrous, women reformers of the 19th century. Wearing silk Turkish trousers, Miss Wright was back in

England lecturing against negro slavery, against the slavery of wedlock*, and extolling her utopian dream. Having absorbed the teachings of Robert Owen, she had purchased a large tract of land in Mississippi, freed her slaves and planned to live there with them where all could enjoy equally the fruits of their labor and prove her theory that the negro, with the same opportunity, is the equal of the white man.

Entranced by these fantasies and having already planned to come to Cincinnati, Mrs. Trollope avidly accepted the invitation to make a long preliminary visit to the new project. Miss Wright, Mrs. Trollope, her daughters Cecelia and Emily, her son Henry, and the refugee French artist Hervieu, who was to be the director of culture, all sailed for New Orleans in 1827 and after much hardship, arrived in swampy, barren Nashoba, Mississippi. Finding little food, heat or shelter, the disappointed Trollopes, accompanied by Mr. Hervieu, moved on to Cincinnatti. More shock lay in wait in this teeming frontier "Porkopolis," where everyone's hogs roamed the streets and sidewalks claiming social equality with the people and exercising their natural "hogs rights" to the uncollected garbage. The natives, she thought, were little better as they dashed about spitting ubiquitously, each solving his identity by loudly declaring that he was as good as the next man, or a damn sight better!

The stench downtown was so bad she moved her sickly family to Mohawk, a suburb of Cincinnati, while waiting for funds from home. They would have starved except for faithful Hervieu, who was able to sell paintings and give drawing lessons. At this point she "conceptualized" the Bazaar; and Thomas, having agreed to the idea, came over, accompanied by the oldest son Thomas, Jr., to sign the contracts, which as a woman Mrs. Trollope could not legally do. After a few months Trollope left for England, promising to provide the merchandise. Mrs. Trollope herself drew the

*When her dream failed, she wound up in Cincinnati as the sedate wife of a school teacher.

plans for the grotesque 4-story rectangular building, 80 feet wide, 100 feet long, and 80 feet high, with Grecian columns, Gothic windows, Egyptian decorations and a Turkish dome, located on 3rd Street near Broadway in Cincinnati. The second floor was the business section and the other floors of the building were to contain a library, museum, ballroom concert hall. and dining room with a balcony overlooking the Ohio River. The merchandise arrived before the place was ready and most of it was sacrificed to satisfy the clamors of the unpaid workmen. Finished in 9 months, the Bazaar opened with a concert, hordes of curious people tramping through it, and five mechanics liens plastered on it! The unpaid mortgage caused its immediate closure and it was sold in court of chancery, presided over by Judge Jacob Burnet, for $7400 to Nicholas Longworth. $20,000.00 had been spent, and only $3700.00 was ever paid on it. The Trollopes had underestimated the cost and overestimated the cultural level of the frontier.

Now destitute and living in one room, they were entirely dependent on Hervieu, who slept on the floor in a storeroom. This gifted artist must have been in love with Frances because he made every sacrifice to support her and her children and find money to get them home, all without hope of repayment. After a long illness suspiciously resembling T. B. which was to carry off Henry and Emily, Frances spent a few months visiting English friends in the East, in the meantime writing furiously on her first book, *Domestic Manners of the Americans*, which was finished on the long voyage to England. The book brought 800 pounds, instant fame, and howls of indignation from America. The English liberals also condemned the book. Without firsthand knowledge, they defended all conditions in the new democracy, just as Bertrand Russell and tha Red Dean defended all acts of the Russian Bolsheviks. Dickens and Mark Twain confirmed most of her allegations, but she was guilty of bitterness, exaggeration, and incomplete observation. She was not invited into Dr. Daniel

Drake's circle and did not differentiate frontier crudity from ordinary poverty and ignorance which was equally present in the British Isles.

Among her complaints, some still valid, were lack of poor laws, indifference to crime (there had not been an execution in Cincinnati up to that time), our puritan blue laws, the isolation of women who were not allowed even at political rallies, the injustice to the Indian, Negro slavery which made domestic service repugnant to white women, and our silly shibboleth that all men are created equal.

Domestic Manners established her as an author at the age of 52. Under the desperate necessity to support the family, moving from England to Holland to find cheaper living, and at the same time nursing, unaided, a dying husband and two children, she somehow managed to write three books in the next three years. During the next 25 years, mostly spent with her son Tom in Italy, she averaged a novel and/or book of travel a year and died at the age of 84.

This impulsive woman of enormous femininity and energy never took herself seriously as an author. As Anthony said, she tended to come to superficial conclusions in her passionate protests against social evils, but she was a woman of her time whom publishers and lending libraries could depend upon for a popular novel a year. But the income from her novels was never enough to cover her bouts of overspending and buying houses in Italy. In these minor crises, she would hurry to her London publishers, contract for another book of travel, collect all possible cash in advance and fly off with friend Hervieu to finish the job.

Like a quarter horse in a two furlong race, she wrote in one breath under strain in her frequent races against the bailiff, but she did have a natural ability. Her best novel was either *The Vicar of Wrexhill* or *he Robertses on Their Travels* ridiculing the bad habits of English tourists and a book which today should be required reading for some American travellers. Her detractors referred to any chronic traveller as a "Trollope," a word which now has a ruder meaning, but she had a large following even if she never was able to gild her reformist ideas with the best romantic fiction.

The Bazaar was a failure but it had the serendipitous effect of establishing the fortunes of the family beyond the wildest dreams of Thomas Trollope. She made a permanent name for herself, but her greatest achievement was to lay the foundation for the success of her son Anthony, the greatest Trollope of them all.

CHAPTER 6

ANTHONY TROLLOPE

The Literary Club 1984

Anthony Trollope is now conceded to be the greatest Victorian novelist in an age which spawned many great novelists. In the last half of the 19th century, reading was the chief leisure amusement of educated people. To whet the demand, novels came out in two or three spaced volumes or serially in magazines, resembling modern soap operas. Trollope, the most prolific contributor, was labelled by critics as a pedestrian writer about the social scene. However, even then contemporary famous authors such as Thackeray, Thomas Reade, George Eliot. and Henry James admired Trollope and lauded his genius in publications which are still on record. On the other hand, recognition by professional critics came belatedly, starting about 1920, forty years after his death, with George Saintsbury, the czar of literary criticism for 50 years. After Saintsbury's stamp of approval a horde of professors of English jumped on the Trollope bandwagon, numerous biographies appeared, and the B. B. C. used his novels for 22 programs, later shown in America on the Public Broadcasting System.

My introduction to Trollope was through a paper read in 1927 at the Literary Club by Simeon Johnson, a local, eminent Victorian, who, like other old members, still wore a short black coat and striped, dark gray trousers. The members loved the paper. Over half of them had grown up during Trollope's lifetime. They had seen the Bazaar built by Anthony's mother Frances only a block away from the Literary Club. Mr. Johnson was born in 1855 only a few doors from the Bazaar, which stood until it was razed in 1882. For many years this building had been abandoned except for furious meetings of the Fifth Ward Democrat Club, of which Mr. Johnson was a young member. This "undemocratic" club once held a presidential election in which the winner and his cohorts subdued the opposition with baseball bats. Mrs. Trollope would have had more material for her book on the manners of Americans. The Bazaar was still in fair shape when Anthony Trollope made a special trip to see it in 1862.

Anthony Trollope was born in 1815 on Kelapel Street in London, had 3 sisters, and was the youngest of four brothers. When Anthony was ready for school, his father, having lost his fortune, sent him irregularly to Harrow and Winchester more or less as a pauper student, dressed in rags, with no spending money. He made no friends. During vacations he lived in a storeroom in his father's office.

As a youth Anthony moved with his improverished family six times in ten years. At age 18, through a friend of his mother, he became a clerk in the London post office. At this point his mother, a step ahead of the bailiff, moved the rest of the family to Belgium, including three children dying of tuberculosis. Anthony, left behind, thereafter rarely had any contact with his family. For the next four years he lived on his salary of 90 pounds a year in lonely isolation with no friends or social activities. This period was not wasted. He spent his idle hours in an imaginary world. In his autobiography Trollope said this practice trained him to construct his novels.

When the position of postal inspector for Ireland became vacant, no one wanted it. It was "beyond the pale." Anthony, feeling that any change would be for the better, accepted the job, the best decision he ever made in his life. Ireland made Trollope. During the next 14 years his job took him over a large part of Ireland. He met, dealt, and associated with all kinds of people. Much of his travel was on horseback. This naturally led him to take up fox hunting, which became a lifelong sport and obsession with him. In all of his novels he managed to include a chapter involving fox hunting.

In Ireland Anthony met and married Rose Hesseltine, an English woman, a move he never regretted. Rose was the ballast for contentious Trollope, copied all his manuscripts and thereby saved him many hundreds of pounds. Without complaint she put up with Trollope's bachelor way of life and his frequent, long absences from home on postal missions. Rose remained serene even about his girl friend Kate Field, an American whom he met on a trip to America and who stayed with the Trollopes on several trips to England. Knowing Anthony, a stickler for the Victorian mores, it is inconceivable that his relationship with Kate was other than platonic, but it was deep. Their correspondence was voluminous, and Kate was his inspiration throughout his life.

While still in Ireland Trollope wrote two novels, *The Macdermots of Ballycloran* and *The Kellys and O'Kellys,* which he sold for 20 pounds each. They were very good novels, but the publisher lost money on them. Anything involving the Irish was unpopular in England at that time.

After 14 years in Ireland Anthony was promoted to a high position in the general post office in London. While holding this post for the next 30 years, he invented the corner mail box and made 5 postal missions to North America and the West Indies, writing a successful travel book on each trip. He is the only writer of note who ever held a near lifetime, full-time position. Conscious of the economic woes of his parents, he regarded his post office job as a financial anchor, retaining it until 12 years before his death, resigning then only out of frustration when he failed to achieve his ambition to be postmaster general.

The lenient hours of his job allowed him to follow a fixed schedule. He wrote from 5 to 8 A. M., worked at the post office from 9 A. M. to 2 P. M., hunted to the hounds on three afternoons a week, and wound up every day at the Garrick Club, where he played whist. Whether at home or travelling on a train, on a ship, or in a stagecoach, he achieved his daily quota of about 3000 words, producing 47 novels and a total of 90 books in about 30 years.

In his autobiography Trollope said novel writing was a trade like any trade. Critics said he lacked the soul of an artist. Another reason he fell from favor after his death was that, unlike Dickens, he had never made public appearances on the platform either at home or abroad. Also unlike Dickens, he never hobnobbed with critics. He ignored their comments whether favorable or unfavorable. This was a mistake. Reporters and I. R. S. investigators are more apt to give sympathetic consideration if you are polite to them.

In the late twenties I acquired and read all of Trollope's novels and many of his other books. I became a dedicated Trollopian, and I was in good company. Even in his lifetime, when critics were downgrading him, leading writers praised Trollope's genius, the ultimate accolade. He was a writer's writer.

When Trollope died in 1882, aged 67, critics and publishers dropped him, but his contemporary peers praised him. Henry James in a long essay said, "Trollope is a natural psychologist without the scientific airs of a Zola; that, better than any other novelist, Trollope could follow the stream of consciousness, feeling correctly what each character thought of himself and what others thought of him. Thus he was not forced to theorize why a person did this or that. Mr. Crawley and Lady Glencora reacted precisely as expected in all situations."

Tolstoy said, "Trollope kills me with his perfection," meaning his craftsmanship and ability to make each word relevant to the story. Tolstoy never met him, but Trollope was known and admired by the Brownings, Charles Reade, and Thackeray. George Eliot said she would have abandoned her half-finished *Middlemarch* except for Trollope's help and inspiration.

Nathaniel Hawthorne said, "My taste is for another class of works that I myself am unable to write. The novels of Anthony Trollope precisely suit my taste—solid and substantial—and just as real as if some giant had hewn a great lump out of the Earth and but it in a glass case with all the inhabitants going about their daily business, never suspecting they were being made a show of." Henry James expressed it another way. He said Trollope was the master of the usual. It is a mark of Trollope's greatness that any reader is entertained by his novels, whether or not they appreciate his genius.

Fellow authors also admired Trollope's business ability. He never sold his novels nor serial rights until the work was finished. He negotiated a lump sum deal and the publisher took his chances. The publishers did well and Trollope did well. Translated into today's dollars, he realized a greater amount than any other writer except possibly a James Michener. He left an estate which, in today's money, would exceed a million dollars.

Comparing writers, especially those of different periods, is interesting but futile. Some like peaches better than pears; some prefer Johnny Bench to Mickey Cochrane. Trollope appeals to me because of the breadth of his life and his realism. His post office position put him in contact with all kinds of people in several countries. He learned politics by running for parliament. He was an avid fox hunter, whist player, and club habitue. Unlike other writers, his novels reflected a firsthand knowledge of the real world. Fortunately he wrote nothing in his young, therefore ignorant, years.

Pope Hennessy's biography, among several, is probably the best. I wrote three papers on Trollope for the Literary Club. Since then there have been many publications about Trollope by critics, authors, and English professors. Knowing my interest in Trollope, my friends, especially George Rieveschl, have sent me copies of these publications. Broward, New York *Times* critic, in a long article said that Trollope's novels were his most enjoyable reading and better sedatives than Miltown. The editor of *History Today* said that Trollope finally rose to the top in a period of literary giants. The centennial of Trollope's death inspired a lot of publications, including three books based on Trollope's letters. The most notable was by Prof. John Hall of Stanford in two volumes which sold well at $87.50. These collections, after 100 years, could have represented only a fraction of his letters, all written in longhand before copies were kept.

You would think that Trollope would appeal mainly to conservative, common sense people with no axes to grind, but his admirers included all kinds of people. Gerald Clarke writing for *Time* magazine said that Trollope's political novels were President John Kennedy's favorite reading. J. Kenneth Galbraith was not afraid to express his admiration. In a long essay in the New York *Times,* comparing political novels past and present, Galbraith said that none equalled the Palliser series. He also said that Trollope, in *The Warden,* created two of the most believable upright men in all of literature: the Rev. Crawley, the perpetual curate of Higglestock, with a horde of hungry children to feed, finally left his poor flock for a better preferment; the Rev. Harding, with no one to support, resisted all pressures and never accepted promotion.

Broward, writing again in the New York *Times,* claimed that Trollope created an irresistible ambiance, rendered the world of his characters better than any Victorian novelist, and had a less theatrical, more convincing responsiveness to places and things than Dickens, accusing Dickens of manipulating his readers by contriving artificial situations and incomplete characters or caricatures.

Edmund Fuller in an article in the *Wall Street Journal* (1975) said that he and his wife, old Trollope fans, often read his novels aloud, a medium for which they are eminently suited.

C. P. Snow (1975) wrote the most favorable and significant if not the most exhaustive biography of Trollopes.. Lord Snow, married to novelist Pamela Hansford Johnson, had a background as broad as Trollopes. Starting as a scientist, he became involved in government affairs and university politics. One senses that Snow would like to be compared to Trollope. At least both were worldly and classically educated yet wrote plainly in contrast to James and Meredith, who often paraded their erudition.

The *Encyclopedia Brittanica* formerly devoted two pages to Dickens and a paragraph to Trollope. Now the space allotted to Dickens and Trollope is reversed. B. B. C. used Trollope's novels to make 22 programs and used Dickens' novels to make four programs. Dickens preached. Trollope espoused no causes or classes. His dukes were dukes, his lawyers were lawyers, and his servants, were servants as they were in real life. In the equally great Upstairs-Downstairs series the servants were given more exposure but the scene was the same. These shows *almost* justify television. The trouble is that only British personnel can produce them.

Trollope's greatest ambition, like that of all prominent Englishmen, was membership in the club of his choice. Trollope chose the Garrick, to which he was elected through his friends Charles Reade and Thackeray. In spite of his bluster, he became popular. Trollope's tongue-in-cheek definition of the "Ideal Club Member" was framed and still hangs over the fireplace at the Garrick. Here it is:

"The Ideal Club Member must cultivate a speaking cordiality with all members, a casual jollity, a willingness to exchange platitudes and to conceal contempt for any member's boring stories, low sense of humor and insane political views. Above all he should never parade his superior knowledge of all subjects except by request and should always be gracious in his disagreements with his inferiors who comprise all other members of the Club."

Let this be a lesson to all club members!

CHAPTER 7

THE SPORT OF KINGS

The Literary Club 1927

Paternalistic modern society is spending vast sums of money for the physical rehabilitation of cripples but is too often overlooking their emotional welfare. The physical constitution of man is not an isolated phase of his being but colors his whole life. A physical handicap or deformity should not be regarded simply as an anatomic deviation, but a potent factor in the emotional stability and social equilibrium of the cripple. Whatever deforms the body profoundly influences personality.

During the ages deformity has had a sinister meaning. From the dawn of history the crippled and the monster have been shunned. The ancient Greeks condemned those with bodily defects. As an improvement on this, legend records that Romulus ordered all children be allowed to live three years unless too lame or monstrous in appearance. The Greeks could not believe Socrates good or wise because he was deformed and ugly. Literature abounds in references to those marred in body and warped in soul. History records many famous personages of this type. Bacon said that "deformed persons are commonly even with nature, for as nature has done ill by them, so do they by nature." The humpbacked Richard the Third (Shakespeare) remarks,

But I, that am not shaped for sporting tricks,
Nor made to court an amorous looking-glass;
I, that am rudely stamped, and want love's majesty
To strut before a wanton ambling nymph;
And therefore, since I cannot prove a lover,
I—am determined to prove a villain.

Byron's tumultous character may have been due to his repudiation of a nature which had visited a club-foot upon him before the day of modern surgery. The "Hunchback of Notre Dame's" distorted mind was due to teasing and torturing, provoked by his twisted body.

The attitude of the pre-modern world toward the cripple was due largely to economic necessity and religious conviction. Deformities were regarded as visitations of the devil and displeasing to the gods. The unfortunates were thought to harbor demons, a punishment for the sins of the fathers. Even our New England forebears were guilty of the destruction of a number of innocent people who, because of deformity, were thought to have the power of witchcraft. Economically, there was little place for cripples, who were unfit for military duty or labor. They had to beg for life itself or for food to sustain life. An increasing liberalism spared life, but reluctantly threw them scraps and crumbs. And so at first they died by edict, later by neglect. At first glance this practice would seem to better the race, but this is not altogether true. There are only a few rare deformities which are inheritable. The majority of physical defects, whether congenital or acquired, are accidental and not associated with mental deficiency, as for instance congenital club-foot and infantile paralysis, an acquired deformity.

Later in history deformed beggars must have thrived because purposeful crippling of children became a common practice and moved St. Vincent de Paul to establish institutions for the care of children. He is still the patron saint of a charitable order of the Roman Catholic Church.

Throughout history (until 1800) the bizarre cripple was a favorite entertainer at court. Thus the sport of gods became the sport of kings. According to Doran in his *History of Court Fools and Jesters*, the Morio was popular among emperors of early Rome—usually a misshapen creature, a monstrous imbecile. Ladies kept them in their chambers, as they did monkeys at a later date, and as they do poodles today. There was even a market for them. At the "Forum Morionum" a frightful, deformed human would fetch $400. Parents often made dwarfs of their children for profit since whole droves of them were retained in the palaces of kings. Many districts of Europe gave employment or free living to one who, by his infirmities and talents, could create the most laughter. Doran thinks this custom originated in the orient. Fools were common in the caliphs' houses and were called "noodles." However the custom must have been worldwide since Cortez, on his first visit to Mexico, found the Aztec monarch surrounded by a horde of hunchbacks, cripples, and dwarfs.

The popes, about the time of Leo X, had misshapen jesters about them, Quero perhaps the most famous. In later European time deformity in a court fool became less and less necessary, and the traveling minstrel often was the court buffoon. Many of these jesters were really brilliant men; for instance Rapere, of the court of Henry I of England, to whom we are indebted for St. Bartholomew's Hospital in London.

Various kinds of deformities have been popular in different epochs. The early emperors preferred dwarfs, other courts desired hunchbacks for entertainers, while still others required more bizarre unfortunates to give them a feeling of sufficient superiority to provide mirth.

Today, among the intelligent, there is a sane attitude toward the cripple. The discovery of the actual causes of deformity, and the demonstration that many can be cured or prevented, has gone a long way toward removing the stigma of centuries. The diversities of modern life, trades, and occupations have given the cripple an opportunity to play a full man's part, as witness the achievements of Steinmetz and countless others.

All human beings, whether crippled or sound, adequate or inadequate, are influenced by the sum total of all their experience. From the beginning life is a continual conflict, physically, mentally, and morally; an effort to adapt ourselves to the conditions under which we must live. The struggle between what we consciously or unconsciously wish to do and what society requires us to do begins in infancy. As we grow older these conflicts become more complex and less sharply defined. If we come out of them successfully, it means that emotionally and physically we were adequate to our experience and that we are the well and the prosperous. If we do not cope successfully with our conflicts, it means that we were inadequate to our experience and that we are the tramps, paupers, criminals, invalids, and neurotics. It is said that everyone has his price. Translating this into the above terms, it means that everyone has a breaking point, given sufficient difficulty with his environment.

Thus the whole question of health and happiness is one of adaptaptation of that which is within us to that which is without us. If we have a disease, it means we have not sufficient antibodies in the blood to confer immunity. If we have a neurosis (an unconsciously imaginary train of physical symptoms), it is due to our inability to harmonzie with our environment. The gastric distress of financial insufficiency is not an imaginary pain, but it has no organic basis. Often the failures in business and in life unconsciously feign ill-health and develop "nervous breakdowns" (some of these are real), indigestion, and backache. In the same manners, anxiety and repression psychoses are formed. War neuroses, often called shell-shock, are the unconscious expression of one's inadequacy to the fear of battle.

To Freud and his school we owe most of our knowledge of

repression neuroses and the ill effects of brooding over imaginary ills and obstacles, although few would be willing to translate these psychoses into terms of sex. However, Freud's definite contribution to our knowledge of functional disorders is helpful in evaluating the mental warp of the cripple and gives us an insight into the peculiar neuroses to which the cripple is subject.

Thus the cleft palate or harelip, untreated, has more influence on social adjustments than almost any deformity. And even with treatment at times the voice is so poor that it requires a superhuman spirit to retain normality. I know a physician whose voice is so influenced by this defect that strangers cannot understand him. But he will smilingly repeat the same statement five or six times, if necessary. He is one of the rare ones with indomitable courage and has surmounted his difficulty. One rather famous misshapen man who often spoke in public would genially preface his remarks by saying, "I am a self-made man." Many examples of this kind show that man has marvelous powers of adjustment, but all too often the mind of the cripple is full of obsessions and inferiority complexes.

Left alone, superior cripples strive harder to overcome their obstacles, while the average or subaverage cripple succumbs to a sense of futility. The thwarting of desires and constant limitations by bodily defects may disorient him socially and spiritually. Most are introverts or microphallics unable to play a character part in life or make the proper social adjustments. Indeed, many of the afflicted tend to become antisocial. Truancy, theft, anxiety, and compulsive neuroses may be the end result.

Antisocial tendencies among crippled children may arise as the result of exclusion from school and recreations, the limitation of occupational activity, the prevention of adventure, romance, and friendships. Probably the most vicious influence on a cripple is the shielding attitude of the parents who restrict play in the usual games of childhood and give freedom from chores and errands. The mother states, "I feel so sorry for Tiny Tim, I hate to make him go to school or do anything." Even at school the same attitude is carried further by the teacher, who often does not punish the cripple for misbehavior and demands less from him in his school work than from the others. Children are often cruel to the afflicted. They are most cruel when they try to be kind to the cripple by letting him tag along, by pitying him and making things easy for him. Obstacles are removed from his path, social qualities are not developed. He is likely to become introspective and depressed and the victim of a neurosis.

If the environmental and inherited fibre be unusally poor, vagrancy, beggary, and criminality ensue. A recent survey of 1000 homeless men revealed 254 of them to be more or less crippled. This is a far higher percentage than occurs in society as a whole. People tend to seek the easiest way. Hency sneakiness and indolence, always showing the world the maimed limb for sympathy and an alibi. Their defects can act as a lever to weaken an already weak personality and drive them into criminality. I was recently called to the jail to dress a nineteen-year-old boy on whom I had repaired a harelip one week previously. He was convicted by the humane society of killing three horses by running sharp broomsticks into their recta. I found later that he only wished to have the harelip repaired to disguise his appearance and save him from prosecution.

The cripple is today a fashionable object of charity. Many clubs sponsor the physical rehabilitation of the deformed. They are culled out of the schools and sought out by the health nurses, officers, and social workers. The International Society for Crippled Children, the Shriners, the Kiwanis, the Rotary Clubs, and the State Welfare Association all are working for the physical help of the indigent crippled child. The handicap Bureau of the Associated Charities attempts to procure suitable jobs for the crippled adult. All the hospitals spend tremendous amounts of money on charity orthopedic cases. Although many of these people would be failures even if not deformed, there are a sufficient number made into useful members of society to justify this work.

Until recent years all efforts were directed toward cure of the physical handicap. War cripples focussed attention on the psychic aspect of this work, and the lessons learned can be profitably applied to handicapped civilians. It was found that education in a trade compatible with their disability should be started as soon as possible in their convalescence before habits of laziness, idleness, and dependence on their pensions developed, and before they became demoralized by the pity of family and friends. It was soon found that their jobs could not be dependent on the beneficence of others. Our paternalism toward indigent cripples may include rehabilitation, but their ultimate happiness demands economic independence.

The children of the well-to-do are the most neglected in this respect, although basically they have greater potentialities than poor cripples unless they are ruined by their environment. We have occupational therapy and special schools for indigent cripples which tend to develop social instincts and adaptibilities, but the well-to-do have private tutors, private nurses, private rooms in the hospital, and are patronized by everybody. They may develop, in the words of Adler, "a useless superiority complex," often becoming either a miserable wretch, determined to wreak vengeance on society or merely a refined beggar or parasite.

If we overpaternalize our indigent cripples and, in spite of all our free reconstructive and educational work, they become complete burdens on society, we cannot blame our system. We must charge this to our desire for humanitarian principles. Whether rich or poor, the cripple who is congenitally inadequate can never be made into a useful member of the community. Except in certain definite cases, such as cerebral palsy, this is a hard matter to judge and a still harder matter in which to obtain a uniform agreement among the many lay and professional organizations engaged in this work. Therefore, we must care for them all.

It is probable that, no matter what the system, and regardless of his advantages, the superior cripple at least will overcome his economic difficulties. The majority have the same mental capacity as any other group picked at random, and if they are properly shielded from psychoneuroses and despondency, if they are trained to do useful work, they become satisfied and happy members of society, removing a weight of despair and self-blame from the hearts of the parents.

CHAPTER 8

FASHIONS IN DEFORMITY

The Literary Club 1929

The tendency to alter or deform the human frame to conform to fashion or religious ideas has been practiced by both barbarian and civilized people. The ancient Greeks were an exception. They worshipped the beauty of the natural. Among civilized peoples deformities have been produced by wearing clothes according with prevailing fashion. The woman has suffered the most because man, faced by the necessity of the full play of his physique to procure a living, has dodged serious mutilation by clothes, although he has not entirely escaped. I shall not presume that men are less ornamental. Among uncivilized people men and women have been equally afflicted because the deformities were purposely done both for the sake of conformity to fashion and as a part of religious rites. Except in one or two instances, their self-imposed deformities did not interfere with physical freedom or health. Many of their procedures were painful, since crude operations without anesthesia were necessary. Domestic animals have often been marred for the sake of style, and in the past children have been deformed, either to increase their begging efficiency or for use as court jesters. Occasionally man has contorted himself for similar purposes. It is the fashion now among malingerers who are suing for damages or compensation to affect a deformity of the spine and backache. In one district in Kentucky during the draft for soldiers in the Civil War, several ingenious, unpatriotic citizens rubbed all the skin off the shin with a stick to obtain exemption.

However, it is proposed in this essay to consider only those deformities which have been practiced over a long period of time by whole nations or tribes of people without any motive whatever except imitation of one another. (This does not include one or two religious practices.)

The origin of most of these customs is unknown. No doubt the cause of new styles was similar to that operating in modern times, except that among barbarous people fashions were not so capricious. Once a bodily deformity was inflicted, it was permanent. As the younger people came to adult life they wanted to look like the older members of the tribe. Thus, for hundreds of years the deformities, probably originally the natural bizarre appearance of a great chieftain or possibly merely such a chieftain's idea of beauty, were emulated and perpetuated. As one chief succeeded another new ideas of fashion were contributed from time to time, and many a young tribesman required several operations before he could become a full-fledged warrior. Likewise, the socially ambitious lady had to endure a lot of doctoring since a variety of bodily perforations and ornaments served as a class index. If their religion required certain bodily changes the perpetuation was even more certain. People tend to conform to common usage and are afraid to appear singular. Prominent people, such as the Prince of Wales or the President's wife, have often set the styles. These fashions have become widespread through the masses because, according to Herbert Spencer, some imitate out of admiration and others to assert equality with both the distinguished originator and their neighbors.

The list of customs among uncivilized and semicivilized peoples requiring distortion of the body is too long to enumerate. It is not my purpose to dwell in detail on these fashions, but it is necessary to name a few of them. The head has suffered the most on the savage altar of beauty. The Australian Bushman thrust a piece of bone about six inches long through the cartilage of the nasal septum. The ordeal of the procedure must have been horrible, to say nothing of the interference with breathing, blowing the nose, and conversation. Many tribes derived their names or nicknames from similar customs. The Botocudo Indians of Brazil cut holes in their lips as children and wore ornamental wooden pendants which were inserted through the artificial hole. Their name was given them by the Portugese and means a "plug" or "stopper". Other Central American tribes use the same idea with variations. Certain of the Eskimos pierced the lower lip in two places and inserted divers devices, probably as a religious observance. According to Bancroft, the worst mutilators of the face were the Thlinkeets of southern Alaska. They were unsurpassed by any nation in making themselves the last word in hideous beauty. They must have had a foundation to subsidize research in ways and means of achieving their results because many of their procedures were ingenious. Holes were cut in ears, nose, lips and chin, through which all manner of pendants were hung. Their chief pride lay in a long curved piece of wood which was placed through the lower lip, pulling the lip downward, uncovering the lower teeth. It is supposed that they spoke of this as their lip-stick. The Bongo women of Africa pierced the ears with several straws or pieces of wood, and after marriage cylindrical blocks of wood through both the upper and lower lips distinguished their unmaiden state. It is estimated that some individuals had as many as a hundred ornaments thrust through the various convenient loose folds of skin about the body. It seems that a great many tribes used more or less the same methods, differing chiefly in the type of ornaments utilized. They arrived surprisingly often at the same effect, although working entirely independently.

Among all people the hair has been a constant object of

fashionable attention since it lends itself easily to a variety of treatment. Most of these practices were harmless except the artificially induced changes of color and the depilatory procedures. It is interesting that some African tribeswomen had a special instrument to black the eyebrows. The women kept their heads closely shaved by sharp stones while the men allowed their hair to grow long and wore it twisted in many bizarre shapes, reversing the usual custom.

As a rule the teeth have been allowed their natural usefulness and beauty, probably because of their necessity, particularly among aborigines. The people of Java, Malaya, Borneo and Senegal are exceptions. Filing of the teeth, usually the front uppers, in various fantastic shapes was widely practiced. Some varied this procedure by filing off the enamel and applying different stains. Others, anticipating our methods of orthodontia, caused the front teeth to protrude, with hideous results. The propensity of negroes for gold teeth is explained by the custom of the people of Borneo, who are said to have bored holes through the upper incisors for the insertion of brass plugs.

On the whole, it is probable that interference with the teeth was never widespread, owing to the intolerable pain which must have accompanied such a destructive procedure. Abscesses at the roots of such teeth were common. This is proven by examination of their skulls, and it would be interesting to know of the incidence of focal infection among them. From our general knowledge of pathology of wild animals and savages such complications were probably rare. Their wounds heal with extreme rapidity and their resistance to their own native bacteria is great.

In lieu of clothes, the Polynesians tattooed their whole bodies. Among them this practice developed into a fine art. Many beautiful symmetrical designs in various colors were produced, and it is thought that our sailors got their ideas on the subject from them. The aboriginal Australian used a cruder form of this art, and the black races were handicapped by the color of the skin. They had to be content with making rough gashes on the skin. In healing, large keloids grew in the scars and were highly prized.

The customs already alluded to are harmless compared to the fashion of artificially changing the shapes of children's heads. This was the most widely practiced of all self-imposed deformities. Savage tribes kept up these practices over long periods of time and were stopped only by extinction or by the power of a superior people who conquered them. Lazy mothers who did not dutifully bind the heads of their children in the prescribed way were ostracized along with the children, but the advantage to the children must have been some recompense. Even among civilized people the none too zealously brought up children of lazy parents often fare better than the closely guarded ones. Of course, many different shapes of the head occur naturally due to habitual positions in which the child lies or to methods of carrying children. The greater number were deformed by design and the process was begun soon after birth while the head bones are still soft, and the process was kept up until a permanent effect was produced. That this is an ancient custom is shown by Hippocrates' account of a barbarian people who had elongated heads brought about by compression bandages during infancy. Hippocrates states that the shape of the head became hereditary with them, thus proving that secondary acquired characteristics could be inherited. Strange to say, the most recent practice of the same kind was commonly seen in France. The French never achieved extreme effects, but it has only been a few years since this custom was abandoned, although it is reported that isolated families still try to mould their children's heads. The Flathead Indians of British Columbia obtained the most remarkable results. The child was placed upon a board and another board was placed over the forehead. The head was then compressed between these boards by drawstrings through the boards until the desired shape was obtained. Other tribes contented themselves with binding the head with bandages, much as the Chinese did the foot. The chief goal was length, and to accentuate this the hair was often piled up and worn on the vertex. Various other people have practiced variations of the above procedures. Some of the Mongolian peoples have left evidence of having flattened the occiput, while other Asians and Africans admired the flat forehead. The negro has never been guilty of these deformities on a large scale. The ancient tribes of the Western Hemisphere, some of the Polynesians, and a few orientals have been the chief offenders. The similarity in the skulls thus treated by the Mongols and North American Indians is one point by which certain investigators have tried to prove their common origin.

We have a poor knowledge of the actual effect of such practices on the function of the brain, but French physicians of the middle of the 19th century noted that even the mild deformities practiced at that time in France caused deafness, epilepsy, headaches and idiocy. The proportion of the inmates with moulded heads in the asylums was very high.

On the whole, the poor savage suffered a great deal by the scourge of fashion. He was tormented and harassed, but as a rule not mortally wounded. We pity him. Before the tears start to flow and a drive for missionary funds is begun, let us examine the doings of modern people of the higher scale and see whether their superior religion has lefted the fetters of fashion from them. Alas, this is not the case, although to our credit let it be said that we are less encumbered today than people have ever been in recorded history, with the exception of the ancient Greek period.

Our nearest approach to such perversities today is our methods of performing sculpture on our domestic animals to satisfy our ideas of style. The bobbing of dogs and horses tails, the recent custom of using martingales on the reins to hold the horses necks in a strained position, are only a few examples. At one time, it was fashionable to cut off a part of the horse's tail and divide the tendons on the under side so that the muscles of the upper side, being unopposed, carried the stump of the tail in a "cocked" position. Cutting off the horns of cattle is not in the above category, as it was for the good of all parties. Savage people often caused the horns of cattle to grow in many bizarre shapes by holding them in twisted positions during the growth period. Artificial selective breeding is usually designed to help the species, but often the opposite has been done. By taking advantage of accidental peculiarities in animals, we have been able by selective breeding through many generations to so increase these variations as to produce many hideous monstrosities such as the bulldog, the dachshund, cats without tails, pouter pigeons and the muley cow.

Returning to modern men and women of civilized countries, we find that they have never spared their own bodies in their efforts to conform to prevailing ideas of beauty. For many of these absurdities we do not have to go further than recent times. Why do men wear tight belts constricting the internal organs and preventing the full play of abdominal muscles, to say nothing of the added discomfort during hot weather? Since the suspender wearers use decoy belts to camouflage the real support of the pants, we must regard the practice as merely conformity to fashion. Sock garters when worn tight cause a congestion of the superficial circulation, and this is a common factor in causing varicose veins. Except for the war which educated men into the comforts of Munson last shoes, we might still be wearing the pointed toe, so-called Englished walking shoe. The deformities such as bunions and callouses produced by these shoes are still carried by a large proportion of the male population (1929).

Several fashions for women grew up in the middle ages. Most of them persisted until a few years ago and one is still with us. Of all the parts of the body requiring mobile and elastic walls for the functioning of the internal organs, the chest and abdomen are the most important. Contraction and expansion of the chest, peristaltic action of the intestines, and the circulation of the blood in the great vessels all are interfered with by any constriction around the waist. For many generations our women actually so tightly squeezed their bodies in rigid corsets that not only was ordinary comfort impossible, but the severest permanent chest deformities resulted. The bottle shaped ones naturally suffered more than the thin, because the ideal of beauty required the waist to be about the same circumference as a husky man's neck. Postmortem examination often revealed distorted livers showing indentations from rib pressure. Although it is hardly conceivable that rational people would subject themselves to such misery, this fashion proves the remarkable adaptabilitiy of the body to adverse external conditions.

The contorted foot is now the last of the fashions in deformity. The Chinese method has been the most crippling, but the American and European women have run them a close second. In China, when the girl reached five years of age, the feet were bandaged tightly in such a way as to draw the toes backward toward the sole and accentuate the bulge of the instep. These bandages were removed about once a month and reapplied over a period of years, until the feet were completely crushed and shortened. Large sloughs of skin, muscle and even toes came away with the bandage and the end result was a rigid, weak stump of a foot, capable of little active use. Until a paralysis of the sensory nerves occurred, the victims could do nothing but lie in bed and moan. All the intrinsic muscles of the foot were made powerless and their gait was about that of one with artificial legs. A mission surgeon stated that some of them would actually be improved by a leg amputation and accurately fitted prostheses.

But what of our own women who weep and pray and give their money for the betterment of the poor benighted heathen? The truth is they achieve similar results except they require a longer period of mild suffering. Years ago someone conceived the idea that the foot should not look natural, that it should be pointed in front. At any rate, the present day woman's fashionable shoe has a toothpick toe and a high heel. If one draws an outline of a foot and places the shoe over the outline, it will be found that the foot projects at least an inch farther than the shoe and that the end of the great toe strikes the end of the shoe. Normally, the foot is triangular in shape with the base of the triangle in front. The shoe is built with the base of the triangle in the rear. The high heel and rigid shank are added to insure the complete destruction of function and production of permanent deformities.

The foot is one of the most complicated mechanisms of the body. The great toe alone has seven muscles for its many different actions and is about 50% of the strength of the foot. There are about thirty joints, some having multiple motions requiring a complex arrangement of muscles and ligaments. The arch is held intact primarily by the pull of the muscles, which, if not interfered with, give the foot the action of a claw. Any shoe will hinder the functions of the foot to some extent, but when the front part of the foot is squeezed into the pointed shoe with the weight of the body thrown upon it by the high heel, pain, loss of function, and a sequence of deformities follow.

It is probable that such a shoe could not be tolerated unless the foot were adapted to this unnatural shape during early youth. The small-boned, thin foot naturally does not suffer as much as the more common wide, thick foot, heritage of our recent agrarian ancestry. When the woman's foot is squeezed into the average modern shoe, the weight is thrown on the front part which has no room to expand. The ball of the foot is crushed together and the toes must overlap one another to find sufficient space. Large callouses appear under the ball of the foot and corns on the tops of and between the toes. The great toe is turned outward, often overlapping or underlapping the second toe. The brunt of the pressure falls on the base of the great toe, and enlargement at this point gradually occurs. The skin over the enlarged joint becomes inflamed and calloused, forming a bunion. The toe becomes semi-paralyzed, due to the restriction of activity and pressuire on the nerves. These deformities are the first to take place and carry with them more or less severe pain under the ball of the foot and at the calloused areas. Later, the large leg muscles running from the knee to the foot are weakened from enforced disuse, since the various motions of the foot are impossible. In fact, in extreme cases, the gait is similar to that required by artificial lower legs. All the springiness and elasticity of the feet disappear between the ages of forty to fifty. The loss of strength in the leg muscles allows the ankles and arches to sag inward, resulting in pain under the main arch and in the calves of the legs. At this point gasoline is thrown on the fire by adding arch supports which usually are as destructive as the shoes. The practice of turning out the toes, which was started by misguided dancing masters, throws the weight toward the inner side of the ankle, increasing the strain and assisting in the production of flat foot. The line of weight bearing is disturbed so that the whole leg and back are put on a strain, resulting in that symptom which is so characteristic of many women: backache. After the ankles sag inward and the front part of the foot is deformed, the feet become rigid and permanently set. The ankles swell and thicken and varicose veins are not uncommon. The great majority of women suffer from these deformities, but the proportion rises with each decade of life. Many of them have as much as 50% disability from mechanical foot troubles alone. The layman regards the high heel as the cause of all these troubles. The high heel does cause shortening of the heel cord and thrusts the weight into the toe of the shoe and is to be condemned, but little harm would come from it if the toe of the shoe were sufficiently wide.

While various forms of treatment will help these deformities, nothing is so satisfactory as their prevention. If the women will wear a normal whoe, that is, one with a solid sole, flexible shank, moderate heel, straight inner line and adequate toe space, man's last vestige of barbarism will disappear. Such shoes are considered inelegant only because we are not used to them. In twenty-five years, the shoes of today will be looked upon with as great horror as a nose-ring. In fact, during the reign of Henry VIII broad-toed shoes were the fashion and as much admired as our modern boots. Women's greater activity and educational propaganda have already brought obvious results. About 50,000 pairs of normal shoes were sold last year in this city (Cincinnati).

On the other hand, the movement is held back by the commercial aspect. The shoe manufacturers want to retain the present style. If the women wear normal shoes, the number of shoes required will be cut in half. These shoes wear longer and fewer kinds of shoes for different occasions and dresses are needed. Men do not spend half as much as women for shoes because they wear only one style. The shoe business has already suffered because people spend all their money for autos and travel on rubber rather than shoe leather. The clothing business in general has suffered because people are dressing up with new autos rather than new dresses.

It is necessary for the intelligent 20% of the population to lead revolution in fashion. The rabble will eagerly follow. I don't believe that any of us regard the present fashionable shape of the foot as intrinsically more beautiful than the natural shape. We only need to remind ourselves that the lipstick of the Bongo negro, the blackened teeth of the Malay, and the flattened head of the Indian were once highly esteemed. If we continue to permit our women to deform their feet, we are not only injuring ourselves but are putting ourselves on the same level with the savages.

Much reform in women's everyday shoes has occurred since this was written 57 years ago.

CHAPTER 9

SURGEONS AND THE HEALING TOUCH

Surgeons have changed in type and physical stature during my lifetime. As a resident in surgery at the Mayo Clinic (1920-25) I remember the large number of staff surgeons and the vast number of visiting surgeons, including many who dated well back in the 19th century. The clinic then was the crossroads of the surgical world. The Mayo Clinic was a Mecca for visiting surgeons. Special provision was made for them to observe operations. When I was chief resident many of them made rounds with me, including Frank Lahey of Boston, who was getting his clinic under way, and Dr. Gallie of Toronto, under whom (and Dr. Star) Drs. Donald Balfour, J. C. Masson, M. S. Henderson and Gordon New studied before becoming members of the Mayo Clinic staff. The mortal sin at the clinic was to be discourteous to a visiting doctor or a patient.

When I finished my residency, armed with letters of introduction by Dr. W. J. Mayo to important surgeons, Mary and I went on a clinical trip for several months to the leading surgical centers of Chicago, New York, Boston, Baltimore, Philadelphia, England and the continent.

At that time the battle between the slow silk technique, exemplified by Halstead of Johns Hopkins and his disciples, and the faster catgut methods espoused by the Mayo Clinic, was raging. Halstead, trained by Kocher in Germany, originated the five-year pyramid system of training surgeons, now generally in vogue, but then in existence only at the Mayo Clinic and in two or three other centers headed by Halstead men, including Harvey Cushing, Halstead's first trainee, who became professor of surgery at Harvard. His disciples were loyal to Halstead, a fine diagnostician, pathologist, teacher and investigator. Some of them abandoned his slow technique, but as late as 1948 I heard Sir Heneage Ogilvie of London remark in a talk at a meeting of the Western Surgical Association that he was invited by a surgeon in a leading east coast center to witness a gall bladder operation at 9:00 a.m. At 12:00 he sent word to the surgeon that he had to leave for a lunch engagement. "That's all right," the surgeon relayed back, "return after lunch to see the finish of the operation." This controversy was gradually resolved. Apostles of both systems adopted the best features of both techniques.

When I got to Baltimore on my clinical trip in 1925, Dean Lewis of Chicago, an outsider not trained at Hopkins, was the professor of surgery. Lewis, attracted by the glamour of the position, was unhappy in the strange environment. He also was unhappy about the $10,000 salary to which he was lmited. I visited Lewis and J. M. T. Finney, who was happily doing private work at the Memorial Hospital. I had a letter to Dr. Finney from his nephew William Finney, a neurologist on the staff of the Mayo Clinic and one of my best friends. It was well known that Dr. Finney had refused the chair of surgery at Hopkins. At lunch he told me he couldn't afford to give up his $75,000 a year income from private practice.

I also spent time with William Rienhoff[1], Dr. Bloodgood, Hugh Young and the orthopedists, Drs. Baehr and Bennett. Dr. George Bennett started as a student in the now defunct Cincinnati Eclectic Medical College, eloped with the young wife of the old dean, ob-

---

[1] In my old age I played gold with Dr. Reinhoff in Florida. In 1985 I became a friend of his son Hugh Young Reinhoff, grandson of Hugh Young, the most famous urologic surgeon of his era.

tained his M.D. at Long Island Medical College, interned at Memorial Hospital in Baltimore, wound up as a partner of Dr. Baehr and became the first to specialize in sports injuries. Meeting Dr. Baehr was especially valuable. About ten years later I had a patient with osteomyelitis of the femur who showed me a clipping from a popular magazine which stated that Dr. Baehr of Johns Hopkins was using maggots to treat osteomyelitis. I called Dr. Baehr, who confirmed the story and was sorry the reporter had jumped the gun before he was ready to make an official report. He outlined the method to me, by far the best before the arrival of antibiotics. I used maggots to clean up 15 cases of chronic osteomyelitis and sent the results to Dr. Baehr, who quoted them in a paper.

In Philadelphia I saw three famous surgeons, holdhovers from the 19th century. Dr. John Deaver at his Saturday Lankenau Clinic, Dr. Charles Frazier at the hospital of the University of Pennsylvania (the first medical school in the U.S.) and Dr. W. W. Keene, aged 95, author of the most used textbook on surgery.

In New York I visited with Dr. Von Lackum at the Ruptured and Crippled Hospital, founded by Dr. Russell Hibbs of Paris, Kentucky, and visited later with Dr. Fred Albee, inventor of the Albee saw used in doing bone grafts. A year earlier Dr. Albee had offered me a partnership starting with the princely sum of $2,500 a year!

I spent two weeks in Boston with Drs. Lovett and Smith-Peterson, but especially with Harvey Cushing, then in his prime. One day while Cushing was doing a head case, I was the only visitor in the amphitheatre when a large man entered. His squeaking shoes smote the absolute silence. Arrogant Cushing was distracted. As the big visitor sat down by me Cushing looked up and said, "Where are you from, Doctor?" When the visitor said "North Dakota," Cushing asked, "Where did you get those shoes?" After a minute, the man, red faced, whispered, "The S.O.B.," and then got up and stomped out. Because of my letter of introduction Cushing was nice to me, inviting me to accompany him to the dressing room before making rounds at Peter Bent Brigham. When he took off his surgical outfit, I noticed a long scar on the right side of his abdomen. "A souvenir of my old chief, Dr. Halstead,"said Cushing. "When the S.O.B. took out my appendix, he split my whole abdomen open."

In Scotland I visited a man I had met at the Mayo Clinic: Mr. Archibald Young, professor of surgery at the University of Glasgow, who finally got the chair after Professor McEwen died at the age of 95, prompting medical colleges to force retirement at age 70. Cushing, one of the first to be forced to retire, was so resentful that he transferred his activities to Yale and left about three million dollars to Yale. I didn't see Jimmie Learmonth, a great friend and contemporary trainee at the Mayo Coniic; Jimmie was still at the clinic at that time. Later he became Sir James Learmonth, regius and clinical professor of surgery at Edinburgh. We visited him on a subsequent trip. When Learmonth died, I wrote the American phase of his life for the British Empire biographical series at the request of Professor Douglas of Aberdeen. In Glasgow, Mary visited the Drs. Riddell, father and son, leading opthalmologists of Scotland. In 1946, Dr. William Riddell and his wife Nan visited us in Cincinnati. While with us, Dr. Riddell took a day off to go to Indiana University to see Professor Herman Muller who later received the Nobel Prize for his fruit fly experiments. If I had known Muller's future fame, I would have gone with him.

In Liverpool I spent a week with Sir Robert Jones, leading orthopedist of the British Empire, whose ancestors were Welsh "bone-setters." (Bone-setter Reese of Youngstown, Ohio, was one of this clan.) Sir Robert showed me the brace shop and original Thomas splint inherited from his uncle, Sir Hugh Owen Thomas. The Thomas splint was universally used for 100 years to immobilize fractures of the femur. He introduced me to patients as his American assistant. As he applied a dressing to a child with a club foot, he told the mother to bring the child back once a week. "Why, Sir Robert," she replied, "I live a hundred miles away." "Oh," he smiled, "it's a beautiful trip, isn't it."

In Leeds we stayed with Sir Berkeley Moynihan, a flamboyant Irishman and greatest surgeon of his era in England, who lived in a magnificent house on grounds of 150 acres, inherited by his wife, located in the suburbs of Leeds. Dr. Moynihan, the greatest gourmet I have ever known, had a greenhouse with fresh vegetables in all seasons. He was proud of his black satin tablecloth, yellow chairs and yellow flowers on the dining table. "Always have yellow in the house and in the landscape," he said. Sir Berkeley showed me the vistas from different places in the house, each with a planned arrangement of trees and shrubs.

Surgery on the continent was cruder than surgery in England. At the Hotel Dieu in Paris, I saw Dr. Hartmann, born in 1846 and still operating. During an operation, when he stopped to explain something to the visiting doctors, he rested his gloved hand on a curtain rod outside the sterile field. Watching another surgeon, I was reminded of a remark Dr. C. H. Mayo made while he was observing a famous Paris surgeon operate. A visitor sitting next to him said, "Dr. Mayo, is he not a bold surgeon?" Dr. Mayo replied, "I don't know. I would have to see the patient awake, holding just as big a knife." Sauerbruch in Berlin also wielded a big knife in contrast to Kocher's painstaking technique, adopted by Halstead of Johns Hopkins.

I met a few American surgeons on my trip but did not get to Vienna, which was still the Mecca for short postgraduate courses. On the continent the attitude toward the patient was different from that in England. In England the doctor was the servant of the patient, as in the U.S. On the continent the surgeon, Herr Professor Geheimrat, was the Czar of the patient and his staff underlings. For a fee he would let a visiting surgeon do the operations on his service over a period of months.

Back in England I joined a society of clinical surgeons who

made trips annually to medical centers. At a dinner in Guild Hall we were welcomed by Prince George, later King George VI. In conversation the prince was normal and charming, but he made speeches with difficulty. He both stuttered and stammered. Clinics had been arranged in several London hospitals and groups assigned to attend them. To the consternation of the English, I was the only one in my group who showed up. The rest were touring with their wives. None were among the leading American surgeons.

In one way or another I observed most of the leading surgeons in the United States early in the century. Except for "Little Man" Keene (5'4"), the surgeons who had gained most of their fame in the 19th century were big, aggressive men, probably because surgery in that era was a rugged calling. We called them the "cattlemen" and the internists the "sheepmen" of medicine. These titles were appropriate. In the west the cattle ranchers wanted big spreads with no fences. The sheep farmers depended on small homesteads with fences.

In contrast, most of the surgeons who came into prominence early in this century were small men, including the Mayos, Sistrunk, Judd and Rankin at the Mayo Clinic, George Crile of Cleveland, Frank Lahey of Boston, and Halstead of Johns Hopkins, along with the eminent men trained by him: Cushing, Heuer, Mont Reid, Carter, Altemeier, Zinninger and Blalock. Many of these surgeons also could be called cattlemen, for they made up for their size by aggressiveness. However, only two had Napoleonic complexes: Cushing, the Czar of surgery at Harvard, and Rankin, who after leaving the Mayo Clinic for Lexington, Kentucky, achieved the presidency of the American Surgical Association, the Southern Surgical Association, the College of Surgeons, and the A.M.A., a record. It is noteworthy that dictators also were small men: Caesar, Napoleon, Stalin, Lenin, Hitler and Mussolini.

Early 20th century surgeons were pioneers who perfected what are now simple surgical procedures. The modern heads of surgical departments are oriented more to research. They have vastly enlarged the scope of surgery. Even before I retired, I referred cases to them which I formerly did and for new operations for which I was not trained. Incidentally, mdern surgeons are men of normal physical stature!

After seeing the leading surgeons and clinics of the western world, I was even more gratified to have had my training at the Mayo Clinic. The big difference was the handling of patients led by Dr. W. J. Mayo himself. The number of patients was enormous, but each patient was individualized at the Mayo Clinic, assigned to a particular doctor who supervised his case throughout his stay, bolstering the confidence of the patient and often leading to a permanent friendship. The patient always had someone he trusted to whom he could write or return to see. Individualization of the patient is still the keynote in spite of the vast increase in size of the Mayo Clinic.

THE HEALING TOUCH

The practice of medicine has not changed at the Mayo Cinic, but elsewhere it has changed since my early years. Seventy-five percent of patients who seek help do not have organic disease. They have phobias or psychosomatic symptoms often caused by family or business problems. The successful doctor cures them because he communicates and establishes an empathy and friendship with his patients. That is why Christian Scientists and quacks can cure so many people. When some doctors enter the room, the patient immediately feels better. This kind of doctor or surgeon has the healing touch. His patients also survive operations and organic disease more often than they do in the hands of equally trained men who don't take the time or don't have the ability to establish the proper personal relationship.

Communication inspires confidence. If a patient does not like the doctor, he will not have confidence in him. He should find a doctor he likes. If he has confidence, he will relax and follow instructions. If he has confidence in the surgeon, he is more apt to survive a dangerous operation. Through the sympathetic nervous system the emotions stimulate the glands of internal secretion, especially the thyroid and adrenal glands, a super cortisone effect which has a powerful influence over the functions of the body. Confidence sets this mechanism in motion. If the patient believes he will get well, he is more apt to get well. I operated on over 600 major cases in the homes of patients with only one fatality, and that was a man who was positive he was going to die. He thrashed himself to death after the operation. If they like the doctor, the family accepts death calmly. If there is a poor result, they do not sue the doctor. I have had three cases of advanced cancer with extensive metastases and know of three more on which all the specialists had given up. Only the patient and the family doctor had hope. Somehow, they got well. No one could explain it.

At present, I am sure there still are doctors with the healing touch, but the conditions of modern practice produce fewer of them. The patient has become an automaton: science and technology have taken over. Everything revolves around the laboratory, machines and computers. Many expensive, unnecessary tests and procedures are done only for protection against malpractice suits, but more malpractice suits could be prevented by a better doctor-patient relationship.

Modern technical diagnostic devices and therapy are fine as long as we remember that the practice of medicine is still primarily an art and not a science. This is especially true in incurable, terminal patients who should be let alone, not bedeviled by heroic temporary measures. Too often, doctors do not extend life; they merely prolong death.

A big factor in the skyrocketing cost of health care and the deterioration of the doctor-patient relationship has been third party payment (Medicare, insurance companies, etc.). Under the old system, when the patient had to foot the bill, the doctor individualized his patients. He did not order unncessary tests. The patient was more apt to refuse unneeded surgery, which has doubled with third party payment. In our present society a certain amount of welfarism in necessary. If extended to everyone, including "free" health care, it would not be free. The cost of health care would be quadrupled. The importance of the doctor would be reduced to that of a clerk, as it is in Russia. The healing touch would be lost forever.

CHAPTER 10

A FRIEND OF MINE IN FRANCE

Literary Club

May 11, 1936

During the past eighteen years I have come into intimate contact with a large number of men who served in the armies of the various nations engaged in World War I. We listened eagerly to the tales of our grandfathers about the Civil War, and now our contemporaries occasionally relate incidents which occurred on the western front. Those of us who were in the army but not in France, as well as the rest of the population, have had an unsatisfied curiosity as to what occurred in the daily life in the trenches. It is with the conversation or lack of conversation of my friends that I wish to deal, as far as possible remembering the comedy relief anecdotes which, after all, produce a clearer picture of men and conditions than reams of narrative. In undertaking this vast work, I shall not discuss war in any of its phases. My only desire is to tell you how soldiers have reacted conversationally and particularly to relate the adventures of one friend and the highlights of his service in France.

In looking back over my contact with several war veteran friends, it is interesting that the amount of information voluntarily broadcast by them was in inverse proportion to the time served. The longer and more grim the service at the front, the less talk about it. As one man explained, the average soldier had a dull routine with narrow perspective, and often whole actions were only a blur in his memory.

While I was in training in surgery at the Mayo Clinic, I came into intimate touch with two Scotch Canadians for a period of five years. One had been an artillery lieutenant and the other an infantry major in the Canadian army. Both were in heavy fighting for three years of the war. They were graduates of the University of Toronto, where they had been in school together for seven years, most of the time as roommates. They were each other's best friend. I often went fishing or hunting sometimes with one, sometimes with both. The war had been over but two years and, like everyone else, I wanted to hear about it. These men were unusually intelligent and seemingly free of any adverse effect physically or otherwise due to their service, except that the artillery man was partially deaf. Indeed, one of them became the champion tennis player of Canada after his discharge from the army. Never once in my hearing did either of them allude to his war record. The only approach to the subject was made on a fishing trip with the tennis star when he remarked that the guide reminded him of one of his best men, killed in a battle, survived by only five of his company. Although fishermen, like sailors, are notoriously poor swimmers, there came a hot day on this trip when I suggested a dip, but to my surprise nothing would induce my companion to get into the water. No explanation was offered. On my return, I asked his friend if they had ever talked over their war experiences. He replied that no word about the war had ever passed between them but that he had heard from another source that his friend, while trying to save a soldier from drowning off the Cornish coast, had himself almost lost his life. This statement explained the hydrophobia but completely ended the conversation on this subject.

Another member of my Mayo group was Dr. Pierre DePage, son of the medical chief of the allied armies, a prominent Belgian surgeon. Pierre, once he discovered that hunting was generally allowed without arrest for poaching in Minnesota, accompanied us on many expeditions, and we were thrown together frequently for several years. Pierre's intensity of feeling toward the war, like the Canadians', was so great that only once in a while a propitious moment would arise to break his silence. On such an occasion DePage volunteered that he had served throughout the war in the Belgian air service. Several years later we visited him and his wife at their home in Brussells. Pierre's wife told us that his mother, who was with the queen on her first visit to America, went down on the Lusitania on a subsequent trip for the Belgian government. This was our first knowledge of this disaster. From the first day I met Pierre I almost asked him a hundred times about the truth of the so-called Belgian atrocities. An opening came on this visit. He stated that, to his knowledge, no one of the civilian population of Brussells was harmed in any way and that his family had lived there throughout the German occupation. There was no plundering except that every bit of brass, including water faucets, was carried back to Germany to make guns.

Pierre reacted much the same as a Prussian friend, Dr. William C. Huebener, now a physician in this country, but one of the crown prince's adjutants in the aviation corps during the war. Even today he shaves his head and never forgets to click his heels. Naturally serious, he broods constantly on the accusation of war guilt against his beloved emperor (not kaiser), would willingly be shot to eradicate this stigma, and on any provacation will talk heatedly and at any length on the subject. When actual fighting is mentioned, he merely shrugs his shoulders and is silent.

At rare intervals circumstances will remove the inhibition to talk. An American born Lithuanian friend was sixteen years old when he and his mother were caught between the Russian and German armies while on a visit to the old country at the outbreak of the war. He and his wife were dining with us recently when he opened up and for two hours held us spellbound with an account of two weeks spent in a cellar, with shells flying thick overhead, the destruction of his uncle's house, the courteous treatment of his mother by both armies, deportation to Russia, fifteen months of anxious waiting in St. Petersburg before their final escape to America by way of Archangel. During this dramatic recital I noticed that his wife seemed as amazed as we. She later told me that she had known something of these events, but that this was the first time her husband had ever talked on the subject in her hearing, this in spite of his natural openness and good humor.

It is expected that Europeans will generally have a fatalistic resignation to war. These people have always had the inevitable shadow of conflict over them, and generation after generation has seen fighting on its doorstep. Military service is a serious part of their lives and partially explains their earlier maturity in comparison to us. The Americans, with their carefree, child-like, prolonged school life, having experienced no foreign invasion and no real combat for several generations, saw the world war as an adventurous picnic under much less rigid discipline than that which prevailed in the foreign armies. While some of our men were in hard fighting, the period was short. And so it is easy to explain the willingness and even desire that my American friends have shown to talk freely about their experiences, although they usually dwell more on their adventures in Paris than at the front. Further, it is well known that our southerners are naturally talkative. It is somewhat contradictory that the only really vindictively prejudiced participant I have known was a southerner, and he had served in the French army for two years before the United States entered the war. I am told that a personal grudge against the enemy is a rare thing among combat troops, but this gentleman must have been the exception. I met him ten years after the war, when a doctor in Tennessee invited me to bring a companion down for quail shooting. My guest had a German name, but his grandparents were American-born. The Tennessean invited the vindictive gentleman to make a fourth, so that we could hunt in pairs, sending my friend with the German name out with him, a most unfortunate choice. When we returned that night we found my friend had preceded us by several hours. My host had forgotten about the fourth man's hatred of Germans. The pair had quarreled and parted almost at the onset and my guest had to find his way back alone. Later I talked to the man who had deserted my friend and found him very agreeable. Probably to compensate for his rudeness, he discoursed at length on his war experience and showed me over a hundred snapshots secretly made at the front. Even my host, who was an intimate friend, had never seen the pictures.

More typically American and southern is the man who really inspired this paper. It is wellknown that the farther south one goes both in Europe and in America, the more talkative become the people. The descendants of the cavalier courtesans in the south have always been addicted to both small and big talk. They have even been accused of boasting and exaggeration, but such accusations are usually made by sons of abolitionists, whose puritanical austerity naturally militates against their appreciation of this gentle comedy. Such people cannot understand that euphony, harmony and mellifluity are necessary to a good story and that facts are of secondary importance. Having been born in a border state, I have no ax to grind. I admit that the form of humor grown from the contact of the southerner with the negro and hillbilly is a delightful contribution to the humor of the world; it needs no champion. To the prejudiced who say that, like old ham, one needs to be raised on it to enjoy its flavor, I commend the stories of Bob Burns each Thursday night on the radio. It has been unfortunate that the literature of or by southerners has been of two extremes, either the rose and lavender sentimentality of *Carolina Low Country* or the distribe and drivel of *Uncle Tom's Cabin* or *Tobacco Road.* While I do not expect to cure this situation, I wish to present something of the life and background of a modern southerner at home and abroad. If, at times, he smacks of Squire Western, no apology will be offered. I must be truthful. But let it be understood that our hero is a gentleman. The off-color attempts at wit in this paper should be attributed, since Sherman's famous comment, to the general profanity of war than to my hero. Witness the recent movies, plays and books on this subject and bear in mind that the author, like Dr. Pottlesmith, is naturally callous, due to his daily contact with all the facts of life. These considerations are offered in explanation, not extenuation, of portions of the paper.

"A Friend of Mine in France" alludes to a southerner, who, like most Americans, never took the war seriously. He was in some fighting, but a few weekends in Paris relieved the grimness of reality. My friend was raised on a large plantation in Louisiana, which, as an absentee landlord, he still owns. Having been away for many years, he went back for a visit, which accounts for an incident descriptive of the man. Looking around the little town he saw many older people whom he knew, but none seemed to recognize him. Finally he spoke to an old Negro who had worked on his father's farm. "Uncle Ned," he asked, "do you remember me?" The negro, after looking intently at him a moment, broke into a wide grin. "Yes, Sir, yes, Sir. 'Pon my soul, if it ain't Big Talking Frank*." In the small town near his old home, he recognized a middle-aged colored woman whom he had not seen for twenty years. After he called her by name, she remembered him and regaled him with all the news of the neighborhood. At length he inquired about her old beau. "He's fine," she said, "I'm still going with him but that man gittin so I can't handle him. Do you remember Brother Alexander? Well, I and Ben goes as usual to meeting to last Sunday night and Brother Alec preached a wonderful sermon. He told us about

*Frank McEwen, born in Nashville, Tennessee, served in World War I in the same outfit with Larry McPhail, Grantland Rice, and Leeke Lea. A steel salesman for Republic Steel Co. - married Penelope Hardy of Louisville. Died in 1941.

all the good things that comes to black people this time of year, crops laid by, days short, rabbit season close with fried meat and gravy in the skillet and maybe a fat old possum in the pot and he said. Pretty soon the white folks going to kill hogs. And then you'll have spare ribs and hog jowls.' I reckon Ben just couldn't stand it any longer. He riz right up in the amen corner and shouted, 'Hallelujah! Brother Alexander, go on with them *greasy words.*' "

I hasten to add that in presenting this paper I am indebted for much material to the leading character, the favor and flavor of whose intimacy I have long enjoyed. In relating the true adventures and characteristics of my friend I am violating no confidences. I have heard him repeat them to casual groups on numerous occasions. In fact he is almost as noted in the south as those raconteurs extraordinary Riley Wilson and Tandy Ellis. I suspect he is as well known privately as Irvin S. Cobb is publicly.

He has the double standard moral outlook of the old South. Although the worst thing he can say of a man is "He doesn't know a lady from a woman," he may in the next breath tell the story of the travelling man who, in bed with his wife after having been away from home for several months, was informed by her that she had a touch of pregnancy. "Well," said he, not much shaken, "who was it? Jack Jones?" "No." "Sam Johnson?" "No." "Rube Smith?" "No." "Hank Riley?" "No." This was too much. Getting madder every second, he kicked her out of bed. "I don't mind the pregnancy," he shouted, "but what hurts me, my friends aren't good enough for you."

The estimate of the French people which our soldiers brought back varies from those who found them small and profiteering to others who thought them generous and warm-hearted. Many have said that in the next war they will fight only if the French are on their side. After hearing the pros and cons it is evident that the same group would have had much the same experience among the people of Ohio, Canada or China. It was simply a case of the reaction of individuals to individuals. The man who was tactful got real service. The southerners, born politicians, generally liked the French. The following incident is one which endeared the French to my friend. As lieutenant he was dispatched with a squad to a nearby sector for certain supplies. It was a two-day trip back of the front in an army truck. Stopping in a town, the soldiers were quartered nicely in a barn, but my friend looked in vain for a suitable place to sleep. At length he saw a French officer, who invited him to his quarters. It was nearing dinner time when they arrived at the house in which the Frenchmen had been living. There they found a second French officer with two charming young French women. Dinner was served with a profusion of champagne, and after dinner the gaiety continued. My friend, speaking French, entertained in his best style with many stories embellished for the occasion. The French were delighted. At a late hour the wine, as the Chinese say, began to die in them and our hero, striving as always to be the gentleman, retired to his allocated chamber in order to equalize the party. He had just gotten into bed when all four of the revelers came into his room.

Amid much clatter and many protestations on the part of the American, both women were put into his bed for the night, thus proving to him forever the highmindedness and generosity of all French people.

In the same officers' training camp with my friend in America was Dr. S. P. Kramer of Cincinnati. One evening during retreat an officer, bare-headed, with his blouse open, was seen nonchalantly walking across the parade ground, smoking a cigarette, entirely oblivious to the occasion. "Who is that 'Son of a B'?" asked the commanding officer of his adjutant, who happened to be my friend and probably the only man present who knew Dr. Kramer. "Just a damned doctor," he replied. The commanding officer only stared with contempt as Dr. Kramer's meditative ambulation continued triumphantly, not even the lowering of the flag and the playing of the national anthem causing him to pause.

This evidently was the general attitude toward the doctors, most of whom could not or would not understand the soldier part of the game in World War I.

But discipline was enforced many times and once resulted in the arrest of a private, a boy whom many of the officers had known back home. One day near noon several of them were making their way into the mess tent. The path extended above a muddy ditch in which a number of guardhouse detail were doing penance consisting of digging mud with a pick. Recognizing their young friend among them, they stopped. Every time the pick struck, mud flew all over the boy, into his eyes, etc. Looking over the fence, he said, "Why John, they can't make you do that, can they?" "No, sir," he replied, "they can't make me do it, but they can make me wish I had."

No love is greater than that between friends who help one another make money or go through many dangers together. War produces an external callousness which would seem to disprove this statement. If evident mourning at the passing of a friend seemed absent, it was because of the frequency of this loss which was relegated to the background by the all-absorbing idea of each individual that he would be the next. The finest illustration of this effect occurred one day while the officers of the flank regiment were waiting at headquarters for a regimental meeting. Some, including my friend, were hanging around the entrance. The tent was well protected behind a hill, although a great many shells were passing overhead.

There was a general silence as each man with his own thoughts idly gazed on the limited horizon. Over the crest of the hill appeared one of their number. They recognized "Piggy" Jones, lifelong friend of several of those watching outside the tent. Either thinking he was late or to get out of danger, he was coming in double quick, when, still far up the steep bank, a bullet struck him in the head. He catapulted forward over and over and rolled to the bottom of the hill. No sound from the crowd. Each at least pretended to be unmoved. As the rolling, tossing form of the dead man approached the bottom of the ravine, the speed of the lifeless body increased. At this point one of the spectators made this only remark: "Did you see that bastard bounce!"

CHAPTER 11

AN EARLY SCENE

The Literary Club
January 26, 1948

How many living people can picture accurately the appearance of this part of the country as seen by the first white man? Except for a few who have had sufficient interest to piece together the snatches of description left by original observers, practically no one has the proper conception. Almost everyone thinks that Kentucky and Ohio were completely covered by dense forests. Of course this was largely the situation, but there were many open areas, especially in gently undulating central Kentucky. In fact,there was an area, still called the barrens, at least fifty miles in extent in western Kentucky which had no growth except wild grass and a few bushes. Though the pioneers left us few written records, some early travellers gave good accounts of this region. On the heels of the first settlers came two French scientific observers, Michaux and Rafinesque, whose journals furnish us descriptions of the original flora. Imlay, Jerediah Morse, General Levi Todd, Filson, Harrod, and others left valuable independent observations with almost no disagreement. Two distinguished historians, John Mason Brown of long ago and our own contemporary, the late beloved Judge Samuel M. Wilson of Lexington, have both brought to light much conclusive documentary evidence to widen our knowledge of the original scene and allow us to understand the agricultural destruction of this region.

Let us imagine ourselves in company with the first white man descending the Ohio River. We have abandoned our raft at the site of Maysville, climbed the bluff, and arrived at the spot where the town of Washington will stand. The year is 1775 and the season is early spring. For the past month we have travelled through mountainous country covered by forests. The picture now changes abruptly. We have suddenly come upon a vast undulating plateau with alternate woods and open areas. Spring, which comes early here, heightens the contrast. As we proceed we find the lower areas covered by a dense growth of cane, the stalks sixteen feet high and up to two inches thick. Some stalks are barren and some covered with leaves, and yet others, partly decayed, have fallen to the ground. We shall learn later that a stalk of this cane lives for two years, having no leaves until the second year and that cattle will fatten on it as they would upon grain. The dead stalks have decayed and formed black loam which averages 6 feet in depth. Scattered through the canebrakes and on the uplands are the finest and largest trees and the most variegated vegetation ever discovered by man in the temperate zones of the world.

Great white, red, and burr oaks, butternut, walnut and shagbark hickories, fine stands of sugar maple and black locusts, a few wild cherry, and the monarch of all, the yellow poplar or tulip, known to reach two hundred and twenty feet in height and ten feet in diameter, covered the areas of richest land. In the shade were found the dogwood, redbud, hawthorn, pignut, pawpaw, and cucumber trees now in the first bloom of spring. What a contrast to the smaller trees we had seen on the mountainsides to the east. We had thought the pines and oaks of the hill region, with the undergrowth of holly and laurel, beautiful, and we admired the fine beech and cedar groves, though we realized these trees meant the cold, freestone land beneath. Up to this time the largest stands of timber had been near the streams, as is usual in wooded country. As we progressed toward the heart of central Kentucky we saw enormous sycamores, sweet and black gum, also catalpa, cotton-wood, silver maple, pin oak growing along the banks of the Licking and Elkhorn; but here the upland trees were even larger than those along the rivers, a tribute to the incomparable fertility and water-holding capacity of the soil. As we approached the largest streams, the country was hilly and broken and the soil consequently thinner, as evidenced by occasional areas covered by sassafras, hackberries, and chinquepins, clusters of pawpaws and, standing out in the open on high ground, numerous persimmon trees. Beyond the hills of the Licking the country becomes mildly rolling and the open areas, almost like big meadows, are more frequent. Travel is now very easy because we follow the buffalo trace, passing the sites of future Paris and Lexington. After the eternal shade and semidarkness of the primitive forests, we welcome the sunshine of this more or less open country. Herds of grazing buffalo thunder away at sight of us, and we examine more closely one of their favorite meadows. We make our most astounding discovery, the story of which caused one of the greatest agricultural migrations of all time in spite of almost insurmountable obstacles. Kentucky Blue Grass! Grass in large patches in the open areas growing up through the decaying debris of last season's weeds and cane. If this were May, we would see the tiny bluish bloom from which this grass gets its name. Interspersed amidst the grass were clovers and trefoil and a profusion of flowers. The explanation of this phenomenon seemed simple: the dense growth of cane smothered out bushes and undergrowth. Buffalo in vast numbers grazed and trampled down the dead and the living cane on their way to the salt licks, allowing the sun to strike the ground-producing perfect conditions for ground vegetation, impossible in the woods. Through thousands of years of struggle, the hardy grass and legumes developed, so that at least in the spring and fall they prevailed over the weeds, which would only grow in the hot months when the grass was dormant. Of course these patches of grass were small, but an experienced farmer could see how easy it would be to have large pastures almost ready made. The earliest explorers such as Gish and Lewis, traveling chiefly on the large streams, reported on the fine hunting and climate; but it remained for the long hunters, Boone, Harrod, and others, penetrating the interior of central Kentucky, to carry back glowing tales of the land, causing a land rush which, considering the hardships and dangers, was greater than any gold stampede. And the settlers were not disappointed. Here was not only the richest soil but in addition a moderate climate, abundant water, and natural food for man and animals. Once established, life has ever since been easy for the central Kentucky landowner.

What made this type of farming relatively easy? The natural grass which was found growing in the open areas by the first settlers. It appeared to them like their own grass at home and was first called English grass. This has been identified by botanists as Poa Praetensis. For many years there were conflicting theories as to the origin of this grass, some claiming it to be native and others that the seed was introduced. Judge Sam Wilson, after years of painstaking work, was able to prove the presence of grass before the settlement of Kentucky. Many people later probably did bring different kinds of seed which may have had some effect in shaping the final product. Even this is doubtful since there has been little change noted for over a hundred years. Capt. Christopher Gist found grass north of the Ohio River in 1751 and George Renick, a first settler, recorded that the Darby Bottoms near Circleville, Ohio, had a growth of native grass. Morse, Todd and Imlay all described the original vegetation and each mentions the presence of grass in central Kentucky. The clinching evidence uncovered by Judge Wilson was contained in the testimony given by eighteen witnesses in a land suit brought in Lexington in 1780. Each witness testified that he saw English grass growing in a certain field in 1775 near which one of the litigants claimed he built a cabin.

A later gentleman, Senator Ingalls of Kansas, the Louis Bromfield of his time, in a bit of grandiloquent oratory said in part:

Next in importance to the divine profusion of water, light and air, may be reckoned the universal beneficience of grass....Grass is the most widely distributed of all vegetable beings, and is at once the type of our life and the emblem of our mortality. Our earliest recollections are of grass; and when the fitful fever is ended and the foolish wrangle of the market and forum is closed, grass heals over the scar which our descent into the bosom of the earth has made, and the carpet of the infant becomes the blanket of the dead. One grass differs from another grass in glory. One is vulgar and another patrician. But the King of them all, with genuine blue blood, is Blue Grass. There is a portion of Kentucky known as the Blue Grass Region, and it is safe to say that it has been the arena of the most magnificent intellectual and physical development that has been witnessed among men or animals upon the American continent or perhaps, upon the whole face of the world.

CHAPTER 12

WATER

Ohio University
November 28, 1949

Water, the single element most necessary to life, the medium from which all life evolved, covers most of the earth and comprises up to 90 percent of plant and animal tissues. An animal can lose all its fat and over half its protein and still live, but 10 percent dehydration will cause death. Water is not merely an inert fluid medium for living tissues but an integral part of their structure and activity. Water regulates heat, lubricates joints and intestines, and, because of its solvent and ionizing qualities, is a transporting medium. Transcending all these functions, the most vital and least studied role of water is nutritional. Plants and animals can absorb needed minerals only as they are transported in solution in water. A plant receives all of its minerals from water and an animal, about one third. If soil is deficient in any element, the water is deficient, the plants and animals are dificient. (Horses from poor land will not be Derby winners and men from poor land will not become members of the Jockey Club.) A trained farmer can diagnose deficiency in a sick plant by its appearance. In man and animals lack of manganese produces sterility; too little iodine, goiter; not enough iron and copper, anemia; lack of cobalt causes "cobalt disease"; magnesium (seldom lacking) is concerned in digestion and formation of teeth and bones. A book could be written on the functions of sodium chloride, calcium, and phosphorus, and everyone has heard about the necessity of fluorine to form sound teeth.

Even more important is the interrelated action of some elements. No amount of iron without the presence of a minute amount of copper will prevent anemia. Less well known are the results of excessive intake of certain minerals. In normal animals, most minerals in excess of requirements are promptly excreted, but too much fluorine causes loss of teeth, too much iron may cause rickets by precipitating phosphates, too much iodine may cause hyperthyroidism, too much salt must be denied certain people with heart and kidney ailments to prevent swelling of the tissues. Thus it is obvious that we must not be overzealous in doctoring our public water supply. Both man and animals absorb minerals best from natural water which requires no treatment except in limited areas of known deficiences and excesses. Under identical conditions otherwise, beef cattle at the University of Kentucky gained almost twice as fast on natural spring water high in minerals as on treated Lexington city water obtained from a reservoir. Related to this is that both the efficiency of grain fermentation and the quality of whiskey vary with the mineral content of the water used. In dry periods, city water is substituted for the usual well water by the bakeries and distilleries of central Kentucky. Formulae for whiskey and bread must be changed and dicalcium phosphate added. In spite of these precautions, the product is still inferior when treated water is used.

There are several reasons why the Indians, by common consent, set aside Kentucky as their hunting ground. According to Imlay, they told early settlers that the meat tasted better. The soil and water of this region still contain an abundance of calcium, phosphate, and trace elements. It is no accident that here lambs without supplemental grain feeding bring premium prices. Thoroughbreds are produced in every state of the Union; central Kentucky, raising only 20 percent of the total, wins 85 percent of the important stake races. Universally conceded but, we hope, not prejudicing the veracity of the author, liars have always been the most eloquent in this highly mineralized area.

The quality of water is even more important to the sick man. Because of the limited intake of food, the body must rely more on water as a source of its mineral balance. Throughout history man has sought cures through healing waters. The Indians told the white man that the Saratoga waters would cure disease. During the nineteenth century, people came all the way from the East by stagecoach to Blue Lick Spring, Kentucky, where, in the wilderness, there was a hotel accommodating three hundred people. This water was bottled and had an international sale. Many people still go to health resorts, as they say, "to cleanse the system and purify the blood." The author himself confesses to a liking for some of these waters. If not directly cured, many people are benefited by the change, rest and psychologic effect of purging. Most of the profession regards this form of therapy as commercial exploitation, but recent unprejudiced observations at the non-profit Saratoga Spa indiciate these waters give measurable help in certain diseases. The Milford, Ohio, water controversy is an example near at home. At any rate we have learned the hard way that such widespread and long-practiced popular beliefs cannot be dismissed without serious investigation.

One of the great boons to man was the discovery of bacteria as the cause of certain diseases. The protection and treatment of our drinking water has removed the scourges which occupied 75 percent of the time of the horse and buggy doctor. But removal of bacteria and other sources of infection from the water leaves us with many unsolved diseases. If the cause of an infection cannot be determined, we call it a virus. How many such viruses are water borne and unprevented by our present methods of water purification? In addition to indispensible trace elements, how many known and unknown vitamins, how many natural antibiotics, how many favorable bacteria, and how many needed radioactive elements are all contained in the best natural drinking water? If we are to get these bio-elements, we must look to water as the source since we eat largely cooked food and by this process kill much of our natural protection. We know that plants, animals and man thrive best on a fertile soil. We think this is due in great part to better nutrition, but we are now finding that fertile soil contains more fungi, antibiotics, and benign bacteria which kill pathologic bacteria. Good land also contains all the needed minerals, water soluble vitamins, and probably many more undiscovered bio-elements. For various reasons many degenerative and other diseases are on the increase. Most of our population is drinking what is regarded as safe city water. The $64 question now is, what are the effects of drinking this safe water that has first rushed down eroded, unfertile hillsides into a river carrying the outflow of privies, garbage, sewage, and industrial pollution, and finally is treated with chemicals to remove virulent bacteria? Even before treatment such water must be deficient in minerals and other bio-elements. After treatment, it is not highly potable. Animals instinctively will not drink creek water if natural well water is available. Both animals and man will drink a greater quantity of good untreated water. Our brood mares at Forest Retreat, when turned out, will ignore a pond or creek and go to the far end of the field to get to a tank of flowing spring water.

The people of America are the largest protein eaters in the world. It is said that a man lost in the desert with only a canteen of water and a beefsteak will survive longer if he throws the beefsteak away. The more meat consumed, the more water required to carry away the end products of metabolism. To be healthy, Americans of all people need the most abundant and potable water supply because they are the largest meat eaters in the world.

More controlled observations on these fundamentals are needed. Even intelligent people are slow at times to understand primitive facts. Two old maid school teacher sisters lived in virginal seclusion. Each sister owned a big tom cat, their only companions. These cats were never allowed out except when chaperoned by the old maids. Each night the sisters would read or sew while their respective pets slept on the floor at their feet. Promptly at 9:00 P.M. they retired leaving the cats locked in the house.

Social privileges and experiences were as unknown to the cats as to the old maids. Miraculously, one of the sisters got married. The second day after she left on her honeymoon, the one at home received this telegram: "Sister, I don't care what you do with your cat, but you let my cat out."

(This chapter consists of a talk given at Ohio University by invitation of Louis Bromfield at a meeting of "Friends of the Land," November 28, 1949.)

CHAPTER 13

THOMAS B. METCALFE

The Literary Club
March 30, 1936

About the year 1795 there arrived in Nicholas County, Kentucky, a proud young Virginian, riding a noble steed. He was given to boasting and confident of the fleetness of his horse, he bantered the neighbors for a race. It was well known to a few that a couple of the best racers in the county had been repeatedly run against one another and were of about the same speed. A poor boy of that neighborhood had, for the amusement of the owners, ridden the two—he riding both horses, Roman style, at the same time. The Virginian was notified that, if he would ride himself, they would run two horses with one rider against his and would bet what they could afford. The challenge was accepted and a meadow in a creek bottom (on my present farm) selected for a half-mile race. The day arrived; the three horses were brought forward. For the rider of the two appeared the boy, about half grown, barefooted, bareheaded, dressed in tow linen shirt and pantaloons of the same material. The dress was not assumed for the occasion but was the best his purse could bear. He was endowed with a well-formed head, a keen penetrating eye, a fearless but cheerful countenance; and was animated with a noble zeal for the occasion, believing the honor of Kentucky was at stake.

The riders mounted, the boy having one foot on each horse. The signal was given. Away went the racers at full speed and for about two hundred yards, it was uncertain who was ahead. The boy, in running near a stump, three feet high, did not guide exactly as he intended; the stump was leaped by one of the horses, which greatly disturbed the equilibrium of the rider but did not throw him. The Virginian's horse dashed ahead, the other two ran with great fleetness and at six hundred yards it was neck and neck. At the end of the race, the pair of horses was a full length ahead, amid the huzzas of the multitude. The young Virginian paid his losses without a murmur; a big treat was proposed by those in luck and accepted by the crowd. The successful rider was looked for, but could not be found; unaccustomed to applause, he had disappeared.

This story was taken from Collins' *History of Kentucky,* published in 1845, revised in 1874, easily that state's greatest storehouse of factual and fanciful lore.

Aside from the identity of the boy rider, the most striking point unconsciously made by the story is the effect of weight carrying on the speed of a race horse. The Virginian undoubtedly had the best horse, but his horse was carrying between one hundred and fifty and two hundred pounds, while the two horses ridden by one rider, who weighed about a hundred pounds, divided his weight between them, giving the pair a hundred pound advantage. This was offset by the perilous position of the young rider, and the interference of the stump simply prevented a runaway race for the couple. Credence is added to the tale by the comment that the Virginian later beat each horse when ridden one at a time by different jockeys.

The incident would never have been recorded except for the later renown of the sixteen-year-old boy who rode the pair of horses. He was Thomas B. Metcalfe, a prominent figure in Kentucky's political life a hundred and fifty years ago. Born of poor parents who had emigrated in 1780 from Virginia to Bourbon

County near Millersburg, young Metcalfe was apprenticed to a stonemason, his own uncle, at the age of sixteen. He not only learned this trade but also the fundamentals of architecture and building, although called upon to support several younger brothers and sisters. Except for a period served as militia officer in an Indian war, his twenties and thirties were occupied in building enterprises. The fame of his talents spread abroad, and proof of his genius is found in the many well-preserved structures, usually of stone, standing in Fayette, Bourbon, Nicholas and Mason counties. The courthouse at West Union, Ohio, still in use, was erected by him 175 years ago. One of his best efforts was the courthouse at Paris, since replaced following a fire. The bank at Millersburg, now restored and occupied as a residence by Mrs. Norton, librarian at Transylvania College, was built by Metcalfe before he was twenty years old (1799). He was responsible for the beautiful design, which includes an artistic doorway and cornice. The hammer he used on this building is still proudly exhibited by one of the old residents.

Among the numerous houses built and designed by Metcalfe, the most important is his own home, located midway between Lexington and Maysville on the famous pike connecting these two cities. When these buildings were constructed, there was only a trail through the dense forest, the famous Limestone Trace, made by the buffalo travelling for centuries to Blue Lick Springs for salt. Hence the name, Forest Retreat.* The old halfway tavern and post-barn are still standing at the foot of the hill below the house, landmarks of the stage coach days. Mr. Metcalfe's grave, marked by a single shaft, is about three hundred yards behind the house, only a few miles from that of Garrard—the only governors of Kentucky not buried at Frankfort. It is easy to understand that political offices would seek so capable a figure. Early in his career Mr. Metcalfe gained his beloved title, Old Stoneham-

*Ed. Note. Forest Retreat farm was purchased by the author in 1934 and the Governor's home restored. The name, Forest Retreat, was suggested by Henry Clay.

mer, when he was presented with an ebony handled replica of this tool at Chillicothe, Ohio, on the occasion of the delivery of a speech by him in behalf of William H. Harrison, presidential candidate. He afterwards carried it with him during all his own campaigns. Like his friend Henry Clay, he was conservative at a time when the radical paper money party was in the majority. He served his district many times in the assembly and his state in both the United States Senate and House of Representatives. When elected governor in 1828, he was the only successful candidate of his party for any office in the state and was able to control a hostile radical legislature. As governor, he caused to be built the first paved road west of the Alleghenies. This highway connected Lexington and Maysville, following the Limestone Trace, *luckily* passing in front of his home. It is still a marvel of road engineering. The numerous double arch stone culverts and bridges are still in perfect order; the original width is ample and the course is free of sharp turns because it was built to connect Lexington and Maysville by the shortest route. Blue Lick Springs of Indian battle fame; Mayslick, birthplace of Daniel Drake; and historic Washington are on this road, which held for years the carriage travel from all points west to the East. Governor Metcalfe also built the old State Capitol, which now houses the Kentucky Historical Society.

After a busy political life, Governor Metcalfe's unusual abilities were honored by his appointment to a specially created office: Director of State Public Improvements.

CHAPTER 14

FARM PHILOSOPHY

Literary Club
March 30, 1959

Many years ago I noticed there were usually a few early arrivals on meeting nights intently reading in the Literary Club library. Commenting to an old member on this laudable custom, I hoped that I too could find the time to read the papers I had missed. My club ideals were slightly shaken by the reply: "Those fellows! They are only reading their own old papers." I plead guilty to this bit of egotism, not to say narcissism. But it was accidental when I ran across a paper entitled, "Shall I Buy a Farm?" read before the club 20 years ago. I was amazed that I still agreed with its conclusions, the chief of which was that land is not as effective as good common stocks in a personal war against inflation. Since this was written, common stocks have gone up three times as much as land. Stocks produce dividends, have a ready market, and require no management, while farms show deficits, are nonliquid, and require personal attention. These things were said when some investment counsellors, having had their clients in common stocks in 1929, were now advocating Georgia land purchases.

Secure in the knowledge that doctors have always been given up to be the best advisers in business matters, I said in this fine paper that, if after all these warnings, a man continued to have the pioneer obsession that everyone should own land, one of three types should be acquired:

(a) Good productive farm land in a location where, if necessary, one would like to live or a plain corn-hog farm under professional management.

(b) Land of any kind with residential or business expansion prospects.

(c) Cheap marginal land with lumber, mineral or oil considerations combined with fishing and hunting possibilities; and that in any case amateur funds invested in either land or horses should be expendable if not expensible.

Ordinary farm land in most locations does not meet the requirements. An amazing number of men, ignorant of farming, have bought such farms and turned them over to hired men or crofters for management. This is the same mentality that prompts people at the races to bet on "good things" offered by seedy strangers. After the ensuing disillusionment, these citizens damn, respectively, farming and racing and call all connected with them crooked. The same kind of people blamed Mellon and Hoover when their paper profits evaporated in 1929. They never questioned their own judgment.

Except on a subsistence level, farming is a business subject to the same rules as other businesses, about 85 percent of which fail to make a profit. Farming is also a profession, an art, and a demanding avocation if combined with the production of purebred livestock. Under the spell of prices obtained by old establishments, the neo-farmer is chagrined to find that it is one thing to produce and another to sell and that he has involved himself in the world's most competitive enterprise. Neither the King Ranch, Calumet Farm, the New York Yankees, the Chicago *Tribune* nor P&G were made in a day and yet the big, new farmer expects immediate profits. Yawkey spent $10 million and 10 years before he won a pennant; Warren Wright went through 10 years and 10 trainers before he got Ben Jones and Whirlaway; King Ranch required 77 years to find oil, 65 years to find "Monkey," the genetic wonder from which Santa Gertrudis cattle were developed, and 83 years to breed the Kentucky Derby winner Bold Venture. Only after decades did Col. McCormick cash in on the King of England, Franklin Roosevelt and Andy Gump, and with all his millions Marshall Field could not defeat the *Tribune* establishment. Ben Ali Haggin with 500 mares on 13,000 acres near Lexington left some very fine barns but no imprint on thoroughbred pedigrees. Joe Widener invested $40 million and 40 years trying unsuccessfully to breed a Derby winner. John Madden, with little capital, bred six Derby winners, and during the same period Arthur Hancock and Hal Price Headley (founder of Keeneland) made large fortunes in the business of farming and racing without ever breeding a Derby winner. Widener, who devoted only his money to breeding, would not have been interested in Headley's results. The Philadelphia magnate was like Willie Dupont. Someone asked Mr. Dupont whether he got a thrill out of winning bets on his horses. "Unfortunately no," he said, "I never wager. All I could win would be money, and I already have that."

From these examples we make the trite observation that material success requires not only some capital of one's own or the modern substitute of using someone else's money, but also brains, dedication, and time. The cynic, usually a poor man, would say that the proper knowledge of tax laws is also needed. But even with all of these assets, many projects fail without timing and luck. Luck is said to be the result of bold, intelligent and repeated effort; but I submit, and there is a certain academic status for the idea, that some people are born lucky.

It seems that certain humans and animals possess a sixth sense, something like radar, which enables them to choose the proper crossroads on the way to their objectives. Dogs, carried hundreds of miles from their homes, have been known to return, and horses if given their heads will bring their lost riders back, usually by a shorter route, ignoring the longer trail by which they went. Such instances are well documented.

Unless one thinks he has this rare "sixth sense," he should refrain from bold extracurricular ventures. With this quality, plus some unneeded funds, plus the willingness to devote his spare time to serious effort, one may have a cure for his usual illusions of retirement if a farm is acquired early enough. Of course, a doctor, if successful in an avocation, must be prepared to pay a heavy price for it. People, as patients, do not tolerate extraneous activity on the part of their doctor, who, to cut down on his prac- tice, needs only (a) to talk about retiring or (b) to engage suc- cessfully in a conspicious hobby, be it farming or winning golf cups.

Whether he wins or loses financially, the amateur farmer does have potential artistic and spiritual compensation. Also, livestock produces a valuable byproduct, manure; in other words materials for conversation and Literary Club papers. Besides, he can always gain satisfaction from tidying up the place, improving soil, and watching the greenness of a pasture intensified by the rays of the setting sun. We have only a few rural areas which compare aesthetically with the countryside of Europe (parts of New England, the Pennsylvania Dutch Country, and central Kentucky). In most places one sees fallen down wire fences and out-buildings, weeds, and eroded, treeless hillsides. Our average full-time farmer blames the appearance of his farm on lack of time and capital. After we had levelled and replanted a large rocky field, one of my irreverent neighbors said, "Think what the Lord could have done if he had had all that money!"

Robert Frost, the poet, loved his New England farm. He said a farmer must enjoy the "tentativeness" of things. A retiree needs fear and worry to keep his glands of internal secretion working and his body in good health. For this a retiree can use the ten- tativeness of farming. If he likes it and can afford it, he can't lose, regardless of profits or losses. With proper management, personal or bought, he will win. Management is the soul of any business.

CHAPTER 15

SOME FOIBLES OF MAN

Man constantly encounters problems, both physical and spiritual. In any situation self-preservation is the chief concern of all living things. Man is no exception. That is why man is selfish. Voltaire said, "He does best by the world who does best by himself." Selfishness is fine if it does not damage others or the world in general.

Even man's religions are selfish. The results are not all bad whether good deeds and charitable deductions are for business or social climbing or bribes for a ladder to Heaven. Many people, otherwise intelligent and down-to-earth, indulge in prayer. Prayers are good if they are humble. At worst they are harmless even if many are selfish and illogical. God gives man intelligence to handle his affairs. It seems presumptuous to inundate the Deity with personal problems and even more so to ask favoritism at the expense of another. The preacher "who went out a hunting all on one Sunday morn" and encountering a charging grizzly bear, prayed, "Oh Lord, if you can't help me, please don't help that grizzly bear," obviously believed in prayer even if he asked only for neutrality.

It took a good old country "boy" living near my Kentucky farm to put prayer in the proper perspective. This born again Baptist preacher went to a Baptist convention in Los Angeles and decided to return a day ahead of his reservation. All seats for both days were sold, but he was able to exchange tickets with a colleague. He arrived home safely. His friend's plane crashed, killing all on board. In his prayer at the meeting on the following Sunday he was giving thanks to the Lord for changing planes when he suddenly stopped, rose and said: "Folks, I just thought of something. Let's leave the Lord out of this. What was He a-doing for the brother who took my seat?"

Man is confused about his gods and even his friends. Jews and Indians believe that god is a spiritual force which controls the universe. Other Western men believe in a personal god. In his confusion man says the dog is his best friend. This is not true. This fine animal has long been a sentimental favorite but is a prime asset only to blind people, Eskimos, and quail shooters. The horse ranks higher among men's animal friends. At first only a source of food, the horse has been man's closest ally at war, at work, and at play for nearly all of the last 5000 years, as proven by Blegen's excavations of the various levels of Troy. Bees deserve a high rank. Bees, through cross-pollination of legumes, plants and trees, are responsible for most of the world's food supply. Grass, whose virtues were grandiloquently described by Senator Ingalls in his classic speech, also is high on the list.

But, of all living things, trees are the greatest assets to man and the Earth. Trees are self-renewable and require little labor. I devote the next chapter to them. As I said in a previous book, an Arkansas sheriff had a different view of the greatest thing in the world. When told that a risque show was about to hit town, he snapped his red suspenders and said, "I'll be there. If they utter one off-color word, I'll run 'em out of town." The show opened with the sheriff in the front row and a leading man sitting on stage reading a newspaper. Suddenly a voluptuous blonde rushed in gushing, "Oh, Hector. What is the greatest thing in the world?" Whereupon the sheriff jumped up, pointed his finger at the actor, and said, "Young man, if you answer that question,

I'll throw the whole company in jail".

The sheriff was close, but he was wrong. The greatest thing in the world is trees. The greatest benefactor is the man who plants or preserves the most trees. The Indians worshipped trees. In this connection I later quote my grandmother who was half Shawnee. The inscription on her tombstone reads, "Daughter of Tecumseh." Court records attest this and the family believes it even if Sam Johnson warned that lapidary inscriptions are not made under oath. Johnson anticipated the spirit of this whole book.

CHAPTER 16

TREES

The Literary Club 1984

"Poems are written by fools like me,
But only God can make a tree"

So said a poet, Joyce Kilmer. There are better assistants to God than I am. Some people may even appreciate trees more than I do. But I am a cut above some people. A stranger, riding on a train to Kentucky, seated next to an old native lady, remarked on the beauty of the landscape. "You mean them old hills and trees", she said. "They's all right for tourists and picnickers, but they's hell on mules and women."

Many people's appreciation of trees is the level of their appreciation of music. They know nothing about music, but they like the noise music makes. They know nothing about trees, but they like trees — as long as trees don't get in their way.

Man has many valuable allies in the animal kingdom, but the Earth's most valuable product is in the vegetable kingdom. It is trees.

Without trees there would be no life on Earth for there would have been no oxygen. About 400 million years ago mosses were the only living matter in an atmosphere of carbon dioxide. There was no oxygen, but there was photosynthesis, which created first ferns and then forests out of carbon with oxygen as the by-product. Thus trees made all life possible. They furnish material for a thousand uses; their rotted leaves create topsoil; trees ameliorate the climate, help purify the air and beautify the landscape. Acting as lightning rods, they sacrifice themselves to save people and buildings. Geologic changes buried trees, creating our gas, coal and oil.

For 300 hundred million years the globe was so warm that boundless forest covered the Earth from pole to pole. Forty million years ago trees were about the size and variety found today. About one million years ago the temperature at the poles drastically fell, burying the polar regions under ice, causing a succession of glaciers extending into the temperate zones. The trees grew back by contiguity after each glacier, the last one, occurring only 22,000 years ago, forming the present Ohio River.

When the white man first came to Ohio, a squirrel could travel from Lake Erie to Cincinnati without touching the ground. By 1955 the wooded area of Ohio had shrunk to 6 percent. Now it is up to 25 percent. *The next time you are in the library look up Gilbert Imlay's original description of the Ohio Valley as the first settlers saw it. He reported a hollow sycamore which would hold 32 men. Collins, in his *History of Kentucky,* reported an apple tree on my farm eight feet in diameter.

The Indians lived in this region 15,000 years without damage. They adapted themselves to the environment rather than the environment to themselves. The Indians believed the Great Spirit dwelled in all living things, especially trees. In the sounds made by the wind in the trees they heard the voice of the Great Spirit speaking to them. The rustling of the green leaves of spring, the dry leaves of autumn, in leaves moistened by dew and the winter wind in the bare branches, all made distinctive sounds varying with the type of tree and intensity of the wind. The medicine men

* Quoting Steve Sandfort, Cincinnati Park Systems

used the variations of these sounds to predict the weather and future events. I have never heard this discussed, but I have it on the authority of my great grandmother who was half Shawnee. I remember hearing her say, "Those oak leaves sound like falling weather is coming."

The Indians worshipped trees, especially certain ones. They insisted on signing so-called treaties with whites under ancient trees. Some of these trees remained landmarks, such as the Logan Elm near the Scioto River. Chief Logan refused to sign the treaty after Lord Dunmore's war, but he made a famous speech under this tree. There is nothing wrong with the Judeo-Christian religion that a touch of Indian philosophy would not help.

When Imlay passed down the Ohio Valley on the Kentucky side, he came upon an isolated pioneer. "You must be happy here, surrounded by all this beauty," remarked Imlay. "Beauty, Hell," replied the pioneer. "I'm surrounded by Indians and all those damned trees." Except for the Germans, the early settlers in the hills around Cincinnati were urban English or Scotch-Irish with no horticultural background. They used trees for forts, furniture and houses. Otherwise trees were enemies hiding Indians and preventing cultivation. In most areas they cut down all the trees, rolled them to the bottom of the hill and burned them, leaving the waterways barren for erosion. When I got my original farm 50 years ago, it hadn't been as hard hit as most, but there were gullies you could hide a truck in. The pioneers plowed a field until it gave out. You can still see some of the pioneer hillsides near Cincinnati, now covered with rocks, briars, cedars, and locust trees. Later, iron ore furnaces, requiring an acre of trees to a ton of ore, and still later, lumbering, completed the devastation. The second growth consists mostly of less desirable species. There are a few original trees in parks, in such places as the Red River Gorge, and on Bluegrass estates where they never plowed fields in sight of the house. We have four pristine trees at Forest Retreat, two oaks, a sycamore and a silver poplar. We recently lost a

300-year-old silver poplar, three times the maximum age of this kind of tree.

Cincinnati has had some famous old trees. One is a bur oak, said to be 500 years old, still standing on Lew Gatch's place in Milford. Another was Lea's Oak, which stood so long on Glenmary near Brookline in Clifton. This tree, discovered by Thomas Gibson Lea and classified by Bartramas Quercum Leana, was a cross between a shingle oak and a black oak. A hybrid, its acorns were sterile and only a few others were ever found.

Cincinnati has been a favorable place for trees, located near the terminal moraine, adjacent to trees in Kentucky. Kentucky was the finest forested area ever found by man. The central region was park-like with a scattering of large trees in the cane meadows. Eons of rotted vegetation on this plateau of rocks, high in calcium and phosphate, spewed up by a geological fault, produced the Blue Grass section, so called because the native grass had a blue bloom in May.

As Cincinnati developed, trees on the steep hills were undisturbed by cultivation and housing, especially in Buttercup Valley and other places. But it was a tree conscious citizenry that made Cincinnati a city of trees. Beginning 140 years ago trees were planted or preserved in Spring Grove Cemetery, Burnet Woods, the Zoo and city parks, especially Mt. Airy Forest. Cornelius Hauck planted a small arboretum; Stan Rowe planted a large private arboretum and also founded the Nature Center. The canal and old markets preserved open spaces for trees on Court Street, in Piatt Park, and on Fountain Square. The city has recently augmented a street planting program. Golf clubs, especially Camargo and the Cincinnati Country Club, have extensive tree planting programs which make them informal arboretums. If pressure should occur to take over these clubs for other purposes, the trees will be a deterrent. Trees have saved several inner city golf courses.

This preservation and planting was sparked by such leaders

as Dr. John Warder, R. B. Buchanan and Stan Rowe, park board members such as George Stimson and Gus Nippert, and professionals such as Spring Grove's Cliff Runyan, who helped start the tree planting program (native arboretum) at my farm. Famous pros still operating are: Fred Payne and Steve Sandfort of the park system and Jim Berry, Cincinnati Nature Center.

Cincinnati's first nationally known dendrologist was Thomas Gibson Lea. He discovered Lea's Oak and classified all the plants of the city. In the first half of this century we had Lucy Braun, professor of botany at the University of Cincinnati, under whom I made field trips in 1914. Her book, *The Deciduous Trees of Eastern North America,* is a classic. *Sycamore Shores,* a book by our old member, Clark Firestone, also is interesting.

Dr. John Warder was the greatest tree man in the history of Cincinnati. In a previous club paper, I described his career, his tree planting on his Scarlet Oaks place in Clifton, at Spring Grove Cemetery and on his North Bend estate. Dr. Warder founded the American Forestry Association, which recently held its centennial meeting in Cincinnati in honor of Dr. Warder. He founded the President's Grove in Eden Park and was co-founder of Arbor Day, an annual practice called Tu-b Shevat, observed by Jews for hundreds of years.

Like Dr. Warder, the present Garden Club of America is promoting the planting of a greater variety of trees. We haven't enough trees with bright red or yellow foliage.

The greatest modern enemies of trees and wildlife are bulldozers, chain saws, and, worst of all, motorized mowers. A half of each large yard should be left wild. All other areas, consistent with their use, should remain unmowed. Trees are great competitors. When attacked by pests, some trees can secrete a pesticide. Trees grow in spite of weeds, and the lowly weeds are underrated. They add organic matter, potash, and nitrogen to the soil, provide food and shelter for wildlife, food for earthworms and other life in the soil, and ground cover to prevent erosion.

We must return to the ancient Greek view that anything which fitted a purpose was beautiful; for example, an untouched landscape and normal shoes on women's feet.

So what is the greatest thing in the world? The greatest thing in the world is trees. The greatest philanthropist is the person who saves or plants the most trees.

CHAPTER 17

RARE NIGHTS AT MY CLUB

Members soon learn the highlights of the club's history, but few have known the full story. it lies in the activities of its members, their impact on the club, their achievements of local and national significance and the 1,500 books they have written. To do it justice would require a man, acquainted with the club's traditions and oral legends, who would spend months researching the minutes, the 8,000 papers, the guest book, the memorials, and such outside sources as old newspapers, diaries, and biographies.

A full paper could be written on the renaissance of the club in 1864, when 42 leading citizens were made new members through the efforts of Reuben Stephenson, Charles Dexter and A. T. Goshorn, who later was knighted by Queen Victoria for his direction of the Philadelphia Exposition.

The lifelong devotion of Rutherford B. Hayes to the club is also a lengthy story, which is better told in Williams' biography than in our own records. Hayes never lost touch with the club and gave two dinners for it in the White House. Hayes took several members to Washington, but some were already established there in distinguished careers, including Cleveland Abbe, who, at the Cincinnati Abbe Observatory, started the first daily weather reports and later developed the U.S. Weather Bureau; Ainsworth Spofford, who directed and made the Congressional Library; and Dr.

John S. Billings, famous librarian, founder of the Index Medicus and president of the A.M.A.

President Taft also entertained the club, but he sent a limited number of invitations. The secret was so well kept that some members never knew of it and, as far as I can find, this is the only mention of it in our records.

Many of our best moments were provided by famous guests, some of whose names are not in the guest book, including Dr. W.J. Mayo, Charles Raven, chancellor of Cambridge, Cassius M. Clay, Ralph Waldo Emerson, and others. Some came before the guest book and some were not even mentioned in the minutes, but the circumstances of their visits have been handed down to us orally and in the written reminiscences of the members. Only one nonmember has ever read the main paper, but many have spoken informally.

Dr. Lawrence Carr in a paper vividly recalled the visit of Booker T. Washington (1903), who, after the regular paper, made an impressive address in which he described at length the program at Tuskegee and, Dr. Carr said, asked nothing for his race other than a chance to obtain an education. Dr. Carr also mentioned the visit of Joachim Miller, "Poet of the Sierras," who recited his "Bird" poem and told of his mountain home. Guests such as Oscar Wilde before his disgrace, Opie Read, Thomas Henry Aldrich, General Noyes, Walter Hines Page, and others deserve a full paragraph.

Joe Jefferson was a frequent guest after his performance at Pike's Opera House, and Charlie Wilby often spoke of him. During the last 4 years of Mr. Wilby's life, the writer frequently called for him at his home in Walnut Hills and carried him to the club. On one of these trips, he recounted the time Jefferson was introduced to Judge Yaple, a great wit, who loved to look like Shylock. The great actor stood amazed at the resemblance and forthwith offered him the part in his upcoming *Merchant of Venice*. Concealing his pleasure, Yaple said, rather sternly, "Sir, you were introduced as Joe Jefferson. I assume your real name is Joseph and I am surprised you don't use this famous name, whether you deserve it or not." Jefferson admitted his defeat and drank many toasts to Shylock and Joseph.

Cassius M. Clay, the "Lion of Whitehall," was present at the 4th (1854) anniversary dinner. The presses on which he printed the *True American* had been moved to Cincinnati from Lexington and he was the guest, probably of his Yale friend, Alphonso Taft, but there is no record of his remarks that night. Since Hayes was president of the club and Salmon P. Chase also was present, it is easy to guess that slavery was the keynote.

This author's two rarest moments were the visits of Amos Alonzo Stagg in 1926 and Victor Reicherts' recent guest, Robert Frost. Mr. Stagg, Walter Camp's first "All American" and still in his prime, told us of his long tenure under President William Rainey Harper and correctly predicted the demise of his Y.M.C.A. kind of football. There was a physical resemblance between Frost and Stagg, and both were long lived. "Teetotaler" Stagg lived to be over a hundred but Frost made it only to ninety, possibly because of his drinking. Frost, aged 86, had two martinis before dinner and listened attentively to the paper. In his talk afterwards he said the difference between Rabbi Victor Reichert and St. Jerome is that St. Jerome studied the New Testament to show how much one needed the New while Reichert studies the Old Testament to prove you can get along without the New. He also recited a couplet "Forgive me, O Lord, my little Jokes on Thee, and I shall forgive your great big joke on me." In the guest book he wrote, "I dared not be radical when young for fear of becoming conservative when old."

On one of the greatest nights in its history the club had two famous guests, the lifelong abstainer George Cable of "Creole Days" fame and Mark Twain, who loved his liquor. After the regular paper Cable spoke briefly and was followed by Twain, who spoke only about Cable, first praising his literary genius, then kidding him unmercifully. "Gentlemen," he said, "You don't realize you are harboring a ferocious man. In his hometown the men fear for their lives as well as their wives." All of which Cable seemed to enjoy until Twain asked the club never to invite him again with Cable, because, he said, "this man drinks so much there isn't enough left for me." At this, Cable, live with rage, jumped to his feet and said, "Sam, you are a liar! I have never in my life touched a drop of your poison." The secretary reported that it took quite a time to cool off Cable and convince him that Twain was joking and also indirectly apologizing for his own overindulgence.

The club's greatest coup was brought off in its very first year, when it induced Ralph Waldo Emerson to come here for a series of 5 public lectures. The members all belonged to the Young Men's Mercantile Library Association, and to attract more attention than the young Literary Club could provide, the lectures were advertised under the auspices of the better known organization.

Emerson never met with the club, but the club met twice with him. One day they took him on a wine drinking picnic to Fort Ancient, and on a Sunday night they gathered in his suite at the Burnet House. Hayes in his diary says the three hour-session was almost entirely devoted to London Clubs and English writers. In the fashion of the day, Emerson had spent more time in England than west of Boston and knew all the British literary figures. His favorite club was the Athenaeum, and his favorite writers were Shakespeare, Wordsworth and Scott, whom he called truly creative, adding that we had never had a single creative genius. The discussion ended on the inevitable Transcendental note. When asked about his new antipuritan, Unitarian philosophy, Emerson seemed vexed and dismissed it by saying that the Transcendentalist was a self-reliant man with his own brand of immortality. They had guaranteed only his expenses but were able to give him $560.00, and he seemed delighted, saying he would place it with his brother, a broker in New York. The lecture series also was put into a profitable book.

At the fifth anniversary dinner a delightful imaginery letter from Emerson was read by artist Ben McConkey. Here is the gist of it:

"Gentlemen,

I accept your kind invitation to eat supper with you at your fifth anniversary celebration. I do not mean I shall leave Concord by steam and rail and present myself at your feast in person. That would be a mere sensuous performance. Hence you perceive I accept in the transcendental sense, the only practical sense, for the ideal alone is, and the actual is not. Therefore, I and not you shall eat the supper and though you shall seem to pay for it, yet not you, I shall pay for it. Of course, the pecuniary consideration would be of no moment to you, as I am well aware, having myself, on a former occasion, furnished suppersfit for the Gods which the Cincinnati public accepted, nearly gratis.

P.S. Man is an endogenous Microcosm!"

Obviously fake letters from Carlyle and Thackeray were also read later in the evening, but the Emerson spoof at first took in some of the audience, including Henry Blackwell. Mr. Blackwell, a long-time member, was married to the feminist Lucy Stone, a native of Massachusetts and friend of Emerson. He was proud of his famous wife and wrote papers in favor of woman "sufferage." He hated always to be introduced as the husband of Mrs. Lucy Stone and was one of those against participation of women in any club affair.

Before the Civil War we met each week throughout the whole year, and the big event of the summer was an informal Fourth of July outing, with patriotic speeches. When summer meetings were abandoned, an outing on the last meeting in June became a permanent substitute. Preceding the Fourth of July celebrations, there were annual arguments culminating in a vote on liquor versus women. If the drinkers won, it was unthinkable to invite the wives, but when the dry Hayes forces prevailed, the ladies participated. Fifty years later there were three wineless

Ladies Receptions in the club rooms, but it was eighty-odd years before the first and only woman ever attended any part of a regular meeting. She was the widow of member Everhard Jack Appleton, a poet and newspaper writer, whose family had donated Harvard's Appleton Chape. When the chapel was razed, Havard sent one of its stained glass windows to Mrs. Appleton. She gave it to the club, where it was placed in the wall of the library, and no one could think of an excuse to keep her away from the dedication meeting.

There have been humorous papers on ladies vis-a-vis the club, but it was a twice-divorced, newly married member who coined a certain classification* of women. The president, on behalf of the club, publicly extended congratulations to him on his new venture, whereupon the much married member rose and said, "Gentlemen, many of you are curious to know why I had to shuck two wives before finding an ideal mate. The explanation is simple. My first wife was a blond, over-sexed chorus girl and my second was that rigid, Grandin Road intellectual. The first was all ass and no class and the second, all class and no ass."

*This incident was apocryphal, not in our records.

CHAPTER 18

RUTHERFORD B. HAYES
AND THE LITERARY CLUB

The Literary Club

One hundred years ago today at the 27th Anniversary Dinner of the Literary Club there was great excitement. All the talk was about the election only days away. The excitement was over the Republican candidate for the Presidency, Rutherford B. Hayes, a member of the club.

The club never had a more devoted member nor one who contributed more to its development and to the atmosphere which gave it immortality. He never willingly missed a meeting. During his three terms as governor he often slipped down on Saturday night, had two meetings at the White House as President, attended two anniversary dinners as ex-President, and remained a member until his death in 1893, though he moved from Cincinnati in 1873.

There is much untapped material on him buried in our archives, there are three papers on the "disputed" election, but, strangely enough, no member has ever written a paper on Hayes. In this centennial year of his election to the Presidency, I thought it timely to assemble (before much of it is lost) information relating to his membership in the club and his career in Cincinnati.

Sponsored by John Zachos and Stanley Matthews and elected two months after the club was founded, he at once became a leader in its activities and in recruiting prestigious older men such as Salmon P. Chase and Alphonso Taft, who first paid no attention to the upstart organization.

It was a period, extending to World War I, when patriotism and Christian mores were rigidly defended if not always practiced, when one drank much or nothing, when one literally observed the Sabbath or went to Hell, which explains why, as a boy, I preferred to visit my drinking uncle who permitted us to go fishing on Sunday and why it still worries me that I prefer the company of an Adlai Stevenson but always vote for a Cal Coolidge. There would have been no such ambivalence about Hayes.

At that time and in my own memory the Fourth of July meant the reaffirmation of patriotism to all responsible citizens, and it was on this serious basis that RBH conceived and led the first annual Independence Day Literary Club outing held in 1850 at Latonia Springs, with Ainsworth R. Spofford the designated orator and Wm. Guilford the poet. Most of the later outings were held in the ancient Mound Builders Fort at Plainville.

This event became second in importance only to the Anniversary Dinner until the Civil War, and drinking was a part of it. After Hayes' marriage his wife and Lucy Stone, the woman's rights wife of Henry Blackwell, wanted to attend these affairs. This was permissible since they were not official meetings, but the presence of women precluded drinking. It became an annual contest between those who wanted wine and song and those who wanted women and song, Hayes, though not a "teetotaler," voting with the "drys" who thought the occasion too solemn for alcoholic revelry.

Hayes was a perennial leader in these outings, but his contributions were more restrained, more in the present fashion, and his favorite declamation, requested on many occasions, was Webster's oration on the Union in reply to Hayne. His club contemporaries and his political opponents were far more fiery and flowery. Nor could it have been said of him, as it was of club friends Salmon P. Chase and Sen. Tom Corwin, that his pertinacity in argument was inextinguishable and his beliefs utterly impregnable. Hayes took reasoned, often middle positions and, as a leader throughout the debating years of the club, was apt to be the peacemaker.

Years later he said the Literary Club had the single greatest impact on his career, specifically that:

1. The club was his greatest intellectual experience.
2. The debates prepared him for the hustings by sharpening his knowledge of the issues and by training him in public speaking.
3. The months of basic training in the volunteer Literary Club drill unit, the Burnet Rifles, under West Pointers R. W. Burnet and Gen. John Pope (fellow club member) and Sgt. Richman, prepared him for advancement in army rank finally to major general.
4. That the members of the club were his most powerful and active supporters in all of his political campaigns.
5. That members of the club encouraged him to locate in Cincinnati and that his various law partners were members of the club, as were the judges who referred court cases to him that started his practice.

Hayes more than repaid the huge debt by his unswerving lifetime devotion, by the wisdom of his leadership in the formative years in creating a nonactivist, sociable "Liberty Hall" and seeking the brightest minds from all walks of life to inhabit it, regardless of their politics or religion. The club has forever profited by the name Hayes and others made for themselves, which, along with the soundness of its traditions, have given it longevity. RBH also repaid the individual members of the club, many of whom were importantly involved in various phases of his career. (All names hereafter mentioned were members of the club.)

Hayes, Legal and Political Career

After graduating at Kenyon and the Harvard Law School, practicing law for five years at Lower Sanduskey, and staying out of the Mexican War (for health reasons on recommendation of Dr. R. D. Mussey), he was encouraged by his Kenyon college schoolmates John Zachos, W. K. Rogers, Stanley Matthews and Manning Force to locate in Cincinnati, at first sharing with John W. Herron two rooms on 3rd Street, one used for their office, the other for Hayes' bachelor's quarters. Within a year, after brief association with W. C. McDowell followed by a partnership with W. K. Rogers, Hayes and Rogers entered the firm of Richard Corwine, a leading attorney of the city. When Rogers temporarily moved to Minnesota and Fred Hausserauk became minister of Bolivia, Hayes took Hausserauk's place in the firm of Markbreit and Hausserauk, the leading German attorneys of the city. Since Hayes spoke German and was anti-"Know-Nothing," the Germans liked him, thus broadening his legal and political base, enabling him to become city solicitor (1858), his first public office, for which he had the support of Aaron Perry, Geo. Hollister and Fred Hausserauk, members of city council, and the influence of Stanley Matthews, Alphonso Taft, Manning Force, and Richard Corwine.

One secret of Hayes' success was that he retained the admiration and support of his friends and former associates in all his moves upward. By birth, inclination and schooling he was a gentleman, and by his ability and legal education he was a lawyer's lawyer. Many of his early cases were court appointed by Judge R. B. Warden, Stanley Matthews and Donn Piatt. He was associated with Salmon P. Chase and Timothy Walker in defending a fugitive slave, and many of his best cases were referred by other lawyers. After the war he was associated with the firm of E. F. Noyes and R. H. Stephenson and lived off and on in Cincinnati until 1873, but public offices and the war practically ended his legal career.

Hayes and all the Literary Club members volunteered for the Union Army at the outbreak of the Civil War at a special meeting on 4/17/61 organized by Hayes. A unit was formed and drilled intensively until individually they were called for duty. Unlike almost all volunteers, Hayes served throughout the war, was wounded three times, the only President, except Monroe, ever wounded in action. While in the army, refusing to take a furlough to campaign, he was elected to Congress in Cincinnati with the backing of the army in the field and such local powers as Taft, Kittredge, and Stephenson.

During his two terms in Congress his great accomplishment was to found the modern Congressional Library by combining the previously puny Library of Congress with the Smithsonian Library, selecting Ainsworth R. Spofford to head it and, both as Congressman and President, insured the development of a great library by enlisting two more members of the Literary Club to help Spofford: Gen. Manning Force, who was induced to add his father's famous library, and Dr. John Shaw Billings, founder of the New York Public Library among his varied achievements.

Members of the club were also mainstays in Hayes' three successful races for governor and for the Presidency. E. F. Noyes, Murat Halstead, Judges Herron, Force, Warden, Taft, Matthews and others, especially Wm. H. Smith (head of the Western News Syndicate which became the Associated Press). Noyes had lost a leg in the Civil War, but this did not subdue his activities. Benjamin Rush Cowen (elected to L. C. in 1887), Chairman of the State Republican Committee and nationally known for his work in the Department of the Interior, was beaten for the gubernatorial nomination by R H, but Cowen nevertheless ran Hayes' campaign.

One hundred years ago (1876) the Republican National Convention was held in Music Hall (Cincinnati) and several prestigious delegates and members of the local committee on arrangements were members of the club. Noyes placed Hayes in nomination. After the early ballots the vote stood: Blaine-285, Conkling-99,

Morton-125, Bristow-113, Hayes-61, others-69. At this point Ingersoll made his famous "Plumed Knight" speech, setting off a
wild, long demonstration for Blaine. It was now time for the supper recess. When the chairman ordered an evening session, the
head of the local committee ruled that a night meeting could not
be held because the lights were out of order. Further balloting
had to be postponed until the next day. In the meantime the Hayes
forces (especially Smith, Herron, Matthews, Hollister, Force and
Noyes) worked all night cooling out the delegates, convincing
them that neither Blaine nor Conkling could get a majority and
that Hayes, with his untainted, moderate, religious image was
the candidate best equipped to bring victory to a party that had
lost its majority in Congress on account of the corruption of the
Grant administration. Grant himself, only indirectly to blame, had
taken recent steps to improve public confidence by appointing
Alphonso Taft attorney general and by stopping military rule in
some sections of the South.

The Hayes forces did their work well, especially two newspaper
men. Senator Morton, influenced by Smith, and Bristow,
influenced by Halstead who had been backing this liberal
Republican, threw their votes to Hayes, who narrowly won on
the seventh ballot. The turning point was the switch of the
Mississippi delegates headed by George Settle, black friend of
W. C. Cochran.

It was another in a long series of narrow wins for Hayes, who
never had the luxury of a "laughter." However, in all of his campaigns, even in the one he lost, he always outran his party. If
there was any intrigue, and there certainly was much infighting
by both parties in the presidential nomination and election, Hayes
cannot be blamed personally for, as was customary then with candidates, he stayed out of it, remaining in Columbus until the eve
of his inauguration.

I heard W. C. Cochran say one night at the club that even
though he was a member of the local committee on arrangements

for the convention, he was never sure whether the lights were sabotaged as claimed by opposing delegates but he was sure that if a vote had been taken directly after Ingersoll's speech, there would have been a stampede to Blaine and that if the convention had not been held in Cincinnati, where Hayes had so many powerful friends, he would not have been nominated.

The Literary Club and the Disputed Election

After the election in 1876, when both parties claimed the electoral votes of Oregon, South Carolina, Florida and Louisiana, Congress (in which the House had a Democrat majority and the Senate a Republican majority), set up a 15-man electoral commission, 5 from the Senate, 5 from the House, and 5 from the Supreme Court, composed of seven Democrats, seven Republicans and one supposedly neutral, to decide the validity of the votes of the four states. By a vote of 8 to 7 in each instance, the commission awarded all four states to Hayes, giving him the Presidency by one electoral vote.

Literary Club members including Noyes, Hollister, Morton, Taft, W. H. Smith, Force, Cowen, Matthews and others were involved at a high level, not only in the campaign but also in the dispute which was not decided until March 3, 1877. At the proceedings of the electoral commission Hayes was represented by Stanley Matthews, Judge Tilden was represented by George Hoadley and Sen. Oliver P. Morton was the leading Republican member of the electoral commission. Hayes stayed out of the controversy, received the news of his election while enroute to Washington, and was sworn in the next day by Chief Justice Morrison R. Waite, grandfather of Henry Waite, a member of the Literary Club.

The picture of Hayes which hangs in the Literary Club was presented to the Club by Edmund Dexter on 3/10/1877, three days after Hayes took office. On 4/28/1877 J. W. Herron and Alphonso Taft proposed RBH for honorary membership. One speaker referred to him as "His Excellency," but the Democrats, few but vociferous, erupted in opposition and the secretary reported a stormy meeting. One said Hayes should be called "His Fraudulency," that anyway there was too much "Hayes" in the club. Another accused John Herron of angling for a federal judgeship, but the main argument was that the constitution did not provide for honorary members. Thew and Nathaniel Wright contended that anything not contradicted by the constitution could be acted on, the vast majority agreed, RBH became the first honorary member. Later a provision for electing honorary members (now 52) was added to the constitution.

On 10/28/78, three days after the regular Literary Club anniversary dinner in Cincinnati, RBH had a second dinner at the White House especially for members living in Washington, nearly all there through presidential appointments. Others in the capital, including Senator Matthews, couldn't come, and G. Thos. Ewing, Jr. and Donn Piatt, Democrats, still bitter over the election, wouldn't come. At the dinner were five nonmembers: Mrs. Hayes, Mrs. Rodgers, Gen. and Mrs. Hastings (the President's daughter) and Webb Hayes. The members living in Washington were R. B. Warden, W. K. Rogers, Cleveland Abbe, T. C. H. Smith, Ainsworth R. Spofford, and Aaron Dutton. Those from Cincinnati were Secretary S. P. Butler, Dr. R. D. Mussey, C. F. James, Henry Reed, Henry Borden, R. H. Warder, J. E. Hatch, and Wm. Guilford. Secretary Butler did not comment on the sparse attendance but said that nearly all of the members at one time or another during the Hayes administration visited the White House, where the "open Sesame" for an immediate audience was "The Literary Club."

After the "wineless" dinner, the ladies retired, Spofford acted as chairman in the absence of President Eugene Bliss, and Dr. R. D. Mussey, Cincinnati's all-time most famous surgeon, read a budget consisting of poems by Rogers, Butler and Guilford and a humorous paper on Hayes by Judge James. The preponderance of poetry reflected the lingering but steadily losing literary fashion of the day. However, prose was still regarded as second rate, novels still regarded as sinful by the churches, and poets were the aristocrats of letters. On this occasion some of the poetry was in blank verse, some called "blankety blank" verse, and the rest was at best ad hoc, but the dinner was a legendary club event.

With the help of Mr. Watt Marchman, director of the Hayes Library at Fremont, Ohio, at least 14 members were found to have been appointed by Hayes to positions important enough to require Senate confirmation. Among them were W. K. Rogers, his secretary and public relations man, a job now requiring hundreds of men, E.F. Noyes, ambassador to France, and Stanley Matthews to the Supreme Court. He appointed others that did not require confirmation and several as governor, including his brother-in-law, Jos. Webb, to be superintendent of Longview.

RBH offered other appointments which were not accepted. Senator Oliver P. Morton of Indiana declined a cabinet position because of ill health, dying six months later. John W. Herron declined the offer of a federal judgeship to prove he had not been angling for the job (his grandson, Robt. A. Taft, inherited his stubbornness). Alphonso Taft declined any appointment because of age. Some Literary Club appointees were Mugwumps and at least two were Democrats (Gatchell and Warden). Many of the appointed jobs were highly desirable, especially the surveyors of customs which went to Stephenson and Smith. Smith, who headed RBH's press campaign, would have been White House press secretary had such a position been thought of in that day.

Literary Club members appointed, requiring confirmation by the Senate: (year elected to L.C. in parentheses after each name)
1. Anderson, Thomas McArthur (1858), son of Larz Anderson. lt. col. in the U.S. Army.
2. Bailey, David H. (1857), from Wilmington, Ohio. Consul general at Shanghai.

3. Gatchell, H. B. (1851). Supervisor of census for the First Census District of Georgia.

4. James, Charles P. (1851). Associate justice of the Supreme Court of the District of Columbia.

5. Leake, Joseph (1852). Attorney of the United States for the Northern District of Illinois.

6. Matthews, Stanley (1849). Associate justice of the Supreme Court of the United States.

7. Noyes, Edward F. (1857). Envoy extraordinary and minister plenipotentiary of the United States to France, who resigned.

8. Partridge, Charles A. (1854). Postmaster at Waukegan, Lake County, Ill.

9. Rogers, William K. (1852). President's secretary, special adviser and liaison with the press, the Congress, and the public, a job now done by hundreds of men.

10. Smith, Thomas Church Haskell (1852). Paymaster of the U.S. Army with rank of major.

11. Smith, William Henry (1861). Collector of customs for the District of Chicago. Smith was an anti-"Know-Nothing" genuine liberal.

12. Stephenson, Reuben H. (1849). Surveyor of customs for the port of Cincinnati.

13. Ward, James W. (1856). Postmaster at Corpus Christi, Texas.

14. Warden , Robt. B. Board of Health of District of Columbia.

Appointments not requiring confirmation:

1. Guilford, Wm. (1850). Clerk of Treasury Dept.

2. Dutton, Aaron (1854). Clerk of Dept. of Justice.

3. Force, Manning F. (1850) and Billings, Dr. John Shaw (1860). Consultants to the Library of Congress.

All the Literary Club appointees were able men and were confirmed without controversy.

Hayes crossed party lines many times to select men best suited to critical positions and best calculated to quiet the turmoil that again threatened the Union. One example was the appointment of Confederate General David Key of Tennessee to be secretary of the treasury. Nor was he afraid to appoint men to his cabinet who might overshadow him, including Carl Schurz.

During the first two years no president ever suffered the villification heaped upon him by a hostile press, by a hostile Congress, by Democrats in general who thought they had been robbed, and by his own party because of his independence in making appointments, because he sided with Democrat Geo. Pendleton on Civil Service reform, and because he stopped military rule in South Carolina and Louisiana, which gave the Democrats the disputed governorships of these states and solid one-party control of the South.

Among the most virulent critics of Hayes was Donn Piatt, a contemporary (1857) member of the Literary Club, who was publishing a magazine in Washington at the time of the election. Piatt's accusations against the President were so extreme that the attorney general indicted him for inciting rebellion. Hayes squashed this indictment and pardoned many others who actually plotted the overthrow of the administration.

The union of the states never faced a greater threat. If Hayes had been less diplomatic, if some leading Democrats had shown less restraint, if the country had not recently suffered through a bloody, inexcusable war, and if the south had not run out of resources, many think the country was ripe for another civil war or "Mexicanization" of the government.

Facts live. Campaign oratory dies. The facts are that Hayes did what his Literary Club supporters said he would do. He conducted clean administration, advanced the merit system, buried the bloody flag, helped education, backed sound money, helped enfranchise and educate negroes, all of which insured Garfield's election and would have reelected RBH had he obtained the nomination.

I have heard and read much speculation about his non-renomination, a rare instance in which the incumbent was not renominated. Everyone takes for granted the inextinguishable ambition of politicians but I doubt whether Hayes wanted another term, and I doubt whether Boss Conkling could have prevented his renomination (as was claimed) if Hayes had wanted to make a fight for it. Hayes had said all along that he would not stand for a second term, but (like the man who didn't want to go to a party but was insulted when not invited) RBH must have been disappointed when he was not asked to run.

His executive actions were those of a statesman, not calculated to please either the bosses or the rank and file of the party. He was getting old and tired of the battle of Washington and probably felt he had little to prove. Certainly his support of Garfield was not the reaction of a jealous man, nor were the philanthropic and statesmanlike activities of the rest of his life indicative of a disappointed or bitter man.

RHB studied Greek at Kenyon and for the L. C. once wrote an essay on Plato's admonition to elders to contribute their wisdom and means to the common good. He gained nothing financially from the Presidency, but was well to do, having inherited the large fortune of his foster father, Uncle Sardis Birchard, who was rich enough to have given Fremont a $50,000 library. RBH also reaped profits from land investments with Billy Rogers in Minnesota and the purchase of several thousand acres of West Virginia land for twenty cents an acre that later turned out to be prime coal and timber property.

In the use of his financial means and energies, RBH, in the years of his retirement, set a "Platonic" example which should be followed today by thousands of men of attainment. His activities were an extension of his lifelong ideas and interests, the development of his library (said to have been the best of any Presidents except possibly Jeffersons), involvement in education as trustee of Ohio State University and other educational projects, especially those for the underprivileged, both black and white.

In all his political and philanthropic life and in raising to maturity (three died in infancy) one daughter and four sons (all of whom and their descendants have been outstanding citizens), his wife was a partner, influential counsellor and loving ego sustainer.

When they were married in December 1850 at Lucy's home (141 W. 6th Cincinnati) one member said that, aside from the Hayes and Webb relatives, nearly all the male guests belonged to the Literary Club. His wife was a fine homemaker and, as the first First Lady to hold a college degree, she was interested in education for women, women's rights, moral and civil causes, temperance, missionary work, soldiers' homes, etc. Effective but not a follower of such radicals as Susan B. Anthony, Frances Wright and Lucy Stone, Lucy Hayes set a flawless example of the proper role of a President's wife, unsurpassed by that of any other First Lady.

Hayes, a Presbyterian, did not join Lucy's Methodist church, but the result was the same. He attended her church and Methodism set the tone of the White House. It was the only administration without alcohol, with daily morning religious services and with Sunday night hymn singing led by Vice President Wheeler and members of the cabinet.

A year after his wife's death RBH made his last visit to the Literary Club and was welcomed even by the die-hard Democrats, mollified by the fairness of his administration. In his remarks Hayes again said, as he had often said before, that he was indebted to Cincinnati for his wife and that he owed his success to the training, experience and stimulus in the club, especially between 1850 and 1861, and to the support and influence of its members in all of his campaigns, and that in all three of the law firms with which he had been connected, his partners were members of his beloved Literary Club.

What was RBH like as a man and as a President? Fortunately,

the truth emerges after prejudice, bitterness and opinions die. He was influenced, as all husbands should be influenced, by the fine moral, social and religious instincts of his intelligent, compassionate wife. He said he was influenced by the debates in the club on the issues of the time, and a study of the secretary's minutes showing the way he voted on the merits of the questions proves that in the decisions of his political life, he consistenily followed his youthful convictions.

Actually, RBH was a mature, highly educated man (age 28-40) when he took part in every debate held in the club. Here is the way he voted on a few of the questions debated:

	Hayes	Majority
Should univerisal education be furnished at public expense?	yes	yes
Should capital punishment be abolished?	no	no
Is the Monroe Doctrine right?	yes	yes
Is communism the ultimate destiny of society?	no	no
Ought the rich pay a higher rate of taxation?	yes	yes
Should traffic in alcoholic beverages be prohibited?	yes	no
Is the stage destructive of morality?	no	no (by one)
Should the U.S. try to get the whole continent?	no	no
Is "Manifest Destiny" defensible?	yes	yes
Should the press be totally free of legal restriction?	no	no
Should women have the right to vote?	no	split
Does a Devil exist?	no	no

Were the biblical miracles literally true?	no	no
Are human actions predestined?	no	no
Did Christ make any new revelations of truth?	no	yes (by one)
Is the Genesis account of creation geologically true?	no	no
Is orthodoxy defensible against rationalization?	no	no
Is slavery constitutional?	yes	yes
Is the Fugitive Slave Law constitutional?	yes	yes
Is the Know-Nothing movement beneficial?	no	split
Is the colonization (Liberia) of slaves worthy of support?	yes	yes
Should the Fugitive Slave Law be repealed?	yes	no (by one)
Is slavery justifiable?	no	no
Is extreme agitation against slavery advantageous to the cause of the slaves and the good of the Nation?	no	no
Is the extension of slavery dangergous to the durability of the Union?	yes	yes
Is the Kansas-Nebraska bill and Clay's compromise (1850) the best solution?	no	yes

The Club and Hayes favored Fremont for President in 1856.

The final debates were on the 64 dollar question: "Should the secession of a state be prevented by the coercive power of the federal government?" Debated in five sessions after which the club voted not to vote. The vast majority, including Hayes, were in favor of coercive measures *short of war.*

Like all great Americans (Washington, Lincoln, etc.) RBH was both a liberal and a conservative. In his feeling on current social needs, on religion and on education he would be classed today a liberal. On fiscal and economic matters he was a conservative.

Quoting old members whom I knew in my early years in the club (who personally knew Hayes) and reading incidental comments about him in club papers, RBH was described as genial, quiet, never dogmatic, well organized, a sound thinker, a good speaker, a fair debater and always a gentleman. In three long, scholarly papers written for the club on the "Disputed Succession" (one of them by southern Democrat Rouse) Hayes comes out clean, and he conducted a clean administration. If an administration is gauged by its success in meeting the problems of the time, by its integrity, and by its progressive policies, the Literary Club regarded RBH as one of our great Presidents.

Eslie Asbury
The 127th Anniversary Dinner of The Literary Club Oct.25, 1976.

CHAPTER 19

LOUIS BROMFIELD

The Literary Club 1986

Louis Bromfield was one of our most popular novelists. He was a significant person in my life. This chapter is based on many personal contacts with him, his daughter Ellen (Mrs. Carson Geld), and his lifelong secretary and alter ego George Hawkins.

Louis, born in 1896 near Mansfield, Ohio, sprang from a long line of farmers from whom he inherited his love of the land. His father abandoned farming but was forever helping farmers restore rundown land. Bromfield spent a semester in the Cornell Agriculture College and took brief courses in journalism at Columbia before entering World War I. During two years of active combat as a member of the French Army, he acquired an admiration for the French peasant. He marvelled that a French farmer could make a living on as little as two acres. They wasted nothing. They collected the garbage of the cities and made compost piles. Farming the same land for 1000 years, they have added a foot to the topsoil. Our farmers with large farms have lost half of the topsoil.

Returning to New York after World War I, Bromfield worked at various jobs, mostly as a newspaper writer. His first novel *"The Green Bay Tree,"* published in 1924, was a huge success. Other best-sellers followed. Movie rights to them were sold. Sam Goldwyn enticed him to Hollywood to write scripts for $2,500 a week. He became wealthy but didn't like Hollywood. He longed for France, where he moved in 1925, acquiring his beautiful home, Presbytere de St. Etienne, in which he lived for the next 14 years. He wasn't alone. Many famous writers lived as expatriates in France between the wars, including Edna Ferber, Somerset Maugham, Scott Fitzgerald, and Edith Wharton.

In 1930 Bromfield returned to Hollywood. After a year he decamped to France without notice. Goldwyn sent George Hawkins to induce him to return. Instead, Hawkins remained with Bromfield. There was instant rapport. After a few days, Bromfield saw Hawkins' potential. It was the greatest decision either man ever made. Boswell stayed with Sam Johnson only to write his biography. Hawkins did everything for Bromfield, leaving him free to write. Until Bromfield's death 28 years later, both in France and especially later at Malabar Farm Hawkins handled the finances, planned the large parties, met the press, and dealt with publishers and movie producers. His most important job was to type Bromfield's novels, written in longhand. Bromfield told me that George was the only person who could decipher his manuscripts. "I couldn't read them myself," he said.

Hawkins kept himself in the background except on one occasion. That was when his friends Lauren Bacall and Humphrey Bogart were married at Malabar Farm. Soon after, on a visit, I asked Bromfield why these movie stars decided to be married far from Hollywood. "I encouraged it," he said, "for two reasons; one was to please George; the other for the publicity that Malabar Farm and *Friends of the Land* would get out of it."

Realizing that war was inevitable, Bromfield moved his family and Hawkins back to the United States, acquiring a large tract of rundown land near Mansfield, Ohio. He named it Malabar Farm after a famous place in India. He had lived a carefree life in France off the wealth received by the sale of his novels and movie scripts in the U.S. He never admitted it, but I know he was conscious of his debt to his native country and his need to justify his repatriation. That is why he developed Malabar Farm to exhibit and promote land conservation and restoration practices.

He loved France (where he was decorated with a Croix de Guerre and later made a chevalier of the Legion of Honor), but he never regretted his return to the States. He continued to write novels. For the rest of his life he also crusaded for land conservation. Malabar Farm became a Mecca for thousands, some curious and some serious. All were given free lunch and a tour of the farm, sometimes 200 a day. His book *Pleasant Valley,* is the story of Malabar Farm.

In order to further his crusade, Bromfield founded a nationwide organization called *Friends of the Land.* After his death in 1956 the *Friends of the Land,* with the help of the Noble Foundation of Tulsa, Oklahoma, took over Malabar and continued to run it.

I first met Louis Bromfield at a conservation symposium in Cincinnati in 1948. Later, John Hertz (Yellow Cab and Hertz Drive-it-Yourself) and his wife, Fannie, brought Mary and Louis Bromfield to my Kentucky farm for a weekend. At lunch another guest, a newspaperman, overheard Bromfield say, "Bluegrass is a weed." The next day this was a headline in the *Lexington Herald.* Bromfield got undeserved bad publicity. The reporter didn't hear the full conversation. Bromfield said bluegrass suited Kentucky soil but that it would be only a weed at Malabar, where the soil required coarse grasses and legumes.

A month later Hertz flew Mary and me for a Sunday visit to Malabar. The usual 200 visitors had a buffet lunch in the big house. Mary and I, Fannie and John Hertz, Louis and Mary Bromfield and their daughter Ellen were served lunch in a private room. George Hawkins was the waiter. Bromfield was cultivating Hertz to get a big donation to Capitol University (he got it). No more dissimilar men ever lived. John Hertz came to Chicago at the age of three as a Russian Jewish immigrant and parlayed one taxi cab into a fleet of cabs for which he received $45 million when he sold the company to General Motors. He bred great horses, including Count Fleet. However, he would sell his best yearling colt rather than keep the colt and risk racing him in his own colors. I asked him why. "Habit," he replied. "I can't resist a sure profit." He left a $300 million charity foundation. Bromfield made a lot of money but thought of it only as a means of promoting Malabar, soil conservation, Capitol University and entertaining his friends. He had much in common with Addison Brown, Ned Putzell and Norman Herren, who have been at the forefront of civic affairs in Naples, Florida, where I spend the winter months.

After visits to Malabar we terraced slopes and planted 20 miles of multiflora rose hedges at Forest Retreat. Those rose fences are still flourishing. They provide windbreaks, water breaks, beauty, feed for birds, and protection for wildlife. They prevent horses from running into fences, but they have a serious drawback. The rose bushes spread to areas where they are not wanted.

In politics Bromfield was a conservative Democrat. In 1950, when Robert Taft, Sr. ran his last Senate race, I enlisted him to form an independent committee of his followers to support Taft. They did a yeomen job and helped carry Youngstown, a labor stronghold. Bromfield was a great friend of Governor Frank Lausche. When Lausche was in office, I operated on Judge Simon Ross and found that Ohio judges had no pensions. I wrote Bromfield, who intervened with Lausche to correct this injustice.

Another fringe benefit of my visits to Malabar was meeting Ellen, daughter of Bromfield, who married Carson Geld. Geld became manager of a large coffee plantation near Sao Paula, Brazil. When Jose de Mello, head of the Brazilian Jockey Club, decided to visit the horse farms of Kentucky, he brought Ellen along as interpreter. She steered him to Forest Retreat for a day. As a result, I was chosen in 1957 to be "Sole Judico" (sole judge) of the National Brazilian Yearling Show, a three-week trip with all expenses paid and a gift of aquamarine jewelry worth several thousand dollars. (The full story of this trip is recounted in my book, *Both Sides of the River.*)

In 1949 Bromfield asked me to take part in a symposium on water held at Ohio University, Athens, Ohio. Professors, government engineers, and conservationists were on the program. My subject was on the bio-elements in untreated spring water, reprinted as a chapter in this book. During the last years of his life we kept in contact by correspondence. He gave me stories which I used in my book *Horse Sense and Humor in Kentucky,* and I gave him two stories which he put in his book *Pleasant Valley.*

Bromfield was a charming friend and a great novelist. I talked with Sam Goldwyn in Cincinnati, when he stayed with my daughter and her husband James H. Stone, for the debut of *Porgy and Bess.* Goldwyn said Bromfield was the best writer he ever had. As a novelist, Bromfield had much in common with my idol, Anthony Trollope. Both were prolific. Both knew the world. Their products were realistic and credible. Both hated verbosity and sentimentality. By the calendar, Bromfield and Trollope lived only 60 odd years. Actually, they lived twice as many years.

CHAPTER 20

DETACHED THINKING
ABOUT UNDETACHED THINKERS

The Literary Club
March 27, 1950

Random notes with a somatic explanation of modern thinking.

It has been said that a man can be detached about anything but his dog, his horse, and his child (and in that order), and that a woman cannot be dispassionate about anything. Cold reflection shows that this is a vast understatement and that undetached thinking is universal in America among all classes of people, educated, uneducated, and some educators. Readers will, with some logic, also include the author.

First a few homely examples of undetached thinking in connection with wounded pride. Veteran quail hunters have long known they must try to excuse their companion's bird dog however many birds he flushes. Criticism of the dog will mean sudden loss of the staunchest friend, and deadly feuds have started over such disputes. Some men, otherwise intelligent, always blame the shortcomings of their horse on the trainer, jockey, track, or bad luck. Even if consistently beaten by the same horses, they always try to excuse their own beloved animal. Consider the golf foursome, each fighting for a concession of strokes on the first tee, but when they sit down for bridge after golf, the worst dub in the group would be highly insulted if offered a handicap.

The most obvious proof of general undetachment is in the alignment of our voters on the basis of immediate economic self-interest, with no thought of the future by either conservative or radical. Almost all financially successful men are conservatives and the few exceptions are suspect as to motive (the psychiatrist's dream type). That this situation is generally admitted was illustrated by a recent cartoon in the New Yorker. Two seedy characters, presumably intellectuals, were in a hot argument. The winner, executing the coup de grace, asked, "Who the hell are *you, not* to be a liberal?" The New Yorker's admission that professional liberalism often stems from frustration makes this opinion unanimous.

The most impoverished and bitter group in France is the intellectuals. Recently a self-appointed commission of thirty French Communists applied to our government to come here on a peace mission. They were turned down, possibly because there were enough Russian sympathizers in our own State Department. The published list of the would-be visitors showed them to be either writers, sculptors, teachers, or artists, further proof that intelligent people in adversity think at the stomach level and that the ancients were not far wrong when they regarded the stomach as the seat of our emotions. Happily, America is rich enough to pay a living wage to its intellectuals and provides a job in a bureau for the otherwise umemployed among them. Certainly the most fanatic and effective revolutionary is a hungry intellectual of some sort, while some professional liberals are intellectuals merely hungry for the unacquired recognition which they think their talents deserve.

Because we hear a great deal about a few Communists and because the professional liberals make themselves heard out of proportion to their numbers, we are apt to forget that in the United States the vast majority of our artists, writers, and teachers are honest men. As a group and contrary to general opinion, teachers rate highest for their ability to think objectively. This is said in spite of the fact that there are some socialists among them, especially the younger ones, that most have no practical experience, and that a majority are underpaid and justly resentful. In this connection Churchill said it was normal for a boy of twenty to be a socialist but if he were still a socialist at thirty, he was a failure. Churchill did not define how long it takes some men to reach thirty years of age.

Many educators say that in our materialistic, socialistic trend, scholarship in teaching has been pushed aside and that the H-Bomb has completed the rout of classical education. Now we have mostly vocational and technical schools, excellent in their way, into which we try to herd the whole population when most of the students should be doing the world's work. Such education barely manages to raise the average graduate to the level of a radio program listener, making him splendid propanganda fodder. Along with the pure technical courses, the curricula of our universities are cluttered up with numerous studies such as economics, sociology, and political economy. Lacking a basis of proven laws and since the average life of an economic fact is about six months, not one of them represents a science. They are merely words representing the organized opinions of individuals, many of whom have had no contact with the world. Originally well meaning, some have become vested interests for different views. These courses are responsible for much of the undetached state of mind of our college graduates because, under the auspices of a university, inexperienced teachers assume authoritarian status to the impressionable student. They breed one-sided viewpoints because the student is taught what to think rather than how to think. If our colleges must take time which would be better spent on scholarship, classical education or technical training, why not be sure the students hear all sides of modern controversies? Why not throw away the textbooks and simply appoint a committee to arrange discussion groups presided over by a series of able labor leaders, industrialists, bankers, financial experts, and statesmen? Our own university* has done this job well for the public. Why not do the same thing for the undergraduates and, incidentally, save money for better use?

Though our teachers are aware they have become technicians training other technicians, smart educators realize they have the world's best job. Disliking the environment where the stake is money (witness a recent delightful satire at the expense of Mr. Twenty Millions), an educator knows that he always has what the businessman works for all his life but never achieves—namely, leisure, both during his working year and long vacations. The businessman gets only a station wagon, an income tax deduction of his Queen City Club dues, and winds up with a coronary while the teacher, justly, may it be said, lives serenely, if at times complainingly, off the prematurely abandoned wealth of his dull pupils.

Columnists and editors theoretically value realistic and truthful reporting, what they like to call objectivity. How many attain it? God knows they have some excuse because a column several times a week could not be filled without tilting at windmills and knocking over a lot of straw men. Most syndicated columns follow one or another unvarying party line. How can you be impartial and objective espousing one cause? True, most papers have all kinds of commentators but most present an extremist point of view. One columnist sees not even a touch of socialism in the President's program, while another sees in it complete totalitarianism. All of which leads a detached observer to suspect that the columnists are no longer merely ambitious to be good writers and objective reporters, that either they are being paid by the interests that they represent or they are using their columns to advance personal ambitions. Some sports writers of the past were said to be mere public relations men for boxing promoters, etc. To-

* University of Cincinnati

day we have much more realistic commentaries on sports, and it would seem we could hope for more unbiased analyses of important controversies.

Billy Rose, one of our fairer commentators, who usually writes delightful O. Henry-like stories, took time out recently to lambast the harried Mr. Bing of the Metropolitan Opera for hiring Kirsten Flagstad. "By all means bring her over," he said, "along with Schacht to be Secretary of the Treasury, etc." The Kentucky mountain feuds were kept alive by such foolishness because even a non-combatant cousin in the opposing family was regarded as fair game. We can forgive Mr. Rose because I believe it was his first offense and everyone is entitled to one outburst of undetachment.

Walter Lippman, the aging original Frankfurter boy, by many is regarded as a paragon of objectivity and detached thinking. Admitting he is an able writer, this view of Lippman is difficult to understand by one who has read his columns the past fifteen years. Long before and continuing to within two weeks of each presidential election, he would attack the New Deal, lambasting it for its foreign policy, extravagance, ineptitude, immorality, etc. But emotion always seemed to overcome cerebration. Just when it was expected that he would endorse the opposition came the inevitable complete flop. With a heading something like "Time for Decision," he would announce that, in spite of his past carping, on the final decisive level Roosevelt was his man. Admitting his acceptable *Yale Review* style and despite his stratospheric intellectuality, it would seem to this detached observer that he only succeeds in wandering verbosely off into space. But those columns must be filled.

Even the *New York Times,* which attains a high degree of detachment, fell flat on its face in its editorial endorsing Dulles last fall (with tears in its eyes for its great friend Governor Lehman). This editorial seemed quite objective but wound up by hoping that the Republican party would get rid of its Tafts, etc. Note the phrase "get rid of." It is easy to see how the editors might, even on the basis of minor disagreements, oppose any man for office, but it is difficult to explain why a great newspaper could be so unobjective as to want to completely get rid of an able man with whom it had so often been in agreement. Challenged on the matter at a cocktail party, one of the editors said that the decision on the contents of this editorial was reached at a full meeting of the editorial staff and that the vote was only eight to six in favor of it. In extenuation it must be said that the *New York Times* usually attempts to be fair rather than emotional in its policy, going so far as to report in full the German war criminal trials, including verbatim Goering's testimony and brilliant self-conducted cross examination. In fact most newspapers, however distasteful the subject, report faithfully both sides of all controversies, as witness a full speech by Henry Wallace beside a vitriolic antileftist editorial recently seen in the *Chicago Tribune*.

Though deserving of sympathy, our businessmen have been guilty of the most undetachment of any group, though it must be said they lack the irritating "blessed assurance Jesus is mine" attitude of their underpaid opposition, the brain trusters. It has been nip and tuck as to which extremists of these two groups have been the most nauseating in discussions pro and con Roosevelt. Let us just say the industrialist has been comical in his plight of continued prosperity amidst his very real fears and that many New Dealers simply sang "The Vicar of Bray." A New Deal inspired story had a businessman at Belmont Park looking at the race card. Noticing the No. 5 horse in the fifth race, he remembered that the day was the fifth, the month the fifth, he had Room 5 on the fifth floor of a Fifth Avenue hotel. It was a sure hunch. When the horse came in last, he actually felt cheated. Throwing the tickets to the ground, he exclaimed, "Damn that Roosevelt!" The truth is that a combination of natural riches, technology, and the efforts of the average American have made prosperity in spite of both Sewell Avery and Roosevelt.

Why can't everybody recognize Roosevelt for what he was, an able politican, spawned by the exigencies of the times? A re-reading of Carlyle's *Heroes and Hero Worship* will clarify this thought. Since opinions die but facts live, no doubt Roosevelt will attain a commanding place in history for certain domestic reforms, but his stature will be reduced by the failure of his foreign policy. If this is true, it impugns the reasoning of some conservatives, who, for the first time, voted for Roosevelt during the war, fearing to change horses in midstream.

It might be said that some of these examples of undetached thinking could be mere differences of opinion. It is true that one doesn't necessarily need a brilliant mind to be without prejudice, but one does require an honest, judicial outlook unaffected by self-interest, kinfolks, or religion. Seneca said first acquire a competence, then practice virtue. Certainly a competence enables one to think less emotionally, but a competence comes usually with advancing age which should of itself make a man more judicial. Is this wisdom or mere glandular atrophy? The aged Sophocles, evidently believing in the glandular theory, found an old age a "blessing." In Plato's *Republic,* Sophocles was asked how it was with him and love; if he were the man he once was. "Peace" he cried, "how glad I am to be rid of that furious master! Now I have calm and freedom to work and think about higher things."

If undetached thinking is so universal among the well informed and intelligent groups of society, can we defend, explain, and possibly justify it? The explanation part is easy. In spite of centuries of education, the human is still an animal with the primary protoplasmic qualities of self-preservation and reproduction. The intellectual also wants food, shelter, and kids, and it is just as difficult for him to be detached about these things as a businessman. Concluding, our best detachment is implored but forgiveness is not asked because the budget must somehow be completed, even if it means moralizing before a captive audience.

Gettysburg speeches do not fill the bill because one of our members in a delightful satire laid down the dictum that a Literary Club contribution must last just forty-five minutes. Dr. Knight added another requirement, that our papers should keep forty-five old men awake for forty-five minutes. Your author would like to make the definitive comment that a Literary Club paper, long or short, is like sex. When it is good, it is wonderful; and when it's bad, it's still good.

Come to think of it, who the hell am *I not* to be a liberal? (Paper read at the Literary Club, March 27, 1950.)

CHAPTER 21

BLACKS IN KENTUCKY AND MISSISSIPPI

Literary Club 1965

Fifty years ago Prof. Cannon of Harvard and many subsequent scientists theorized that under the same circumstances all races have equal potential. I shall leave the arguments on these questions to the sociologists, anthropologists and Dr. Schweitzer, though I am afraid the anthropologists will not be helpful. They are divided in their opinions like the rest of the population, proving again that emotions often override intelligence and education and that many smart people merely use their brains to rationalize their politics and prejudices.

For detached thinking on the racial issue, one should at least visit the center of controversy. In Mississippi today (1965) this is not enough. A knowledge of history, of the soil of the origins of its people, plus the confidence of various kinds of natives and a comparable living experience are all needed to interpret impartially the present situation. The events of a recent trip stimulated these homespun, nonpartisan, sociological remarks, which are colored by lifelong observation in Kentucky and a smattering memory of Americana.

After the area east of the Mississippi River, comprising present Alabama and Mississippi, was ceded by France to England in 1763, large grants of land were made to prominent Englishmen, who established the famous plantations in the restricted alluvial delta area near the river. Through lumbering, cotton, and slave labor these people became rich and built fine mansions at a time when the southern east coastal states had depleted their soil and were slave poor; however, Misissippi did not become a state until 1817 and the vast hilly, pine woods interior was not settled until well into the 19th century.

Practically all the people who rapidly filled up this area during the land boom of the first third of the century came from the Piedmont directly to the east or, strangely enough, from the rocky thin land areas of New England. Thus they were all native-born Americans, almost entirely pure English with only a sprinkling of Scotch-Irish, since the Scotch-Irish Kentuckians on the move went straight west to Oklahoma or Texas. By 1840 Mississippi became the largest cotton producing state. The high price of this crop created a great demand for slaves and mules, and Kentucky had just what they wanted. Ease of transportation down the Ohio and Mississippi rivers made this traffic Kentucky's best export business between 1805 and the Civil War. Young bucks fetched $1,200, women $600, and mules $250 a span. There was no respect for the brutal dealers, but the owners had no compunctions about selling their slaves, especially the bad actors and those of subpar mentality. Bourbon County, Kentucky, was a center of this commerce, and one can still see the chains and shackles attached to the walls of an enormous basement under a fine old house near Paris, the Grange, where hundreds of slaves were collected for shipment; and thus I presume arose the old Kentucky saying, "Meaner than a Mississippi nigger." (They had a right to be mean).

Slaveholding in Kentucky existed chiefly in the central part and the region around Louisville. This area bred a vast number of slaves. At one time there were two slaves in Bourbon County to every white person, yet, unlike the eastern states of the South, Kentucky never became slave poor since it sold its excess to

Mississippi and Alabama. To be sold down the river, still a phrase in common use, was dreaded by the slaves because it meant disruption of families and brutal treatment. Whether due to the fear of being sold, the paternal attitudes of the owners, or the nearby border which made escape easy during slavery and continuous ever since, the fact remains that Kentucky had little slave trouble and now few integration problems. The NAACP advertised a demonstration in Paris over a year ago, but only the officials showed up for it.

I do not subscribe to the phony myths about happy, singing slaves, and I have seen brutal treatment of the negro in Kentucky, both physical and mental, largely by low-class whites; yet the negro learned to live there in his segregation with a certain amount of personal dignity. Except on the part of the white trash, there has been respect and affection between whites and negroes in Kentucky on an individually earned basis. There was little mixed breeding involving poor whites and negroes, but many highborn whites had secret and often acknowledged negro mistresses and many a light skinned negro bore an embarrassing resemblance to his prominent white father.

The impression is very strong that the biracial situation has always been more difficult in Mississippi. Who can say whether the difference is due to inferior negroes, inferior whites, the background of the whites, or the greater number of negroes in Mississippi? The native American settlers of Mississippi were of pure English descent, largely working people and small farmers. Coming from New England and the Piedmont, they, like the Kentucky mountaineers, had never been in contact with the negro. This is in contrast to the people of Virginia and Kentucky, who were used to servants and have lived with the negro twice as long as the people of Mississippi.

In the coastal states of the South and in Kentucky, many negro men and women occupied trusted positions in the household, many were light skinned, some were educated, and many more were exposed over a long period of time to the civilizing contact with Western man. The wall of segregation here was little higher between the negro and the white man than between the gentry and the rest of the population in England.

Except in the more enlightened very small Delta plantation region before the Civil War, there was never any rapprochement between the negroes and the whites in Mississippi. To the back country whites whose descendants, called "wool hats," became the supporters of Rankin and Bilbo, the negro was always a subhuman chattel on a level with the mule. They never liked him, they seldom saw pleasure in her, and there was little of the kindly interest in the negro so often shown in the eastern part of the South. After slavery and the breakup of the large farms and plantations, in Mississippi the negro's position did not improve. He fared badly in his competition with the poor whites for share cropping and manual labor. When, in recent years, due to soil erosion and automation, Mississippi lost its cotton raising supremacy to Texas and California, the lot of the negro was further lowered, if this was possible.

Neither the mule nor the negro is now needed in large numbers in the rural areas. On my recent quail hunting trip in Mississippi I saw abandoned negro shacks everywhere. If one were still occupied, it was in a state of collapse, surrounded by tin cans and trash, indicating a level of existance no better than that of the unemerged people of Africa.

Negroes, once far outnumbering the whites in Mississippi, still comprise 46% of the population. Many have gone north and many have moved in or near the small industrial centers, the largest of which has only a little more than 100,000 population. Whether due to the limitations of their age-old environment or, as the whites claim, to their lack of intelligence, they have not been widely employed in Mississippi's expanding industry and diversified scientific farm program. Today, wherever they live in Mississippi, large proportions of the negroes are on relief, but their spending is an important factor in the retail trade, causing instances of reverse discrimination. A lady told me that she was standing in line in a supermarket next to a negro woman and her little girl. She merely said, "My, what pretty pigtails," whereupon the negro woman complained to the manager. She said the white woman had insulted her daughter. The white manager requested the white woman to leave, explaining that right or wrong, he couldn't afford any negro trouble. For obvious reasons, most businessmen of the South are moderates.

The destination for my February quail hunt was 17 miles south of Oxford. This area is off the beaten tourist path and out-of-state cars are seldom seen here, especially in winter. My station wagon carried Ohio license plates, and as I drove sedately along the road about a mile this side of Oxford, I saw a state highway patrol car standing off on a side road. After I passed him, the officer gunned out behind me, red light blinking and siren shrieking. I slowed down and as the officer pulled alongside, giving me the once-over, he suddenly saw my crated dogs, laughed and waved me on. Feeling innocent of any traffic violation, I couldn't understand it.

A gas station attendant in Oxford enlightened me. Looking at my Ohio tags, he said, "You ain't from Antioch, are you?" I said, "No, why do you ask?" "Well, I'll tell you, a lot of students from some of them Ohio schools been coming down here butting into our business, stirring up our niggers—a bunch of Communists!! They blamed us white folks for burning them nigger meeting houses; probably did it themselves! See my nigger over there," pointing to a man changing a tire, "He's a member of one of them churches. He ain't too smart, but he's on to their game. Those beatnik bums got no religion, but they suck in those poor niggers by helping them build back their church. My nigger told me when the job was done, they had a free-for-all freedom meeting. After the singing and the preaching, a long-haired white boy took the pulpit. It was like a Hitler meeting. 'What do you want?' he yelled. 'We want freedom! What else? We want jobs! What else! We want food!' This rabble rouser said, 'O.K. but I don't understand you negroes. The white man turned you down, but you follow his religion. You believe in his God and now let's see if his God will give us any sign he believes in you.' Then the bastard raised his hands, looked straight up and said, 'Lord please help these poor people'. He said it three times and of course nothing happened."

"Then he got down to business. He said there was a great movement in the world to help poor people, especially black people. 'Now let's call on the Great World Leader for a token.' My nigger was getting madder all the time. Before he could slip out the door he heard the fellow say, 'Now, all together everyone, Comrade Kruschev, please help us.' What do you think those bums did? One of them, hiding up in the loft, let down three hams on binder twine!"

After driving around the sedate "Ole Miss" campus and reviewing the recent battleground, I proceeded without further incident to my destination south of Oxford. My host was Andy Edwards, a large landholder whose New England forebears had settled in this still remote area over a hundred years ago. Andy, never very talkative, was more glum than usual because only two weeks previously his brother, Charley, a pitcher for the Cincinnati Reds forty-five years ago, had been killed when a drunken negro smashed into his jeep. Fortunately, Andy's son Elwood, a leading lawyer in Memphis, was present, and I enjoyed many conversations with the intelligent, reasonable man. Just before I left, I summoned enough nerve to relate the "ham" incident as told me by the Oxford gas station man. Old Andy was not amused. After a brief silence, he said, "Well, I'm glad one nigger knows what's going on!" Andy's son Elwood shook his head, "Dad, I'm afraid you don't know what is going on," he said.

Elwood later told me that the attitude of his father and the gas station owner was widespread. That is why blacks in Mississippi had more difficulty in the pursuit of civil rights and integration than the blacks of Kentucky.

CHAPTER 22

WILLIAM C. HUEBENER

The Literary Club 1986

Dr. Huebener was a rare German-American, my friend for sixty years. I am one of the few who knows the story of his colorful life. He was a storybook Prussian: he always retained his formal military bearing, shaved his head, clicked his heels, and bowed.

Huebener was a lieutenant in the German Air Corps in World War I, a fighter pilot and adjutant to Captain Herman Goering. The crown prince was the titular head of the German Air Corps, but Goering, only a captain, was the actual operating chief. Huebener engaged in many dogfights and flew observation missions. The recreation of the flyers was wild boar shooting. On flights they would spot boars near camp and then go out on foot to shoot them, providing fresh pork for the mess.

After World War I, Huebener finished his medical education and went with his brother, an internist at Bad-Nauheim who later gained fame when he was called to treat Pope Pius. He lived at the Vatican for six months until the pope recovered and stayed in good health for six more years. As Cardinal Pacelli, Pope Pius visited the Good Samaritan Hospital in Cincinnati, where I talked with him. He was fluent in seven languages, speaking English without an accent.

Dr. John Greiwe, a leading internist at the Good Samaritan Hospital, spent two months each summer in Germany before and after World War I. Dr. Greiwe, his brother-in-law Rudolph Wurlitzer (piano fame), and other German-Americans, including Jewish Germans such as Dr. Goddard Deutsch (H.U.C. faculty), all naturally made pro-German statements before the United States was involved in World War I. They were patriotic citizens, but they were under surveillance as potential enemies after the United States entered the war. Kunwald, director of the Cincinnati Symphony, was interned.

In 1923, on his annual trip to Germany, Dr. Greiwe met Bill Heubener at Bad-Nauheim and induced him to come to Cincinnati as his radiologist and associate. Dr. Greiwe referred his fracture cases to me. Huebener accompanied the patients, bringing along the X-ray films, still wet. This was the start of our lifelong friendship.

In 1925 Huebener was the booking agent for the United States lecture tours of Count Felix von Luckner, the "Sea Devil," who was popular because, as the famous German "Sea Raider" in World War I using a sailing ship, he sank hundreds of ships but never lost a passenger. He left them safe on a ship or on an island. In Cincinnati, in 1925, Huebener took me to hear Von Luckner speak at the Cincinnati Club. After World War II, Von Luckner was in Cincinnati on another lecture tour. The circus was here at the same time. Huebener had us, Von Luckner and Emmett Kelley, the famous clown, as the only guests at dinner at his home. Kelley showed us his clown tricks, and Von Luckner, a master magician, entertained us by tearing two telephone books, etc. The next day Von Luckner, at my request, went to the home of Mrs. James Benedict to autograph his book *The Sea Devil* for young Jimmie Benedict. Von Luckner, opposed to Hitler, moved to his wife's native country, Denmark, where he lived to the age of 93. I had correspondence with him.

All the aerial circus performers were from Germany. Huebener was their doctor. If one of them got hurt or needed an operation, Heubener had them flown to Cincinnati to be under our care at the Good Samaritan Hospital. He often flew to other cities to be with them. This got Huebener in trouble, as I shall relate later.

I am ahead of my story. In 1925 Huebener was one of six men appointed to be doctor for Emperor Wilhelm at Doorn, each serving two months a year. He always referred to him as the emperor, not the kaiser. After he came to Cincinnati, he continued this service every year (until the emperor died), with time out to go to Berlin to have dinner with Goering and other World War I friends. He brought back movie films of Doorn which he showed us and a photo of the emperor autographed by the emperor "To my friend, Dr. Eslie Asbury." (I hid this photo during World War II.) He also brought us Lebkuchen. We named a filly "Lebkuchen." It was lucky. She became the leading filly of her year.

When Hitler first came to power, the emperor, Huebener, and the Prussians regarded Hitler as the savior of Germany and a bulwark against communism. They were soon disillusioned. They opposed Hitler in frustrated silence, though Huebener often voiced his opposition.

He took out his first citizenship papers but delayed getting his final papers in order to keep his annual job with the emperor. When we entered World World II, Huebener was listed as an alien and potential enemy. On Saturday night before Pearl Harbor, he invited me, Dr. and Mrs. Dale Osborne, and Mr. and Mrs. James Benedict (daughter of Hulbert Taft) to dinner, all of us obviously not German. He met us at the foot of the Southern Railway bridge to guide us to a famous German restaurant (Monte Casino) in the south of Covington. He was agitated and on the phone several times during the evening. On December 8 he was taken in custody. The F.B.I. called on me and told me they followed Huebener back and forth across the Ohio River bridge when he took us to dinner. I told them all I knew. I was called to testify at the hearing conducted by the Alien Committee, all of whom I knew, including Raymond Walters, president of the university, and Charley Sawyer. I told them about Huebener's opposition to Hitler and that I regarded him as a loyal American citizen. The only evidence against him was a telegram sent to Goering when Goering was made field marshall and a record of his travels with the circus. He was interned, Sawyer told me, mostly for his own safety. He was so typically Prussian, he was a sitting duck for maltreatment. However, on the way to camp he was hand-cuffed to a proven Nazi, a crowning insult. In a few months he was released through the efforts of Judge Weber, Judge Dammerill and three members of the Literary Club: myself, Dale Osborne, and Ed Schulte, the famous architect.

After his release he became a full-fledged American citizen and acquired an even better practice among all sorts of people, including Jews. Through him I operated on many leading citizens. He also referred several Jewish survivors of German concentration camps for evaluation of permanent injuries. The peace treaty specified that Germany indemnify survivors for permanent damage arising out of injuries sustained during internment. The amount depended on the degree of disability. These people averaged about five feet five inches in height, reflecting the poor diet of the ghetto for centuries. Through Huebener they were referred by the regional German consul at Cleveland. Several, beaten by guards, had disabilities.

Huebener's social friends were people in his position: Prussian immigrants who had made a success, including Allendort (real estate), Paul Klotsch (submarine engineer who developed the Crosley automobile) and Arthur Koeppe, (actuary for the Union Central Life Insurance Company). I enjoyed their formal Prussian dinners at Forest View Gardens, a famous Westwood German beer garden. Many toasts were offered; suddenly someone would catch your eye, stand up raise his glass, salute, and say,

"I drink to you, Sir".

Huebener was a physical fitness buff. Through his association with the circus he learned to ride two horses, Roman style, while standing with one foot on each horse with the horses going at full speed. This feat required extremely strong leg muscles. When he was 70 years old, he fell down a stairs, completely tearing the quadriceps tendon from the knee-cap in both legs, the only case of its kind I ever saw or heard of. The quadriceps is the most important muscle of the leg. A major operation was required on both legs to reunite the tendons with the knee caps. I thought he would be at least partially disabled. Instead he fully recovered and even resumed Roman riding.

Huebener was married twice but had no children. His first wife was a beautiful, athletic, Austrian brunette whom he met when she came to Cincinnati to visit relatives. She fractured the semi-lunar cartilage of her knee while riding. After I operated on her knee, I remarked on her well-developed leg muscles. "Ah, yes", replied Huebener "she's sehr ausgebildet." This marriage was short lived. She went back to Austria. Before World War II he married Verna Reimann, who survives him. Verna, an efficient career woman, was secretary to Holmes Hospital for many years. She was a great help to Huebener, who was careless about finances. Her story about her husband would be more vivid than mine. Bill Huebener helped to improve German-American feeling.

CHAPTER 23

GOLF

Someone said to Sarazen, "Gene, now that you are 83 years old, what is your handicap?" "Distance," replied Gene. This is the experience of all golfers as they get old. Some partially compensate with a good short game; but many pros, for example, Hogan and Snead, lose their touch around the green, although they still hit the ball as well from tee to green. In general, old people lose distance because they lose muscle power, they can't make a good shoulder turn, and they can't concentrate as well. Healthy old golfers can slow the increase in their handicaps by taking isometric exercises, by daily practice, and by checkup lessons from an understanding pro.

I started playing golf at the Mayo Clinic in 1920 at the age of 25. I got there in July. My first diagnostic training assignment was in the section on neurology headed by Dr. "Pop" Sheldon and his associate, Dr. William Finney. Avid golfers, they were promoting and helping build the first golf course, a nine hole layout on the treeless outskirts of Rochester. On Saturday afternoons and Sundays I helped them plant trees and build sandtraps. They let me hit a few practice shots. The club dues were $15.00 a year for fellowship men and $50.00 a year for members of the permanent staff. I joined the club. Jimmy Alves, a native

Scot, was the pro. After watching me hit some balls, Jimmy made me a set of clubs which exactly suited my build and swing. Having played college and semipro baseball, I could hit the ball. With no lessons, using my baseball "arm swing," I scored in the eighties, now and then in the upper seventies, during my years at the Mayo Clinic. In 1985, 65 years later, I went back to the clinic for a hernia and prostate operation. During the week before I entered the hospital, I went out to the golf course, now 18 holes. I recognized nothing. The beautiful clubhouse didn't surprise me, but the trees astounded me. There was practically no rough: the course was limited mostly to fairways bordered by forests of trees, oaks, maples, and evergreens 80 feet high. The course looked as though it had been carved out of a native forest. After I told the pro I had helped plant the trees, I played several times: free carts, free lunch, no green fees. Dr. Waltman Walters was my only living contemporary member.

After I left the clinic in 1925 and located in Cincinnati, I continued golf. I first joined the Western Hills Club, where Johnny Fischer, age 16, was my caddy and my patient with a broken arm. Johnny became the national amateur champion. In 1928 I joined the Cincinnati Country Club (one of the oldest golf clubs in the United States), where I often filled in a foursome twice my age: George Warrington, R. K. LeBond, and Barney Kroger (founder of the Kroger Co.). The absent member of the foursome was John Omwake, founder of the U.S. Playing Card Co. I was taking care of him for a broken hip.

During the thirties my handicap varied from 3 to 7. When World War II came, I was over age for military service. My handicap was my farm and my busy surgical practice. I didn't have time for golf. I quit the game for 24 years, until 1965. My old shoes were still in my locker, but my pet Jimmy Alves clubs were in ruins. I got a new set of clubs, and for the first time in my life I began to study golf, first under our great pro Freeman Haywood, until he moved to Naples, Florida, and then under our present fine pros, Bill Wood and Gary Arnold. After two years my handicap was 14, rising to 18 as I reached the late seventies. Playing with such great friends as Lowell Powers, Bud Hackney, Henry Andrews, Howard Morgens, Frank Mayfield, Duke Smith, Les Gaut, John Thier and Paul Kunkel, I could still hold my own until I was 86 years old. Since then my tolerant friends allow me to hit from the front tees, and knowing I would cheat anyway, they also permit me to improve the lie anywhere. At the age of 91 my handicap is 20 (ladies tees) and 24 (regular tees). I need all of it when I play with Dr. David Simon and John Wiethe, a great Democrat leader. John, an ex-NFL lineman, at age 70 can hit a golf ball 290 yards.

RESORT GOLF

At the age of 70 I resumed golf in order to have something to do on vacations, first in semi-later in full retirement during the past 20 years. I spend several summer periods at the Lake Placid Club, where I played with Charles Heekin, Gus Nippert, Lou Daniels and Jack Mulcahy* (President Nixon's greatest contributor). In 1970 I built a summer house at Biddeford Pool, Maine, along a fairway of the 9 hole golf course which I first played 50 years ago as a guest of Kay and Jim Benedict. In recent years at the Pool my golf mates have been Joe Russell, Fred Rohwedder, Pete Lindsay, Jack Gibson, and the late Eric Bergland and Henry Wetter. My son Arthur and his family took a house at the Pool for the month of August, giving me a chance to play with him. As chairman of the Department of Neurology at the University of Pennsylvania, Art had time for golf only during his August vacation, but he played well. Had he devoted himself to the game,

---

* Mulcahy, a wealthy Brooklyn Irish immigrant, was a loner. He played only in a twosome. He contributed anonymously. One day after golf, without solicitation, he gave me a check for $10,000 for the campaign of Senator Robert Taft, Jr.

he would have outdone any member of the family.

When the Idle Hour Club in Lexington was founded in the thirties, I became and have remained a founder member, playing on rare occasions with Charles Bagyard, Happy Chandler, A. B. Hancock, Ralph Kercheval, Bob Green, and Tom Yocum.

When the Carnico Club was built on the hills at Carlisle about a mile from Forest Retreat, I momentarily held the course record with a 38. I play Carnico about once a year, at times with President Andy Dudley of the First National Bank. Mr. Dudley may not score as well as his brother, Bill the famous pro, but he can hit a golf ball over 300 yards, farther than our friend Wayne Shumate.

WINTER GOLF

At the age of 70 I started taking full winter vacations, buying a condo in Scottsdale, Arizona, where I joined the Mesa Country Club in this Morman community and played regularly with Tom Wake and Dr. Hagyard. During my five winters in Scottsdale I played twice with Jocko Conlan, the famous umpire, and once with Dizzy Dean. Once with Dean was enough. He was a golf hustler. Regardless of the number of strokes he gave you, he would beat you. I played as guest at the Phoenix Country Club through Barry Goldwater, whom I had met during his ill-fated campaign, and played with Joe Hall (president of the Kroger Co.) at Paradise Valley, a plush club where you had to tip four uniformed attendants (auto, locker-room, waiter, cart man).

In 1970 we transferred our winter activities to Florida, first for two years at the Gasparilla Inn, Boca Grande, a delightful place where I played golf with Tony Farese, the pro, Francis Kernan, and Bayard Sharpe, the owner and a ranking senior golfer. For the past 13 years we have lived in the winter at Naples, where we still own a condo. I joined the Royal Palm Club, where I played with my Appalachian friends Don Whitehead, Kyle Tieche, Cecil Horne, and B. Ray Thompson. I played as a guest at the Royal Poincinana Club with Tom Goodloe and Carlo Paterno; finally joining the Hole-in-the-Wall, where I play with Bill Keller, Breaux Ballard, Dr. Frank Mayfield and Bob Telford.

Between club memberships I often played at the Beach Club Hotel course, the best layout and the best conducted public course I have ever seen due to the personnel: Gregg, Les, and Dan (attendants), Jim Duffy and Bill Lowry (pros) and George Maxwell, the best starter I have ever known. I have a standing challenge with George: that he can't put me in a game with anyone with whom I do not have a mutual acquaintance. I haven't lost yet.

HIGHLIGHTS OF MY GOLF LIFE

In 1931 Mary and I spent two weeks with Kay and Jim Benedict at the Hobe Sound Inn, which featured a primitive 9 hole golf course. Gene Tunney, the famous fighter, B. Gates Dawes, founder of Pure Oil Co., and Cardinal Mundelein had the only houses in the area. I didn't see Tunney, but I went fishing with Mr. Dawes, whom I knew through his son in Cincinnati, and I played golf several times with the cardinal and his visiting priests. Cardinal Mundelein, a big, genial man, played well in spite of an abdominal paunch.

In 1932 we were guests in Ft. Lauderdale of the Erkins family, who owned half of the town, including the movie building, the Towers, the only apartment complex, and their home (where we stayed) near the beach about 1/2 mile from U.S. Route 1-A. The only other house in the swampy area, very close across the narrow waterway, was owned by E. J. Tranter, head of the Fasig Tipton Co., which at that time had a monopoly on the yearling auction sales at Lexington and Saratoga. This year the Tranters were leasing their house.

There was no golf in Ft. Lauderdale. I played at Hollywood with Johnny Farrell, the pro and recent open champion. In the depth of the depression, he charged only $10.00 for an 18 hole playing lesson. One day when I arrived nobody except the caddymaster was around. I asked for Johnny. "He just started out with Gene Sarazen and a couple of strangers," replied the caddymaster. I decided to watch the match and joined the gallery of about ten people, four of them small, swarthy men with their hats pulled down over their eyes. One of the foursome was a tall, striking, bareheaded, black-haired man. A fellow standing next to me whispered, "That's 'Machine Gun' McGurn, Capone's enforcer. Those fellows over there are his bodyguards." He didn't look like my image of the gangster who carried his machine gun in a violin case and killed all those people in the St. Valentine's Day massacre. He played golf well, having finished second in the Western Amateur.

That evening before dinner, while my host and I were having a cocktail on the porch, McGurn and his men came out of the Tranter house on to the lawn not over one hundred feet away. I said, "Bert, you have a distinguished neighbor." I was amazed and Bert was horrified. He later told me that this was the only time he saw the gangsters during the month they occupied the house.

Fifty years later Tom Earls and I went to Marco to see the Tony Lima Tournament. Sarazen was alone on the practice tee. After watching him hit a few balls, I said, "Gene, do you remember the day you played with 'Machine Gun' McGurn?" Sarazen, crestfallen, dropped his club and said, "Johnny Farrell fooled me. I didn't know who I was to play with. I was a young Wop trying to get a start. If it had got out, it would have ruined me. You are the only one who has ever mentioned the incident."

Another highlight of my golfing life occurred on a duck shooting trip with Charlie Hagyard to Lloydminster in northernmost Saskatchewan. We flew nonstop in Harold Genter's plane 1500 miles, landed on the tundra, and stayed in a primitive motel. The residents were mostly Indians and Eskimos. One morning on the outskirts of the village we saw a sign on a one-room wooden building: "Golf Course". Nine holes with sand greens were laid out on a treeless expanse. At each green, attached to a rope, was a doormat, used to smooth the putting line. We borrowed clubs and played twice. The caddies, Eskimos, charged 50¢ a round and the green fee was 50¢.

In 1970 I was invited to be the speaker at the annual dinner of the Georgia Breeders and Owners Association. Ed Wade, the architect of the Augusta National Clubhouse, and Cothran Campell, a genuine southern gentleman and Georgia's best horseman were on the committee. I agreed provided, they would hold the dinner just after the Masters Tournament, get me admission to the tournament and the privilege of playing Augusta National. Everything went on schedule. The tolerant members' tees made the course civilized. I shot 84, the same score I made at St. Andrews when (1971) I played the principal courses in Scotland with Betty and Ray Palmer.

In 1979 I was the guest of Cecil Horne at Dryden in the mountains of western Virginia. Cecil, a native, had made a fortune in coal mining. It was C. Bascomb Slemp and John Fox, Jr. territory. The "Lonesome Pine" of Fox's famous novel stands in the vicinity. I played golf at the Lonesome Pine Club with Kyle Tieche and Jim Stallard, mine operators, and Cecil's father, a retired pick and shovel mine worker. Carved out of the mountainsides and valleys, the Lonesome Pine layout was one of the most spectacular I have ever seen.

For the past 50 years (except for the 2-year blackout during World War II) I have played golf at Saratoga with Sherrill Ward, our trainer; Johnny Nerud, one of the smartest of all horsemen; Bob Placek, who played on the original New York Giant Football Team; Chris Chenery, breeder of Secretariat; Ralph Wilson, owner of the Buffalo Bills; Barry Ryan, member of the Jockey

Club; Steve Wilson, founder of Fram Corporation; and Morton Rosenthal, Warner Communications. For years I had a standing date to play the day after the annual Jockey Club dinner with Jack Knight, publisher of the *Miami Herald*. Eddie Arcaro and my son Dr. Taylor Asbury often joined us. Eddie was a fine golfer. Jack Knight, my age, was a poor golfer but insisted on high stakes. Since Jack was a customer of the farm, I tried not to beat him but always failed. One day before we teed off Jack said, "I'm getting a a hernia. I need two more strokes." I said, "Jack, let's go back to the locker room. I'll examine you." He had only a muscle strain, but I couldn't keep from winning $40.00 from him. That evening at a Reading Room cocktail party someone said, "How are you, Jack?" Knight replied: "Fine. I lost $40 playing golf today but I got a free examination."

CHAPTER 24

BASEBALL: NOW AND THEN

Literary Club 1933

Baseball has been onr National Game for seventy years. With me it has been a lifelong passion. Around it has been written by the late Ring Lardner, Damon Runyon and others some of our most original literature. Both the game and the comedy are uniquely American. The worries and mishaps of the baseball rookie, as portrayed in Lardner's "You Know Me, Al," along with his other short stories, are regarded by many as on a par with Mark Twain's tales of another era. Both of these authors have one thing in comon: they depict the average person of the day, although Lardner's humor carries beneath it more subtlety, sarcasm and comtempt. Lardner could paint a word picture of his characters with no label needed. To my mind, Lardner may become one of the immortals of this age.

Lardner began his literary career as a baseball reporter. It was in this connection that he got his early material. His "You Know Me, Al" stories were conceived in the spring training camp of a Chicago Baseball Club and represented a rookie writing home to his friend Al. In one of these letters, written about a week after the team arrived in the South for practice, the rookie says, "Al, tell Ma to wash my overalls. I'll probably be home next week. They're starting to curve 'em now."

This essayist has not had Lardner's advantages. This chapter is based only on personal experiences as an amateur, semi-professional and college player, together with memories gathered by the daily perusal of the sport page since 1905. My interest in life will be low when I no longer look at the box score of the games of the Cincinnati Reds. In this respect I am joined by people of all classes in this city, home of the first professional team, the undefeated Cincinnati Red Stockings of 1869. Big league baseball has been in existence in Cincinnati since that year and the city has been able to hold its franchise, although other cities have outgrown it. In fact, Cincinnati is the best baseball town in either league in proportion to size. Some of our most prominent citizens have been behind the club. Among them were Ashley Lloyd, John T. Brush, Charles P. Taft, Hulbert Taft, Julius Fleischmann, Garry Hermann, and Powel Crosley. Since this was written (1933) other civic minded citizens have owned the Reds: William DeWitt, Louis Nippert, the Williams brothers, Carl Lindner and Marge Schott.

Opening game day, virtually an official holiday, is a more celebrated institution in Cincinnati than in any other city. But the most rabid followers of the Reds are people living outside of Cincinnati in small towns in Ohio, Indiana, Kentucky and even as far as Tennessee. On Sundays for years the railroads have run excursions to accommodate the out-of-town crowds — the women and children going to the zoo and the men to the ball game. As a youth I availed myself of these opportunities. My first visit to Cincinnati (1912) was to see the Reds play. I remember with what intense interest the men daily awaited the arrival of the newspapers in our small town to find out the varying fortune of the Reds.

Aside from the direct financial value; it is worth a great deal to the city to be a big league town. The game has had a good reputation here, although Cincinnati was involved in baseball's biggest scandal, when some of the Chicago White Sox players sold out to the gamblers in the 1919 World Series. The furor which this caused only helps to prove the rarity of dishonesty in baseball. Mr. Comiskey, owner of the Chicago White Six, un- earthed the evidence and threw out of baseball seven players who, had he sold them, would have brought him a quarter of a million dollars. The White Sox never recovered from this blow. Some of these men continued to play the next year on an independent team in Rochester, Minnesota. The author, unbeknownst to the Mayo Clinic, played on this team on weekends, finding it necessary to use a catcher's glove at third base during infield practice. Those fellows threw a ball like a cannon shot.

Only two of the Sox players actually received any money from the gamblers. Cicotte, pitcher of the first game, was given $5000.00 before the game and was promised $5000.00 after the game. Lefty Williams found $2500.00 under his pillow before the second game, but neither of them received the second half payment. "Shoeless" Joe Jackson, outfielder and great hitter, was implicated. Jackson was so stupid and so accustomed to mechanically hitting the ball that he couldn't get over the habit, leading all players of both teams in batting during the series. When reproached by Gandil, ringleader of the "Black-Sox," his only defense was that when he saw the ball coming, he couldn't help taking a cut at it. Some of the accused men were involved only because they knew about the sellout and were banished because they did not report the conspiracy. They did not squeal because they were more afraid of the crooks than the owners. I have known a great many professional ball players, but these men were unusually rough and hardboiled, unlike the average modern player. They were always ready to "bean" or spike an opposing man on the slightest pretext.

I have heard wiseacres assert that the results of baseball games are prearranged. Nothing could be further from the truth. In the first place, no game can be thrown unless several players are in- volved. Even then their efforts may not be successful. The Reds had trouble with one or two men, particularly Hal Chase, who was discovered to have bet against the Reds and attempted to throw the game. At the hearing it came out that Chase and Lee Magee had bet against the Reds while playing Boston. These two men made errors, allowing Boston to score three runs on the Red's best pitcher. All their calculations were upset because Edd Roush knocked a home run with a man on base to win the game, and they lost their money. Such sins are very rare. They cannot be tolerated by the owners because honest baseball plays better than crooked baseball. One often hears the statement that the home team is allowed to win on Saturday to get a larger Sunday crowd. Although the home team has an advantage, the visiting teams in the Major Leagues last year actually won 60% of their Saturday games.

Jockeys are given cold mounts; wrestling matches are admittedly rehearsed beforehand; managers of fighters will often not accept a fight unless the opponent will lie down; but baseball, like cockfighting, is, of necessity, honest. If it were not, disgruntled players would talk, a thing which to my knowledge has not happened, nor has any owner been accused of complicity in any baseball scandal.

On the other hand, the author knows a few instances where, near the close of the season, certain teams have gone easy on other teams. For example, when Ty Cobb was manager of Detroit, with a team hopelessly sunk in the second vision, he used only second string pitchers in a series with Cleveland, who was fighting for a place in the money. Tris Speaker, manager of Cleveland, was a close friend of Cobb's. Cobb didn't care if his friend won, although every game was contested on its merits. Cobb simply wanted to have his best pitchers in shape for the next series with New York, a team also trying for a high position, but very much disliked by Cobb. A natural and human occurrence, but the situation was so obvious that other teams protested. Cobb and Speaker were reprimanded, although the only charge was that Cobb did not present his strongest lineup.

Odd and colorful characters have been a part of the game. Who does not remember old Chris Vonderahe and his manager Arlie Latham? Vonderahe, an old-fashioned Dutchman who spoke broken English, owned the St. Louis team. He was eccentric and comical and loved baseball but didn't know a great deal about the game. Latham, a natural clown and practical joker, led the old man a dog's life, but in spite of his pranks, Vonderahe put up with him because he was a good baseball man and a great drawing card. He was forever firing Latham but would hire him again the next day. Chris attended every game, viewing the play from a specially constructed box-like arrangement in the grandstand. Windows were arranged so that the old man, who was nearsighted, could look out with a telescope to see that everything was going to suit him. He had a bell which he would ring when he wished to summon Arlie to talk over strategy. One day violent ringing of the bell was heard. Arlie ran over to the cage and found the old man greatly agitated, waving his free arm, but still looking intently through the telescope. "Hey, Arlie! Who iss dot new blayer oudt in left field? He's oudt too far. Tell him to come in the ball park." "That's no new player, Boss," replied Arlie, "that's Sheckie, our regular left fielder. Turn your telescope around." Sure enough, "der Boss" was looking through the large end.

Latham pulled a great many jokes on Chris, but for a certain one he was never forgiven. One day he called on Vonderahe formally and told the old man that they all wanted him to know that they appreciated all he had done for them. In token of their regard they had made up a purse with which they had bought him a present. The next Sunday, before the game, they were going to make the presentation. He reminded Chris that, as it would be announced in the papers, a large crowd was expected and that he must have a speech of acceptance ready. "Der Boss," flattered, prepared his speech. Just before the game the umpires and players of both teams gathered around the home plate; two players escorted the boss from his cage to the field. Latham made a flowery speech and presented him with a large be-ribboned box. Vonderahe's voice shook with emotion as, in characteristic language, he thanked his boys for their thoughtfulness. He retired proudly with the package to the cage and the game was in the second inning when the bell began to ring and loud shouts were heard from the cage. "Vere iss Latham? He's fired. He's fired for good." "Der Boss" on opening the ornate package had found his own watch which Arlie had pilfered for the occasion.

Heine Zimmerman, third baseman of New York Giants, who gained dubious fame when he chased Eddie Collins over the plate with the winning run in a World Series game, was illiterate but a good, unscrupulous mechanical player. As you know, if there is a man on third with one out or no outs, he can try to score after the catch of an outfield fly ball. He must not start until the ball is caught, and the decision is often close at the plate. In the days of one umpire, Zim had a habit of stealthily holding a runner's belt just as he was ready to leave the base after the ball was caught by the outfielder. This maneuver would slow the start and the runner was thrown out at home. During a game at Pittsburgh one day, before a large holiday crowd, Zim had thus caused Honus Wagner to fail to score on a sacrifice fly. It so happened that later in the same game Honus was again on third when the batter hit another outfield fly. Honus felt Zim close behind him and, knowing he would hold his belt, unbuckled and loosened it rapidly. He started for home as soon as the ball was caught, leaving Zim with the belt still in his hand to the great merriment of the crowd.

"Rabbit" Maranville, shortstop of the Boston Braves, was the Buster Keaton of baseball. A very smart and aggressive player, his early years in the Major League were full of spectacular episodes. His peculiar mannerisms and clowning antics in the field (carried to great length if his team was either far in the lead or hopelessly behind) together with a mask-like, guileless expression endeared him to all followers of baseball. Not all of his tricks were confined to the diamond. One night a group of the players on his team were playing poker. The room was on the second floor of the hotel overlooking the street intersection, where a policeman was on duty. The Rabbit, watching the game, conceived a bright idea. He opened the window and yelled, "Help! Police! Murder!" at the top of his voice and dashed out of the room, locking the door on his friends. He then ran down to the lobby, and when he saw the policeman coming, he told him to hurry to room 209 as something awful was going on inside. The policeman, reinforced by clerks and others, rushed upstairs and found the door locked. When they banged on the door a great commotion was heard and when the door was not opened promptly, the officer, unwilling to wait until the clerk could get a duplicate key, broke open the door. The policeman was so mad, he took all the culprits to the station and charged them with disorderly conduct.

On another occasion Maranville induced a bell hop in a big hotel to lend him his clothes. As he was about the size of a fifteen-year-old boy, the clothes were a good fit. Donning the uniform, the Rabbit walked down to the lobby and sat on the bell hop's bench without being recognized. Almost at once the cap bell rang. Maranville jumped to attention and the captain said, "Ice water to 406." Grabbing a very large pitcher of ice and water, he rushed up to 406. A big bald-headed, fat man in B.V.D.'s answered the knock, whereupon the pseudo-bell hop yelled "Ice water coming up," at the same time dashing the whole pitcher of water on the guest, who never received satisfactory explanation from the management. They are still looking for the bell hop.

Horseplay, on and off the field, was more common in the days before baseball became a big business. A good part of the color of the game of the past was mere rowdyism; The individual player and owner did not have so much at stake, the umpires and officials of the league were more forgiving, so that rugged individualism among the players was the keynote. Competition was intense because there were at least 10,000 possible candidates for every job. The apprentice went through a hard school and he had to be tough to keep his place. The desire for respectability, the entrance of the college player lured by big salaries, the fear of injury, and the wails of the righteous put an end to the fighting and umpire baiting except among such old-timers as John McGraw.

Another criticism one hears today is that baseball is too perfect; that it is too mechanical; that no team is representative of its city, since its players are bought and sold and may come from all parts of the country. As far as I am concerned, I can't see why such criticism should be made about baseball any more than it should be about the Cincinnati Symphony Orchestra. Does anyone complain that the orchestra is far too professional; that the players do not make enough errors to make the concerts more interesting, and that too many musicians are not Cincinnatians? The author goes to see a game because he loves baseball, not because he loves the Reds.

The baseball writers are all concerned about the future of the game; about what's the matter with baseball. Why blame it on baseball? One might as well ask, what's the matter with the Seventh Commandment?

In reality, baseball seems to have weathered the economic and machine age storm better than most anything, considering the competition of prosperity, depression, golf, movies, autos, necking and allied sports. The magnates have kept their heads and refused to make concessions to the theatrical element. Some 50,000 people attended the first game of the World's Series this year (1933). Winning teams were able to show a profit even with a prosperity overhead. Next year Sunday baseball will be legal in Pennsylvania. If the admission price is lowered, attendance will increase.

Football, as a spectacle, has gone ahead of baseball. But when one considers that there are only a few football games, each one advertised and built up weeks ahead, with the loyal alumnal body in habitual attendance and a little bet down, it is natural to expect a few big crowds. Night games have also added to attendance and it is now possible for clerks and barbers to get their football inspiration. Indeed, shouldn't a municipal university provide thrilling and dangerous entertainment for the benefit of the mob and the Chamber of Commerce? Though the rain is coming down in torrents, though the field is frozen near as a rock, though the temperature is below zero, the show goes on per schedule, all for the sake of a sound mind in a sound body, though if a player gets out with either he is lucky. Our sons are asked to help make these Roman holidays for the love of dear old Alma Mater. They don't tell him that if he gets his leg broken he will be sent to our charity (1933) hospital for treatment because funds are needed for large stadia and proselyting. He is not told that he is not protected even by the Industrial Commission in case of a permanent injury. What, then, is his reward? If so unfortunate as to be a star on a famous team, his sense of values is sure to be overturned. On graduation, he may coast on his fame or play professional football. All kinds of statistics can be brought forward to prove that football makes great men out of boys, but these figures represent the product of a different era, when not only a different type went to college, but when we actually had amateur football in college. The American Medical Association and others made such vigorous protest last year against the forty deaths and thousands of injuries in football that the rules were changed.

Some people love to witness physical competition even if there are injuries. In 1925 I was at the farewell show in the old Madison Square Garden. The old building was to be torn down and the new garden was nearing completion. Joe Humphries, famous announcer and colorful figure in the sports world, was attempting to make a sentimental speech about the old garden. The packed house was impatient for the fight to begin. Every time he would start a sentence, a group of hecklers in the cheap seats drowned him out with cries of "Start the fight," "Cut out the bull." Finally, holding up his hands for silence, Joe made his now famous remark. "The more I sees of youse guys, the more I believe in boith control."

It has always seemed to me that baseball has most of the good points of other games and few of the disadvantages. It is a game which people play and watch for the love of the game. In other words, it is a game and not a spectacle. There are few injuries, and those that occur are usually due to lack of skill on the part of the player himself. I believe it was the famous all-American Owens of Harvard who, a few years ago, wrote some articles for a magazine in which he stated that college football was a thankless grind and that not one man in ten played because he really liked the game. Even Red Grange, "galloping ghost" of Illinois, in a recent article stated that his favorite game is baseball. But enough of this idle detraction of a game which is really attracting more attention every year. If football ever gets by the stage of three monotonous pile-ups and a punt with an occasional pass and a prayer, baseball followers will take more notice. The professional teams are forging to the front through the reputations of college players. After all, I must admit that it is possible that there are a few sour grapes in the fruit, a certain envy on the part of a diehard who resents the success of a rival game. I am afraid that the games for seeing outnumber the games for playing (more spectators than players). While a few magician-like inventors are dominating, not only our recreation, but our whole life, I can think of three hopeful signs. The game of golf is growing popular; recently, I saw a long-haired youth in the rumble seat of a Ford smoking a cigar; and baseball competition between small towns is coming back.

Footnote: In my book, *Both Sides of the River*, I had a chapter on the humor in baseball. My friend Frank Mead loaned Billy Werber a copy of this book. I knew Billy when he was the main cog of the Red's pennant-winning teams (1939-1940). Werber himself is author of a fine baseball book, *"Circling the Bases."*

CHAPTER 25

MY JEWISH FRIENDS

I have had a lifelong close contact with Jews as schoolmates, as my teachers, as patients, as social friends, as clients of my farm, and as fellow members of The Literary Club.

My admiration of the Jews began 83 years ago in Louisville, where my favorite playmates were two sons of immigrants: Meyer Rabin (later a famous musician), whose father was a saloonkeeper, and Muncie Goldstein (later a Harvard graduate and successful New York businessman), whose father ran a dry goods store. Twice, after public school let out, I attended the rabbinical school with Meyer and Muncie. The class recited aloud in unison. I can still hear the buzz.

I entered the University of Cincinnati on a Fleishmann scholarship. Juluis Fleishmann was a great friend as was his sister Louise and her sons, Buck and Chuck Yeiser, schoolmates of my sons at the Cincinnati Country Day School.

In 1915, when the Hebrew Union College had ties with the University of Cincinnati, I was captain of the UC basketball team. The other four starters were Jews; three of them rabbinical students (Goldman, Isserman, Levine) and one (Dave Hachen) a premedic and my best friend, later the popular leader of my medical class and uncle of Rabbi Hachen. The subs were all gentiles. Once when we were about to play Oberlin someone said, "Don't worry. Your gentile team could beat them." Our Jewish players, poor boys from New York, learned to play basketball on the playgrounds. I had never seen a basketball until I entered the university.

In 1920 I met Dr. S. P. Kramer and Rabbi Goddard Deutsch through my father-in-law Dr. A. L. Knight. Dr. Deutsch lived in Madisonville, a suburb of Cincinnati. Dr. Knight was the long-time doctor of the family. To the consternation of the board of the Hebrew Union College, Dr. Deutsch, a German native, remained vehemently pro-German during World War I. In later years I visited his son Herman Deutsch in New Orleans, where he was the publisher of the *Picayune* and also the author of a realistic *History of the Jews* in which he said the Biblical dictum "turn the other cheek" was not merely a moral concept; it was the only practical defense by the Jews against the armies of the East and West who were forever passing through Judea.

Dr. Kramer and Dr. Knight went to Europe together twice, and Dr. Knight was often Kramer's guest at the Wednesday (Jewish) Literary Club. Dr. Kramer would insult his best friend for the sake of an epigram. One night, after a paper by Rabbi Philipson on the persecution of the Jews through the centuries, Dr. Kramer, all 5 feet, 5 inches of him, rose and said, "What do you expect? Two thousand years ago (on the cross) you had your choice between a prophet and a thief. You chose the thief and you have been consistent every since!" After a paper in which a *tall, blond* ghetto hero was extolled, Kramer rose and said, "Aberrant gentile sperm must have got loose in the ghetto."

In Germany, in 1922, Drs. Knight and Kramer met the prime minister, who excused Germany's involvement in World War I and bemoaned her present plight. Kramer replied, "Mr. Prime Minister, one Lusitania 'shooz' killed you." Kramer and Knight were nicknamed Lenin and Trotzky. There was a resemblance.

At the University of Cincinnati, in my premedic and preclinical years, all of my teachers were gentiles, serving on small, full-time salaries without private practice to augment their incomes. In contrast, all my clinical professors were Jews, mostly German Jews of established families, including Joe Ransohoff, Sigmar Stark, Julien Benjamin, Sam Iglauer, Henry Freiberg, Albert Freiberg, and Alfred Friedlander (later dean). They served without salaries and had prosperous practices, but they voluntarily devoted a lot of their time to teaching. Dr. Christian R. Holmes, the dean, married Betty Fleischmann, a fortunate thing for the medical college (benefactions). Dr. Holmes' pavilion plan for the new General Hospital was a disaster which paid off. The large acreage for the plan became a priceless asset of the present Medical Center.

As an intern my "Mr. Chips" was Dr. Albert Freiberg. I voluntarily served an extra period on his service and for 16 months I assisted him at odd times in his office and in operations at private hospitals. Along with Dean Holmes, Dr. Freiberg obtained my fellowship at the Mayo Clinic. I became the first graduate of the University of Cincinnati to take the full five-year training then available in only two or three centers. Dr. Freiberg offered me a partnership, but his son Joe was in the offing. Anyway, I didn't want to limit my practice to orthopedics. Dr. Freiberg, along with other of my Jewish teachers, supported me when I started practice. Along with Dean Stanley Dorst (who married Emma Westheimer, a member of one of the city's most civic-minded families) the Jewish members of the faculty, especially Dr. Julien Benjamin, supported my son, Dr. Taylor Asbury, when he was appointed chairman of the Department of Opthalmology. After 20 years my son was succeeded by Dr. Joel Sacks, who is a cherished friend and ally.

Around 1900 four immigrant brothers, with a poor eastern European background, came to Cincinnati. All soon had big families. Their sons became successful businessmen, lawyers, judges, realtors, etc. Together, with a few friends, there came to be enough Schwartzes to fill an entire synagogue. One of the immigrant brothers and his sons developed the large Schwartz Tailoring Company. Si Rosenbaum, a salesman for this company, was a patient of my father-in-law Dr. Knight. Through Si, Dr. Knight and I had our clothes made by the Schwartz Tailoring Company. A member of the Schwartz family had an abdominal fistula due to terminal ileitis. He had been unsuccessfully operated on three times. I resected the diseased segment of the bowel and he got well. After that I operated on three generations of the four Schwartz families and dozens of their friends whom they referred to me.

I bought the *Daily Racing Form* at the Fountain News Shop, owned by the Bishow brothers. Their mother, an immigrant widow, had supported them as children by scrubbing floors in an office bulding. After I operated on this fine old lady the sons went out of their way to personally bring patients to my office. Adolph Bishow left the racing form for me every day, and I still use the electric coffee warmer he gave me. I did not charge Hebrew Union College rabbinical students for operations. Many years later two of them (rabbis) came to my office and insisted on paying $150 for their operations.

In 1931 my office was next door to Harry Benet's Pharmacy. Harry, with his brother Jonas later developed a fabulous pharmaceutical company. I personally took Harry to the hospital in my car and removed a gangrenous appendix. When I got my farm in 1935, Harry Benet became a lifelong client, as did Arthur Bettmann, a member of one of Cincinnati's most prestigious families. John Hertz (drive-it-yourself) had a farm near mine. We visited back and forth and he let me breed to Count Fleet. I was the only commercial breeder he permitted this privilege because Hertz himself sold his yearlings at auction. Through Hertz I met Robert Lehman (Lehman Brothers), and Eddie Weisl (New York lawyer and personal advisor to President L. B. Johnson). In my early years I had the pleasure of keeping mares for, and selling yearlings to, Joe Straus (Straus-Frank Company of San Antonio) and his partner, Steve Wilson (Fram Corporation). My connection with this four-generation Texas family continues through Joe Straus, Jr.

Forty-five years ago Mrs. Alfred Roberts (Betty Bloch, Bloch Pharmaceutical Company) called me. She had seen my advertisement to sell two mares. She said, "Are those mares good enough to breed to a top stallion?" "Hell no," I replied, "if they were that good I wouldn't sell them." This remark made Betty a life-long client of the farm. When she died she willed me her best mare. She had bought the mare from me as a yearling filly.

About 35 years ago, through trainer Burley Parke, Louis Wolfson bought two yearlings from me at Keeneland. One broke a track record and the other won a stakes at Saratoga. I hadn't met Mr. Wolfson. The next year when I was introduced to him at Hialeah, his first words were, "Have you got yearlings this year out of those same mares?" When I replied that I did, he said, "I'll give you $50,000 each for them." This was a big price. I said, "Mr. Wolfsen, I want to keep you as a customer. It's a deal if your trainer looks at them and O.K.'s them." He had Parke fly to my farm the next day and it was a deal.

When Wolfson's great stallion Raise a Native came along, he let me have a season to him. That summer in Saratoga I said, "Lou, my mare got in foal." "I'll give you $50,000 for the foal," he replied. The foal turned out to be an unimpressive-looking filly. I wrote Wolfson voluntarily reducing the price to $35,000. "You don't have to do this," he said when he sent the check. When Wolfson was taken to court by the S.E.C., Abe Fortas, his lawyer, took a deposition from me. Based on my dealings, I couldn't believe the accusations and said so. Louis Wolfson survived the ordeal and continues to be a leader in breeding and racing.

For many years we have had a fine association with Morton Rosenthal (Warner Com.) and his partner, Al Greene, for whom we syndicated and still stand Naskra, a top stallion; also with his great trainer, Phil Johnson (Jewish), who trains for us and our clients; and with owner Tom Whitney, who buys my books, the ultimate accolade. Harry Isasacs bought his foundation mare Isa from us as a yearling. Sonny Werblin (Music Corporation of America) bought a good colt from us which he named Run Through. From Hirsch Jacobs, I bought a share in Hail to Reason, which became a famous stallion.

I treasure 45 years of involvement with the Hirsch family, beginning with Max and the Revoked episode detailed in my book, *Both Sides of the River*. Over the years Max bought six of our best yearlings for various clients, including Ed Lasker. He trained many horses for us and my son-in-law Jimmy Stone. One year, at the Keeneland sales, Max admired our green alfalfa hay. I shipped him a carload as a gift. He refused it as a gift. He sent me a check for $800 and this note, "I appreciate the hay but insist on paying for it. Keep trying. I might need it." Our association continued through Max's son Buddy and his wife Sandy. We look forward to our annual breakfasts with them at their barn in Saratoga, as we had done with Max.

In 1939 I removed a 3-pound substernal goitre from Morris Brown, a Cincinnati stockyards cattle dealer. After that Mr. Brown and his son bought our farm cattle, followed by Milton Schloss (Kahn Packing Company). One time Milt bought our cattle in the spring for fall delivery. The price of cattle went down in the meantime, but Milt paid the agreed spring price. Stuart Schloss, nephew of Milt, has handled our personal and farm taxes. The IRS has never questioned our tax returns.

Max Gert, who kosherized the meat for the Kahn Packing Co. and headed the labor local, was a lifelong patient. In 1932, when he referred a Jewish friend, he said, "This man is broke, he has a family, and his doctor advised leg amputation." When I agreed with the diagnosis, the man said, "That's it." That night he turned on the gas so that his family could collect a huge insurance policy.

Gabriel Paul, son of a cantor, is retired but for 40 years he was the ablest general manager in major league baseball. He helped elect my friend Happy Chandler to the Hall of Fame and never misses our farm Derby lunch, coming all the way from Tampa, Florida, for the event. Bill Gradison, our long-time congressman, has done us many favors.

I cherish three generations of the Friedlander family beginning with my teacher, Dr. Alfred Friedlander, and continuing now through Bill Friedlander, a fellowmember of the Commonwealth Club. On the intellectual side, my 60 years, association with the Jewish members of The Literary Club was equivalent to an ongoing post graduate course. It started with Rabbi David Philipson and continued with Rabbi Victor Reichert and his son David. Through Victor I had dinner with Robert Frost. Others were Murray Seasongood, mayor, and Alfred Bettman, chairman of the Cincinnati Planning Commission. Some of my best friends in The Literary Club were on the faculty of the Hebrew Union College: Nelson Glueck, Sam Sandmel*, and Eugene Mihaly, the only one living. Bill Miller, a former editor of *Life* magazine, helped with my books. My persent cherished friends in the club are Henry Winkler, Dr. Stewart Dunsker, Dr. Stanley Troup, Joe Stern, Norman Levy, Dr. Martin Macht and Dr. Eugene Saenger.

In sports my friend Al Bunis founded the Senior Tennis Tour, and Phil Meyers was the best end in the history of football at the University of Cincinnati. Phil and Al buy my books, the ultimate proof of friendship. At bridge, in which Jews excel, I have played with the leaders, including Phil Steiner, national champion with his partner Charley Hall; Oswald Jacoby, the most nervous person I ever played with; and Charles Goren, one of the few Jews I ever knew who had trouble with alcohol.

Iphogene Bettmann was my wife's closest friend. Her husband Gilbert and her son Judge Gilbert Bettmann also have been friends

---

*Sam Sandmel, provost of the Hebrew Union College of Cincinnati.

of the family. Iphogene, a granddaughter of Rabbi Isaac Mayer Wise, founder of Reformed Judaism, was a niece of Adolph Ochs of the New York *Times*. Iphogene and Mary went abroad together five times, once with the Sulzbergers.

One of my most interesting friends was the merchant prince Fred Lazarus, Jr. and his wife Celia. Fred was one of the soundest men I have ever known. I served on the Cincinnati Development Committee with him. This connection continues through his sons and their wives: Irma and Fred, Gladys and Ralph. Ralph has been a patient partner in our horses and I have had many pleasant golf games with Fred and Ralph. Irma Lazarus interviewed me on television (PBS). Danny Ransohoff interviewed me three times, once in association with Dr. Albert Sabin, of polio vaccine fame, quite an honor. I liked the programs of Irma and Danny because, unlike many T.V. hosts, they let me do *some* of the talking.

Irma is a sister of Mrs. Carl Strauss. Carl, Cincinnati's greatet modernistic architect, has built three houses for the family. All have stood the test of time and public approval. Polly and John Strauss (Carl's brother, a Yale graduate, owner of a Kentucky farm) are now partners with the farm in yearling fillies.

The Strauss's are great friends of my daughter Elizabeth and her husband Jimmy Stone, founder of the fabulous Stone Oil Company and a member of one of New York's most prestigious Jewish families. Jimmy's father, Jake, was an investment banker and a member of the board of Williams College for 40 years. Jimmy's brothers, Donald and Robert, also have made a great success and are highly respected in upper financial circles. As conservatives, the Stones were great fans of Barry Goldwater, whom I met during his presidential campaign. At that time we were wintering in Phoenix, Arizona. Barry introduced me to his brother Bob, through whom I had entree for bridge and golf at the Phoenix Country Club. When I told my son-in-law Jimmy Stone about this he was reminded of his favorite Jewish discrimination story. Jimmy said "the Goldwater's are part Jewish. My children, your grandchildren, are half Jewish." One day a friend of mine, a member of the Muirfield Golf Club in England, had a guest. Permission for guests to play had to be cleared through the reigning dictator, an austere, retired army general. The member said, "General, my guest was a squadron commander in the Royal Air Force. He was credited with bringing down 40 enemy planes. He was decorated by the Queen and voted the leading citizen of Liverpool, but I must confess, *he is half Jewish.*" The general was half impressed. "Let him play nine," he said.

Jews have a great sense of humor. They can laugh at themselves. Henry Fecheimer told me about a man who bought goods in London and took them to Cohen to have a suit made. After measurement, Cohen said, "Sam, you didn't buy enough goods." The man went to another tailor. No trouble. After he made the suit, the man put it on and showed it to Cohen. "See," he said, "Solomon made this suit and had enough goods left over to make a suit for his 6-year-old son." Cohen laughed. "My trouble," he said, "was *my son is 12 years old.*"

Dr. Sam Iglauer of Cincinnati devised an operation to remove nasal humps and make the nose straight. His fame spread when he operated on Bebe Daniels, a famous actress. Lecturing on the procedure at a meeting of the Academy of Medicine, Iglauer showed photos of his patients before and after operation. In the discussion, a Jewish member rose and said, "Sam, you have made things of beauty of these people and 'goys' forever."

Why these Jewish phenomena? One reason was the reverence of Jews for learning and education. For thousands of years Jews had the Rabbi for a teacher. Other people had no access to education. Herded into ghettos, forbidden to own land or engage in general commerce, Jews were forced to live by their wits. The smartest survived. Crowded into ghettos, exposed to diseases for centuries, the survivors acquired an hereditary immunity to bacterial diseases. I noted this in my practice and it was a general observation before antibiotics appeared. Jews living on the poor diet available in eastern European ghettos were under average in height. Their children, born in the United States, reached the average in height. The humor of these people naturally was urban in contrast, for example, to Kentucky humor which was and is mainly agrarian.

In the free atmosphere of the New World and with the help of Reformed Judaism, Jews are making great contributions to society.

Sam Sandmel wrote a famous book, "A Jewish Look at Christianity." Now a gentile takes a brief look at Jews.

There are all kinds of Jews just as there are all kinds of gentiles with this difference: Jews are smarter. This has been obvious for thousands of years in many countries. In modern times the leading nuclear physicists, the leading international bankers, and many of the leading merchandisers have been Jews. Jews, far out of proportion to their numbers in the population, have been prominent in the arts, the media, and the sciences. In various countries at many times in history, the success of the Jews plus their unique customs and religion, has made them conspicuous. The result was jealousy and persecution by the larger, ruling, non-Jewish class.

Why these Jewish phenomena? One reason was the reverence of Jews for learning and education. For thousands of years Jews had the Rabbi for a teacher. Other people had no access to education. Herded into ghettos, forbidden to own land or engage in general commerce, Jews were forced to live by their wits. The smartest survived. Crowded into ghettos, exposed to diseases for centuries, the survivors acquired an hereditary immunity to bacterial diseases. I noticed this in my practice and it was a general observation before antibiotics appeared. Jews living on the poor diet available in Eastern European ghettos were under average in height. Their children, born in the United States, reached the average in height. The humor of these people naturally was urban in contrast, for example, to Kentucky humor which was and is mainly agrarian.

In the free atmosphere of the New World and with the help of Reformed Judaism, Jews are making great contributions to society.

CHAPTER 26

SHOOTING AND FISHING

In my era city-born boys were not exposed to hunting and fishing. This is why my city friends of later years never took to these sports. My earliest memory of shooting (1899) was the annual Thanksgiving Day rabbit hunt of my father and his brothers in the hills of Nicholas County, Kentucky. I tagged along. They used muzzleloader shot guns. Breechloaders and smokeless powder came later. Clouds of acrid smoke filled the air. There was no game limit. The family bagged more rabbits than they could carry. They piled them up and brought them out later on horseback, but they didn't dent the rabbit population of the briar covered hills. The excess was sold to the country store for 5 cents apiece.

In 1908 I bought, from Sears-Roebuck, my first gun: a single-barrel breech-loading shotgun, price $2.50. For safety, by parental mandate, I could go hunting only by myself. In those days Sunday shooting was prohibited. During my college days I had infrequent opportunities to go hunting. At the Mayo Clinic (1920-1925) hunting and fishing were the main sports. We hunted ruffed grouse in the hills near Rochester. Now and then we raised a covey of quail which survived the severe winters by roosting in corn shocks. We also bagged prairie chickens, now in existence only in remote regions of western Canada.

Among my companions were Jimmy Learmonth, later clinical and regius professor of surgery at the University of Edinburgh, and Pierre DePage of Belgium, son of the head of the Medical Corps of the Allied Armies in World War I. Jimmie and Pierre always marvelled that American farmers permitted free shooting.

Duck shooting was the main fall sport. Many times Morrie Masson and I left Rochester at 1 a.m. to arrive at the northern lake by daybreak. We stayed with Ole Olson, a former patient, who charged us $1.00 a day for bed and meals, but the meals were thrifty. We got weak tea, porridge, and skimmed milk. He sold the cream. Ole, a typical Minnesota Swede farmer, had a magnificent, all-purpose barn, connected by a blizzard guiding wire to a very small house. Once, on a rain-freezing day, Morrie and I were in blinds about 70 yards apart. No ducks were flying. Our hunting coats were covered with a half inch of sleet. "Hey," Morrie yelled, "let's shoot one another. I'll turn around and you shoot me first." The spent shot rattled off our ice covered backs.

In the dead of winter the only sport was rabbit hunting. The rabbits holed up in snow burrows. From the chief of police, I borrowed a ferret, carried in my hunting coat. The burrows had an entrance and an exit. We put the ferret in the hole and those rabbits came flying out at full speed. One time the damn animal caught a rabbit and we had a hell of a job digging him out. One day we tracked and killed two jackrabbits. We were sorry of it. They weighed sixteen pounds each.

In those days the highways, all gravel, were not cleared for traffic during the winter. Everyone in Rochester jacked up their autos. The Swedish farmers used sleds for all transportation. One Sunday, when the temperature rose to 25 degrees, several of us unjacked our autos. Armed with guns, skis, snowshoes, and shovels to clear the snowdrifts on the road, we laboriously arrived at a good spot along the Zumbro River, covered with three feet of ice and 4 inches of snow. In the morning we went hunting on snowshoes, built a big fire and had a hot lunch, and in the afternoon we skijored behind autos at forty miles an hour on the frozen river. Last year when I went back to the clinic for an operation, Dr. Waltman Walters, recalling this event, said it had often been a topic of conversation.

In the twenties pheasants were scarce in Minnesota but so plentiful in South Dakota that they threatened the grain crops. Four of us drove to Redfield for a hunt. By previous arrangement, we visited 3 large landowners who were glad to help us relieve them of the pests. They drove us in farm wagons to half-mile long corn fields. Stationing us at the end of the fields, the farmers and their children walked toward us, the pheasants running ahead of them. Nearing us, the pheasants rose as many as a hundred at a time. We all got our limits in 30 minutes. Two years after I was in practice in Cincinnati, I took two medical friends for a South Dakota hunt at the same farms. Each of us brought back the transportable limit, 21 pheasants, which we saved for a big dinner at the University Club. Dr. A. W. Adson, chief of neurosurgery at the Mayo Clinic, was the guest of honor.

After I got my farm in 1934, I had great quail shooting in eastern Kentucky for the next 20 years. My buddies were two cousins, Hical Asbury and Bernice Ritchie, given to be the greatest quail men in the history of the state. Each of us had the same Indian cross in our pedigrees and we showed it. One fall at Mayfield, Kentucky, I went hunting with "Rip" Wheeler, famous Cub pitcher. I traded Rip two pups by General Jackson, (a field trial champion) for a young Llewellyn setter, part Gordon, which gave him his size. Rip didn't realize what he was parting with. The dog developed into every quail hunter's dream dog, a Man-o-War of the dog world. Jock Whitney sent his bitches to breed to him. I wrote extensively about Mutt in previous books.

In September dove shooting is the sport in central Kentucky. There was a shoot almost every day in Bourbon County. I enjoyed many shooting days at the farms of the Nancocks, Spears and others. When the quail got scarce, I quit hunting them. The scarcity was not due to hunters. It was caused by a growing lack of feed and cover, the greatest enemy of wildlife. Powel Crosley solved the scarcity by rearing hundreds of quail at his big spread in southern Indiana. In the hunting season he put them out there and at Bull Island, his big place near Savannah, Georgia. They didn't fly well and they didn't survive predators to propagate. It was a relief to raise a wild covey.

During the next few years I took quail trips to various southern states. In another chapter I recount my visit to the Edwards family in Mississippi. In Tennessee I shot with General Cavender and Bob Snowden on farms adjacent to the famous Ames Plantation, where the National Field Trials are held. Snowden was a brother to Mrs. Stanley Rowe, Sr. Their father owned Exterminator, sold on Derby eve to W. S. Kilmer, who won the Kentucky Derby with him. In the winters I went to Albany, Georgia, on trips arranged by Henry Goodyear, Georgia's leading realtor. We shot on the plantation of Harold Wetherbee, the largest native landowner, with John Hanes and once on Jim Hanes' big place. I also leased the hunting rights on a large tract of land with my partners (Goodyear, Sapp, Owens).

For the past 25 years the highlight of my life has been my annual shooting trip to Ring Oak, Dave Ingalls' plantation near Tallahassee, Florida — a strenuous week with golf in the morning, shooting in the afternoon, and bridge at night. Most years I flew with Dave Ingalls, Sr., a famous World War I pilot, who loved any excuse to fly his jet, landing us on his own field, two minutes from Ring Oak. In recent years I have flown from Cincinnati with Dudley Taft or Jock Lawrence. Among the guests were W. S. Rowe, Buddy Rogers, Lingie Harrison and Andy Coombe from Cincinnati; Morris Everett, Dr. Howard Rowen, David Ingalls, Jr., "Brownie" Brown and Frank Treco of Cleveland, Louis Hill of Tallahassee, and Angus Wuertle of Minneapolis. This part of Florida is Cleveland territory. Nearby plantations are owned by George Love, the Irelands, and the George Humphrey family, all of whom entertained us. I expect to be there this October.

FISHING

I started bait casting and fly fishing while at the Mayo Clinic. I could write about bass fishing trips to Canada; about trout fishing in the Yellowstone River and Idaho with my Mormon friend, Dr. Rigby of Rigby, Idaho, so named because Dr. Rigby's grandfather settled 11 wives on 11 homesteads in the area; about trips to ponds at Zanesville, Ohio, with Wick Jones and Andy Coombe; about deep sea fishing with the Erkins at Ft. Lauderdale, Florida, where I caught a 7-foot sailfish and played a 250 pound black marlin for 1½ hours; about trips to Grand Lake near Tulsa, Oklahoma, with Forrest Lindsay, Buzzy Minshall, Van Allen, and my favorite son-in-law Jimmy Stone. The oil people had lavish homes on the lake. Visiting one of them, we cruised up to the dock. The house stood on a perpendicular bluff 150 feet directly above the shoreline. I wondered how we could get up to the house. No sweat. There was an underground elevator.

Except for expeditions with Gibb Gay in Thousand Islands near Marco, Florida, I have limited my fishing to the seven impoundments on my farm. One day I killed a mallard which fell in the center of the lake and remained motionless. The problem was to retrieve it. I went to the house and got a casting rod and a plug. On my first cast I didn't get the duck but hooked a 4 pound bass. We had a bass and duck dinner.

CHAPTER 27

A FAMOUS HORSEMAN

Literary Club
November 26, 1962

The greatest rider of all, Francis Asbury, never rode on a race track. His races were against the Devil, who saddled such formidable entries as the Demon Rum, Slavery and Ignorance. Since the Devil's powerful horses were often ridden by leading citizens, Asbury didn't win all his races, but, to beat him, the opposition crippled its stock and was never the same again. Between 1771 and 1816 he rode about 270,000 miles organizing and bishoping Methodism from Maine to Missouri, and this figure is not pioneer exaggeration. It was compiled from his recorded attendance at conferences and from his celebrated daily journal.

Francis Asbury founded the Methodist church. John Wesley founded the movement, always hoped to have Methodist principles adopted by the Anglican church, never resigned as a priest of the Anglican church, and never became a member of the Methodist church. Wesley, a Tory, was against the American Revolution. Regarding the movement as his personal property, Wesley never approved Methodism as a separate church and gave only limited and reluctant help.

Francis, born in 1745 near Birmingham, England, was the only son of Elizabeth and Joe Asbury, a small freeholder. Joe, by a previous wife, had another son, Thomas, who got into trouble with the law. His exact crime is unknown, but his descendants hopefully believe it was no worse than poaching. At any rate, Thomas fled to Virginia at the age of 21, preceding Francis by several years. There he became enamoured of Susan Jennings, daughter of a wealthy cavalier who prepared to take his daughter back to England to foil the marriage. The night before they were to sail, Thomas boarded the ship, killed a guard and took Susan into the wilderness, where they lived with Indians. When they heard the father had moved to England, they came back to the settlement, were married and had at least a dozen children from whom all Asburys[1] in America descend. My country doctor father was named Francis, but I have known five uncles and cousins named Thomas.

The bishop, a lifelong bachelor, had a Welsh-English mother who is credited with much of his success. Since Thomas, his wild half brother, had a different mother, Asbury claims to fame are tainted, but family genealogical nuts are not discouraged by this. Herbert Asbury,[2] the writer, inherited the work of several generations. His charts reveal a succession of mostly ordinary men, scattered from Virginia to Texas, but they do have a certain sociological interest. On the records are a large number of Methodist preachers, teachers and doctors, a few writers; and the rest were chiefly farmers. Due to family and environment, there were almost no lawyers, politicians and businessmen, therefore no very rich men. A family tradition that most Asburys can be identified by their mouth (both literally and figuratively), was brought home to me at a family reunion at Benson Church near Cynthiana in 1926. I attended with an eye to my surgical

---

[1] Carl Asbury, Ft. Meyers, Florida, has published a book on the Asburys in the United States.

[2] Herbert Asbury wrote "Hatrack," a story for which the *American Mercury* was banned in Boston. He also wrote several books on Methodism.
I (the author of this book) was descended from Thomas. Bishop Francis Asbury never married.

practice and found over 300 from far and near, including 50 preachers, all of whom prayed or preached.

Soon after the birth of Francis his mother came under the spell of John Wesley and was a lifelong worker in Methodist circles. She dedicated herself to making her son a religious leader and had she been Catholic would have settled for no less than the Papacy. The boy was taken out of school early because of a brutal schoolmaster and placed as a page with well-to-do people, where he acquired manners and further learning under the family tutor. In spite of meager formal schooling, he made himself proficient in Latin, Hebrew and Greek, and followed a lifelong rule of reading 100 serious pages a day and a chapter of the Bible, in addition to writing his daily Journal. If all Bibles had been lost, it was said that he could reproduce verbatim the whole of the New Testament.

When he was 16 years old, Francis preached a sermon before his local society in the presence of John Wesley. His quiet delivery, containing just enough hortatory Methodist vehemence, appealed to the educated Wesley, who disliked screaming sermons. At age 21, Wesley made him a circuit rider, and 5 years later Asbury accepted his offer to go to America.

No one was better grounded in the new movement, the germ of which had its origin in a Holy Club started by the Wesley brothers at Oxford in 1727. Because of their strict religious rules they were derisively called Methodists, a name always resented in England, but it was 12 years before Methodism really began. In the meantime, the brothers made their only trip to America, Charles as secretary to General Oglethorpe and John as an Anglican minister. This trip, cut short by a controversy, accomplished little for the still unborn Methodism, which had to wait 30 years for Wesley missionaries to bring it to America. Returning to London, unable to use the Anglican pulpits, Wesley preached in the fields and worked with the Moravians, who had impressed him in Georgia. This sect, started by John Hus in secret before the Reformation, had the best system ever devised for spreading a new movement. Their ideas of indoctrination and cells which multiplied by division must have been copied by the Communists. They certainly were used by Wesley after he founded the first Methodist Society in 1739. The Holy Club had served merely to save the souls of the members, but the new evangelical, Arminian movement sought to save anyone high or low who would follow the rules. There was no intention to found a new church. John always remained an Anglican and regularly received the Anglican sacraments, as did Charles, who wrote 300 hymns, many of them still popular today. The movement, a sort of religious Alcoholics Anonymous idea, was organized on the Moravian principle of bands and classes. Wesley's discipline, still the Methodist doctrine, was based on deritualized Anglicanism plus rules of conduct which prohibited cards, drinking, dancing and such admonishments as pay your debts, do not haggle, obey the law, help the orphan, the poor and those in prison. The times called for a religion for the neglected masses, among whom illiteracy, lawlessness, poverty and drunkenness were universal. The intellectuals of the day were absorbed in metaphysical philosophy; the Anglicans were interested in the gentry and the Calvinists only in the predestined elect. Methodism, headed by practical religious liberals, met the challenge to help the masses.

Supreme and able commander, Wesley sent his best cohorts in all directions to form new societies, each headed by a lay leader who issued cards each quarter to members in good standing and ruthlessly expelled the deviators. Though Wesley and his followers were beaten by mobs, the societies and their schools spread over England. Circuits were organized to which Wesley assigned his well-tried itinerants, even sending them to Ireland, whence, in 1766, the first Methodist preachers came to America, followed by Asbury five years later.

ASBURY IN AMERICA

Landing at Philadelphia in 1771 at the age of 26, he found

a fertile field. The population of about 2½ million colonists lived chiefly near the seaboard, but there were no amenities except in the large centers. The outlying majority, scratching out a subsistence, without the benefit of education, religion or law, were completely undisciplined. Drunkenness, ignorance and poverty were general, as in England. There were only one or two small synagogues, the Catholics had a bare foothold in Maryland, the Congregationalists were confined to the elite of New England, and only a few belonged to the Anglican church. Except by certain Baptists and Lutherans, little mission work had been done among the poor whites, negroes and Indians. Bish Sherrill told me that it is still a standing joke that on missions, the Baptists walked, the Methodists rode horseback, and the Episcopalians waited for the Pullman.

When Asbury arrived there were only a few converts, though many were nibbling at the Methodist bait offered by several missionaries, working largely in New York and Philadelphia. Asbury, always the perfectionist, was appalled at the lack of organization and discipline, and "Why," he asked, "was there no one crying Methodism in the Wilderness?"

Asbury wrote his complaints to Wesley, who made the future bishop his general superintendent. His youth and his refusal to allow the unordained missionaries to give sacraments got Asbury into trouble and caused Wesley to send Rankin to take over in 1773.

The Oxford educated Rankin became unpopular with the preachers when he objected to their shouting sermons and was disliked by the people because of his sympathy with the crown. The brewing revolution was loudly denounced by Wesley and by all the Methodist Evangelists that had come over from England. Several were jailed as suspected spies, but all, including Rankin, managed to escape to England as the war broke out. Asbury remained neutral and was protected by Judge White, a large Delaware landowner who, though a known patriot, was temporarily jailed for harboring the suspect. For two years Asbury quietly continued his work and study, organizing numerous societies in Delaware. After the interception of a letter in which he predicted victory for the colonists, he went everywhere unmolested, even by the Indians. He often read as he rode, and one day after unconsciously riding through a fighting zone, he found a bullet hole in his hat.

The war years were fruitful ones for the Methodists during which Asbury, by general consent, again assumed the leadership. Membership quadrupled and circuits were set up in the eastern states, but the battle of the sacraments again broke out. Asbury and Wesley held that official offices were vested only in ordained functionaries and ordered the faithful to use the Anglican clergy for Baptism, Communion, etc. Wesley's Toryism and the wartime disruption of the Anglican church deprived the people of its services, led to open rebellion.

Asbury quickly called a Northern Conference and having maneuvered through a resolution to suspend the sacraments, rushed to the Southern Conference where the revolt was hottest. Prominent in it was Phillip Gatch, who later moved to Milford, Ohio, and was kinsman of our own John Gatch. After many bickerings, so sweet to church hierarchies, Gatch and others were won over and the Northern resolution ratified.

Having solidified his leadership and sensing schismatic rumblings, Asbury wrote Wesley, requesting a properly ordained representative to lay hands on his American disciples so that they could officially render the ordinances. Wesley, in his eighties, took the controversial step, over the objections of his high church brother Charles, that established the Methodist as the first Episcopal Church in America. He chose to send Dr. Coke, a graduate of Jesus College, Oxford, and former official of the Anglican Church, who had been chimed out for preaching Methodism.

Armed with a letter designating himself as Bishop and Asbury as general superintendent, Coke arrived in 1784 accompanied by Elders Whatcoat and Vasey. Fearing the temper of the colonists who wished to break all ties with England, Asbury, the practical politician, carefully prepared for a general conference at Baltimore by sending trusted lieutenants to brief the itinerants.

On Christmas Day, 1784, Asbury was ordained, made elder the next day and consecrated on the third day. The term *bishop* was not used but assumed by the Americans, who made it official at the next conference. The jealous, aging Wesley was infuriated at the use of the title and berated Asbury by letter. He addressed him as "Dear Frank," leading to the apocryphal story that our own beloved member, Brother F. J. Moore[1], got his nickname the same way.

Dr. Coke preached a lot on his eighteen trips over from England but never did any episcopating. Remaining spiritually loyal but breaking completely with Wesley in conducting church affairs, Asbury became the czar of Methodism. Under him membership grew from almost nothing to nearly 300,000. His method was to send into a settlement his most ferocious exhorters to apply the last of Methodism, after which he would come with his itinerants to form a new circuit. Radiating from his eastern strongholds, circuits were set up in Tennessee, Kentucky, Mississippi, Missouri and the Northwest territory. Even in tough New England many doomed Calvinistic lambs were brought into the fold. At first, denied the use of buildings, Evangelist Lee and Asbury preached to thousands on Boston Commons and finally formed a solid organization extending to Maine and Nova Scotia.

The Bishop rode 6,000 miles a year over this vast domain, moving his itinerants like pawns, organizing conferences, dedicating churches and putting out ecclesiastical fires. On numerous trips to Ohio he visited Dr. Tiffin, a physician, later Ohio's first governor, who formed the first Methodist Society in the state, at Chillicothe. In Cincinnati he dedicated churches in College Hill

[1] Member of the Literary Club.

and Mount Washington. At Milford he always stayed with his great ally, Phillip Gatch, who with Dr. McCormick founded the second church in the state. He established three colleges and over a hundred academies in the backwoods where there were no schools. Many of these schools still exist; and many more today, including hundreds of churches and hospitals, and countless children are named after Bishop Asbury.

One of his first acts as bishop was to make the Sunday School[1] a part of each church. The need of Sunday Schools for printed tracts was the cause of one of his greatest contributions, the founding of the Methodist Book Concern in Philadelphia in 1789. It was his pet project, whose scope was enlarged to produce hymn books, bibles and other church literature, and is now one of the largest of all printing houses.

Asbury also made social evils the concern of the Lord and started Methodism on its career as the church militant. He was the first to wage a relentless campaign against the demon rum. Drams were taken freely at log rollings and barn raisings in those days, yet he made prohibition a part of the discipline, a move no other Christian church has ever made. Many of the clergy and others had to be purged to make this law effective.

Next to liquor he regarded slavery as the greatest curse of the time. He treated negroes as human beings, welcomed them to the church and often carried with him a certain negro preacher whose sermons, painting a vivid picture of sinners tormented in Hell and the faithful living in mansions in the skies, made him a great favorite with both white and black.

Asbury converted many prominent people who became his personal friends and gave generous contributions to the church. He had inteviews and correspondence with Washington and succeeding Presidents on slavery, and addressed both houses of Con-

[1] The first Sunday Schools were set up by Wesley in England. Classes were held in barns. His objective was to teach the ignorant to read so that they could read the Bible.

gress and numerous state legislatures, proposing law for gradual emancipation.

Because of his attitude toward slavery and because he forbade his preachers to own slaves or make whiskey, Methodism grew slowly in the South but finally gained a large membership of especially the hill people. Methodism had numerous upper class members but, because of its non-Calvinistic doctrine, promising a beautiful eternity without physical toil; its natural appeal was to working people. It was a practical religion, bringing discipline and education directly to the doors of the masses, as it had done in England.

Wesley, always in good health and good spirits, lived to be 89 years old, while Asbury, always in bad health and never known to smile, miraculously lived to be 71 years old. He carried on his work in spite of the afflictions of Job, suffering constantly from chronic bronchitis, asthma, swollen legs and skin eruptions, all obviously due to exposure and avitaminosis, brought on by his fasting two days a week and the bad food on this travels. Even when acutely ill he insisted on riding to the next appointment, though many times he had to be tied to his saddle and in his last years was forced to use a cart. His diet guaranteed a low cholesterol level, but he must have had a strong constitution to survive his rigorous program.

In 45 years he covered the east over 80 tmes, the south 50 times; made 23 trips into New England, one to Canada and 20 over the mountains. He missed few settlements and became known personally or by sight to a greater proportion of the population of a nation than any man in history, before television. His last trips, on which he was accompained by the local elder and a coterie of intinerants, were triumphal processions. Great crowds of the curious and the faithful assembled to see and hear the venerable saint, and as he tottered or was carried to his cart after the sermon, the multitude invariably broke into tears. On such a trip he died in 1816 trying to get back from Kentucky to a

Baltimore Conference. His estate of $2,000 saved from his $80 a year salary and recent gifts went to the Methodist Book Concern. His letters, books and mementoes are on display at the Drew Seminary. There is an imposing statue to him in Washington and I remember Dr. Fenneman's paper on it in 1927. Fenneman quoted from the dedication speech of Calvinist Cal Coolidge, who said the bishop was the single greatest influence in building a new nation.

I actually knew one man, Uncle Willis Snapp, who had seen Bishop Asbury. Living to be 112 years old, he alone revelled in this distinction for many years. Uncle Willis ran a horse mill near my present farm in Nicholas County, Kentucky, and when I was seven years old my grandfather took me and a sack of corn to the mill. Patting me on the head, the old man said, "Ben, this boy might grow up to be a bishop."

* Uncle Willis Snapp was my great-great-uncle.

CHAPTER 28

RACING AND THE BIBLE BELT
Thoroughbred Record-7/14/73*

Legalized racing is conducted in all civilized countries of the world and in the United States except in certain Bible Belt states: Virginia, the Carolinas, Georgia, Tennessee, Alabama, and Texas. The purpose of this chapter is to trace the history of racing, to show why racing is prohibited in the Bible Belt states, and to propose the kind of racing bill which would be acceptable to these states.

The superior breeds of the horse came from Asia, Asia Minor, and Arabia. Blegen, in his excavations of the various levels of Troy, found bits and bridles and established 3000 B.C. as the date when the horse was first used for purposes other than food. There is evidence of racing involving mounted Bactrian and Arabian horses before the Bronze Age and the wheel, after which, beginning around 2000 B.C., there is well-documented history of chariot racing and gambling with bookmakers, especially in Greece and Rome. The Mongol hordes, in "blitzkrieging" Western Asia and Eastern Europe, used Bactrian horses which became

*Among practicing horsemen, few indeed equal Dr. Eslie Asbury in the ability to translate ideas into prose. During times past we have been privileged to publish some of his articles, others appear occasionally in periodicals of varied interests, from medical journals to epistolatory annals. In addition, he is an after-dinner speaker in considerable demand. Recently he presented a talk before the Georgia Thoroughbred Association, the theme of which is of interest to racing people throughout the land. Excerpts from that address are printed here. (Editor, The Thoroughbred Record)

crossed with Arabians. The Crusaders, and later others, brought stallions of these superior breeds to England and bred them to native English mares. The result was the Thoroughbred, a horse superior in size and performance to either parent. Three hundred years ago, the new breed jelled into the produce of three stallions on the sire side, Matchem, Eclipse and Herod, from whom all thoroughbreds in the world descend.

Like the atom bomb, we owe to war the development of the race horse. When the crossbow at the battle of Crecy ended chivalry and the use of a heavy horse to carry a 400-pound knight in armor, the need was for a light, fast cavalry horse. At this point, the thoroughbred came along to fill this need and, man's nature being what it is, it was natural as a sideline for the proud breeder to stake his horse against all comers. By selective breeding over a period of 300 years, the height of the thoroughbred has increased a foot and his speed doubled from 20 miles to 40 miles an hour. England not only developed the thoroughbred but exported him, along with the traditions of racing, to all countries, especially to our southern colonies, whose plantation owners were English and whose back country and Piedmont sections were settled by Scotch-Irish, *always in opposition to the English and in control since the the Civil War.*

Until the Civil War all thoroughbreds were imported by southerners, and thoroughbred breeding and racing was limited to the South. For 200 years, racing was legal and widespread in Maryland, Virginia, the Carolinas, Georgia, and later in Tennessee and Kentucky.

President Washington, Jefferson, Jackson and many famous citizens, including Henry Clay, were prominent in racing and breeding[1], and the Charleston Jockey Club was a prestigious body.

---

[1] President Grant owned a stable of 22 race horses before he was elected. Vice-President Curtis (part Indian) had been a professional jockey. Even F.D.R. "improved the breed" in his own way. Harry Hopkins, an inveterate bettor, had a special wire to the White House over which he placed his bets, often inducing the President to join him. The wily Yankee never risked more than $2.00.

With the passing of the colonial governors, racing began to lose out in parts of the South. The War Between the States almost finished it[2]. The thoroughbreds and part thoroughbreds gave the South a superior cavalry, but many were lost along with pedigree records. Fortunately, the majority were in the upper South and most survived.

SPREAD OF LEGALIZED RACING

I am a great admirer of the "wool hat" politicians and their followers, the Baptists, and my Methodists, who have dominated the South since the Civil War and often helped northerners such as Senator Taft save the country, but the idea of racing means so little to them that Georgia newspapers notice only the Kentucky Derby. In some ways they are like the great Yankees who moved west with the frontier and, through their control of government and education, prevented racing in the North until they were outvoted by more liberal recent immigrants.

Meanwhile racing prospered over the world. The pedigree of the thoroughbred is the only universal language. In any country I have visited I found influential friends eager to communicate. Abroad racing is universally on a nonprofit basis and always in the hands of leading citizens. In England, under the Jockey Club, with such stewards as Lord Derby and the Duke of Norfolk, it is the most prestigious sport. In South Africa and Italy racing is high-class, and the biggest purses in the world are raced for in Japan and France. It is the most popular sport in Australia and Ireland, where the government actually subsidizes it to promote the breeding industry. It rivals soccer in all South America, countries, where the proceeds also go to charities, after the jockey clubs take out enough to provide for the members the most lavish amenities I have ever seen. In Russia, even though the govern-

---

[3] Lexington was hidden in a swamp for two years by his slave groom.

ment takes 47 percent out of each bet, the people support it because, I suppose, it is "the only game in town."

As racing became legal in various parts of the United States, gamblers and commercial interests too often were in control, and racing commissions were composed of political hacks who knew little and cared less about racing. Doping, ringers, and cheating were commonplace. In spite of well-conducted racing in New York and Kentucky, it was an uphill struggle to obtain the present well-merited confidence in racing. The Harrison Narcotic Act helped. The Jockey Club and other leaders became influential, and soaring pari-mutuel revenues made it in the interest of both the tracks and the state to exert strict supervision. Now, professional gamblers and criminals cannot own stock in tracks, cannot get licenses to race thoroughbreds, and are not even allowed into major tracks. Of course, wherever there is money, someone will try to cheat, but I believe racing is the cleanest of all professional sports. Today, bankers, businessmen and pillars of the church own and breed horses, and the important tracks are under the control of leading citizens.

OPPOSITION TO RACING AND GAMBLING

If racing is now on a good basis, if gambling per se is not a moral issue, and if the combination of betting and racing is accepted as a legitimate sport of the world, why is it illegal in Bible Belt States?

(1) Our puritanical and Calvinistic background.

(2) Bad past history of racing in certain places.

(3) Prejudice and ignorance about the potential advantages of racing and breeding.

I am proud to say I am not a professional economist and, although *I have given up all ideology in favor of being right,* I hope I am an enlightened conservative or at least an "extreme moderate." I can remember when 85 percent of the people were needed to supply the essential goods and services; when an insurance salesman was regarded as a parasite; when a depression meant that the majority could not get enough clothes, housing or food. Social-minded capitalism has not only exceeded the demands of the "manifesto" of Marx and Engels; it has freed labor of cruel toil (how I hated as a boy to pitch the hay), and I guess that now 20 percent could produce our essentials. The pressure of production which is necessary to keep factories and business prosperous and to keep essential producers employed; the pressure of the demands of added leisure; the pressure to provide income to the whole population to buy and consume the vast output of essential and nonessential products and services, are the real reasons behind the expansion of recreational businesses (golf, racing, professional sports, amusement parks, etc.), government spending, the number of government employees, and *Welfarism,* as well as the expansion of other nonessential services. This is another justification for the spread of racing.

The last and most important reason that racing is still illegal in the so-called Bible Belt has been the presentation by the wrong people of wrong bills which give no assurance to the average citizen that racing is in his or the public interest (bills, I, myself, would not vote for).

THE PROPER RACING BILL

We must convert honest opposition. Calvinists, Methodists, Baptists and other Protestant churches fought the excesses of their time. They are *my* people and they are sincere people. They built this country, they established colleges which are still among our best, even if the founders never dreamed they would descend to partisan policies and become leaders of liberalism. I have only one thing against our ancestors. They put a drop of "bluing" into our washtub of culture. They wrote church laws into the laws of the land and some irrational blue laws that violated the rights of their neighbors. The Methodists led the prohibition effort, and while it was a failure, prohibition at least carried the logic that drinkers endangered others. Laws against honest gambling have no such justification. They attempt to repeal the nature of man. Everyone gambles. The peach grower gambles on the weather, a Kansas farmer I knew sowed a carload of wheat and didn't get a biscuit, and insurance companies bet you against fire and death. The amount one eats or spends, drinks or gambles on the races or on stocks and bonds is each individual's problem. Laws to protect one against mistakes of judgment are impossible.

The world has always recognized that wagering is an integral part of racing. The sport consists in staking your horse against other horses, and those that bet are temporary part-owners of a horse. The association of racing and wagering is so ingrained that many states have legalized gambling *only* on horse racing. The age-old worldwide established custom of going to the track and betting on a horse is as logical as going near naked on the beach. Betting with a downtown bookie is not a part of the sport of racing. It is as out-of-place and just as illogical as wearing a bikini on a public street.

Owning, breeding and racing horses has never been regarded as immoral by most leading people of the world. Even Cromwell kept up the Royal Stud and stopped racing for only six months (the only time in history it was ever stopped), and then only to prevent the Cavaliers from massing together. The continuity of the industry and sport was so essential that no country[4] interrupted it during the world wars. Our submarine men took pictures of Japanese races through periscopes, and racing continued in Germany until April, 1945.

In his diary George Washington kept an account of all his wagers, and his records of his importations, and those matings, as well as those of Andrew Jackson, are valuable for our stud

---

[4] In the U.S. for four months during World War II, transportation of horses was banned.

books. Barney Baruch and Admiral Cary Grayson bred and raced extensively and persuaded President Wilson to permit racing during World War I. Mrs. Woodrow Wilson boarded mares with the Graysons in Virignia. Sam Riddle gave Mrs. Grayson and Mrs. Wilson seasons to Man o' War, and I was present when they sold their yearlings at Saratoga.

If producing a good horse has challenged the leading people, and if the proper conduct of racing and breeding has been proven to be a constructive industry over the world, how do you get racing in Georgia or Texas or Virginia? In my opinion, to obtain permission to run pari-mutuel betting, the backers will have to present assurance that this activity is in the public interest. A bill will have to be proposed which any legislator can vote for without alienating his constituents, and which he can justify to be in the interest of all citizens. You can go about it the Texas way and fail, or you can go about it the right way. Texans are merely transplanted Georgians and Kentuckians. They assume a man is either *a Baptist or an outlaw!* The average man equates racing with legalized outlawry, an activity which enriches gamblers, track owners and the Mafia and does nothing for him or the community. The backers of the first Texas bill did nothing to dispel the fears of the people. A few years ago, a second bill with better backing was proposed. A committee came to Lexington and invited six of us to dinner. They asked for financial help, a big mistake which gave ammunition to the opposition, claiming outside selfish influence. I had made a special trip from Cincinnati to attend this dinner, and when I found they were backing a routine racing bill, I left after one drink and drove back to Cincinnati. As predicted, they lost again.

Legalized racing provides a discriminatory privilege to conduct gambling. Therefore it is a questionable vehicle for free enterprise. Racing should be conducted in the public interest. All profits should go to education or other good causes. Nonprofit racing attracts leading people to be owners of horses. Attendance at the races becomes fashionable. Employment is created for thousands, many unsuited to modern industry.

Keeneland, established 50 years ago, was the first nonprofit operation. Following the Keeneland model, nonprofit racing was installed at Belmont, Saratoga, Acqueduct, Aksarben, Delmar, Fairgrounds and Delaware tracks, where it is flourishing.

High-class free enterprise racing is still conducted at the California, Illinois, and Florida tracks but with increasing difficulty under the harassment by the horsemen and the politicians. I believe even religious fundamentalists would not oppose a nonprofit racing bill in the Bible Belt states.

CHAPTER 29

THE THIRD WORLD OF RACING

The Third World of Racing is the backstretch populated by thousands of people on whom the care of valuable horses, the security of fine barns, and the integrity of racing finally depends. Billions have been spent on race tracks, breeding farms, and the importation of the best bloodstock and jockeys; owners go all out to breed or buy the best horses and hire the best trainers and riders. The Jockey Club trains capable officials, fine citizens without salary help manage non-profit tracks and serve on racing commissions, yet all of these expenditures and noble efforts can be nullified by poor backstretch employees who, through ignorance, spite, carelessness or contrivance may mishandle horses or burn down a barn. This is no reflection on the many hard working, loyal grooms and exercise personnel; but the demand exceeds the supply. As a result, only a few fortunate stables retain the best help, leaving the vast majority to shift as best they can.

These trite but true statements are best understood by trainers. During 50 years, the author has known well possibly 100 established trainers and found them a remarkable group of men. Though many grew up without education or privilege, I found them equal or superior to the people of any calling. Like doctors, they have troubles that go with their jobs. Usually the more successful the trainer, the fewer his occupational complaints, but the loudest, most universal complaint has been "bad help," so bad that many have curtailed their stables or quit the business.

In England trainers have a "headquarters" which they occupy the year around, permitting the help to live in one place. Racing there has been a way of life for centuries, and many "Head Lads" are available who are proud to follow in the footsteps of their forebears and are capable of training and disciplining backstretch personnel.

In this country, considering the adverse living conditions, especially for family men, and the vast distance between race tracks, it is remarkable that trainers have as much good help as they do. The most successful horsemen who have trained the fillies of our own stables over the past 50 years (including Sherrill Ward, Howard Oots, Babe Wells, Mack Miller, Woody Stephens, Homer Pardue, Billy Hicks, Rusty Arnold, Stanley Reiser, Max Hirsch and Gib Gay) all had either a foreman or at least one groom or exercise boy whom they modestly claimed was indispensible to their success. If short of such help, the trainers of the small stables (such as Ward, Pardue, Hicks, Gay) did not feel it beneath them to help rub or exercise their horses.

The few great grooms and exercise boys, accidental products of their environment and natural ability, receive no more public credit for their efforts than the fine linemen on football teams who are responsible for the success of famous halfbacks. It would be a contribution to a vacant area of turf history if a book were written about unusual "backstretchers."

GROOMS, DOCTORS, GARDENERS

One of the greatest grooms who would have to be included was the late Clifford Gatewood, known as "Dink," a black man. Dink worked for Babe Wells for 30 years. Babe said he always came up with the best horse and easiest-to-train horses in the barn. Dink talked constantly to the horses ("Come May they gonna pin them roses on you") as he groomed them and somehow they always felt well, ate well and "bloomed" in training. In other words, they seemed to train and race more willingly and to remain "good" longer than the average horse.

It has long been known that some doctors, whatever their specialty, have a high percentage of cured or satisfied patients. The exact mechanism of the psychosomatic effect some doctors are able to achieve is not established, but it must be the result of better communication which instills confidence and sets in motion a train of stimuli which favorably activate the various glands of internal secretion and the sympathetic nervous system. Acupuncture has little scientific basis, has been overtouted and lends itself to false hopes for cure of organic diseases and to quackery — but the apparent success of acupuncture in certain situations only further proves the profound effect of suggestion and communication which is valuable in handling both functional and organic conditions.

Peter Tomkins and Christopher Bird have recently written a book, *The Secret Life of Plants*, in which they conclude that all living things, including plants, have emotions and respond to conditioned reflexes. They claim that some horticulturists — those with a "green thumb"— communicate with plants and get results superior to those of others. Jim Fitzsimmons said, "No horse was born mean, not even the most obstreperous sons of Nearco and Man o' War. There are only two kinds of horses: (1) good actors, and (2) those that had been mistreated." Thoroughbreds are not plow horses. They are smart, have quick reactions, and the greater their inherited power and energy, the more easily they are upset by the actions and tone of voice of their handlers and the greater patience and delicacy required to develop their potential. It is not necessary to "love" horses but to understand their psychology, and the trainer's attitude sets the pace for the barn. More than once in making rounds of a stable, the author has heard a trainer say, "Look out for that mean hussy. She'll bite or kick you." Many a "mean horse," lost intentionally in a claiming race, has "bloomed" in the new barn. Whirlaway could have been a failure in lesser hands. Ben Jones' handling of this horse was a classic example of conditioning the reflexes, which is a good part of what training is all about. Trainers like Jones also conditioned the reflexes of their help. For example, an "outlaw" (the horse had been hit over the head with a twitch stick) from a famous farm was delivered under deep sedation, carried out of the van on a tarpaulin, and deposited in the hallway of Hunter Moody's barn. Two days later Moody was driving this horse in a cart around the trotting track and he later won stakes races.

Fred Hooper (the author sold him his first stakes winner 44 years ago) is a most successful, statesmanlike, down to earth owner and breeder. At the 1974 Jockey Club Round Table Conference Mr. Hooper had this to say, "Next to breeding sound horses, I believe the most important thing is to keep horses happy. I never go to my barn without petting and talking to each horse. Horses receive too little or bad care. Proper care, I think, prevents the necessity of medication, to all of which I am opposed because there is no way to control it." A well-trained groom can detect early trouble and is the first line of defense against crippling injuries.

This preamble, in fact the whole chapter was written in the hope of stimulating the production of more and better backstretch help, racing's greatest internal problem.

A POSSIBLE JOCKEY CLUB TRAINING PROGRAM

Several years ago at breakfast at Max Hirsch's Saratoga barn, Max (because there were three Jockey Club members) suggested that the Jockey Club should start a backstretch training school at Belmont Park. The matter was proposed to Jack Kennedy, who was then the executive secretary. After some inquiries, he reported a favorable reaction. However, Mr. Kennedy died soon thereafter and the plan was not pursued. The author discussed this idea with Chairman Nicholas Brady, Francis Kernan and others.

I still hope the Jockey Club will sponsor a backstretch training program*. Backstretch schools would attract a better class of boys and girls than the dregs, which too often, trainers must depend upon. Youngsters, ambitious for careers in the horse world, would have a place to start; graduates of these programs would have a status which the present backstretch employees do not have. The problem deserves consideration– by the Jockey Club, the Trainers Association, and the American Horse Council.

*Progress has been made since this article was published 15 years ago in the *Thoroughbred Record*. The Kentucky Breeders Association, among others, has established a backstretch training program.

CHAPTER 30

MAN O' WAR

Literary Club
January 26, 1948

A few will remember him as a tall, long-legged foal running beside his dam in the wooded pastures of the old Nursery Stud, like other foals except for his extra height and his long legs and his presumption that the world was his.

There are a few left who will remember him as a striking yearling which might make a good steeplechase if he failed on the flat. He was a trifle large, his head was too high, his forelegs forked a bit wide. Beside the sleekest sale yearlings he seemed thin and hungry. But there was a powerful frame and a proud spirit, and he had a proud name to go with it.

In later years there would be a hundred stories of those who recognized in him the spark of greatness. There would be a dozen tales of those who were on the point of buying him, but something or other happened (Riddle bought him for $5,000 as a yearling).

Some will remember how the eyes of the clockers widened when they began to catch his workouts, and how he went to the post at odds-on the first time he ran, and every time thereafter.

They will certainly remember that after six successive victories he came out of a pocket a little late to win the Sanford Memorial from Upset, which had the added advantage of a 15 pound weight concession. In the years to come this defeat would have to be explained a million times; it was so hard for people to believe that it could have happened. Most have forgotten that for the witnesses at Saratoga that day, the race actually added to the reputation of the horse, and confirmed the belief that the American turf had come upon the greatest figure in its history.

The horsemen who saw the racing of that memorable summer in New York will call to mind this colt of Sam Riddle's, how he reminded old-timers of his fiery sire, only bigger and wider and stronger, and how they joked with Sam that he had rung in a four-year-old. They will recall his imperious disregard of men and horses, his impatience with restraint, his stubborn laziness that had a way of bursting into a yellow flame of speed, and how he bolted down his feed and gave himself the bellyache.

They will remember how he came out the next spring and cut his way through the ranks of his opposition until there were no ranks left. How finally it became difficult to find even a token of opposition for him and he still went about running races faster than they had ever seen run, even when there was no need for him to get out of a gallop. How they matched him against an older champion, a great horse, and saw disappear the last hope of finding anything worthy to come on the track with him.

Some others will remember the day he came back home to Kentucky and under colors for the last time, and was cantering along the stretch of the old Kentucky Association track, the faint light of winter gleaming on his golden coat.

The horsemen who came from all over the world to see him in his prime at Faraway Farm will remember him vividly — the massive body, the wide sweeps of muscle, the great chest and abnormally wide spacing between his forelegs, the die-cut perfection of his legs and feet, the slight dip of the back deepening with the years, the high head, the imperial air, the feel of power and mastery. They won't see another like him.

The millions who have gone out to Faraway to see him will remember the look in his eye, the dignity with which he held himself for their inspection. They will remember that it was hard to tell whether his coat was red or yellow, and that there were faint little spots here and there.

Finally they will all remember his most worshipful fan, the groom who patiently recited for all visitors the glories of the greatest attraction in the history of Kentucky: "He was foaled March 29, 1917, at Maj. Belmont's place, right over there. Mr. Riddles bought him for $5,000 at Saratoga as a yearling . . . A man come here and offered a million dollars for him, and Mr. Riddles said, 'No, lots of men might have a million dollars, but only one man could have Man o' War.' " Man o' War was America's greatest stallion.

Mr. Riddle was jealous of Man o' War, limiting him to 25 mares a season with a stud fee of $5,000, four times higher than any other stallion. He easily could have covered 50 mares, but Riddle wouldn't allow the Whitney's and Wideners to breed to him. He feared their good mares would get foals who would beat him on the track. No other stallion owner ever took this view. He would let Elizabeth Graham and Mrs. Woodrow Wilson have seasons, and, being unknown, I finally got a season to Man o' War.

The day after Man o' War died I went to Faraway Farm. Mr. Riddle, age 91, was sitting by the fire, crying. "There will never be another horse in that stall," he said. But there was: War Admiral, a son of Man o' War. I came to call to get a season to him. Hundreds applied. I got one every year and sold the yearlings for large sums. Later, at Saratoga, Mr. Riddle said, "Asbury, you are getting rich off of me." He still let me breed to War Admiral.

Note: Much of this chapter was taken from an article by Joe Estes in the *Blood-Horse* magazine.

CHAPTER 31

LOUISVILLE

"Doctor, you know more about Louisville than I do," said Breaux Ballard during a recent bridge game in Naples, Florida. Even if he was joking, this was a compliment coming from Breaux, whose family, starting with William Clark, younger brother of unmarried George Rogers Clark, has produced leaders since Louisville was founded. Among them were Bland Ballard, the famous Indian fighter, and Meriwether Clark, founder of the Louisville Jockey Club and builder of Churchill Downs on 100 acres owned by his uncles, John and Henry Churchill. I knew Breaux's prestigious father, Breaux, Sr., through Ike Lanier, Lyter Donaldson, and Judge Richard Hill, his schoolmates at Centre College. I know Breaux's son, also named Breaux, and knew U.S. Senator Thurston Ballard Morton, later head of the American Horse Council. One of my long-time friends in the horse world has been Warner Jones, a top-rank breeder, son of Breaux's aunt, Mina Ballard Chambers. I first met Warner at Saratoga, where he was a guest of the Hancocks. Aged nineteen, he had osteomyelitis of the heel bone. Mr. Hancock asked me to see him. Later, Warner, his mother, stepfather Henning Chambers, and Mr. Threlkeld, Warner's adviser, spent a Sunday with us at Forest Retreat. Jeff Wood (graduate of Berea), sales manager of

Procter and Gamble, was also a guest. Roosevelt was about to run for a third term. Mr. Chambers bet Jeff Wood a case of Bourbon that Roosevelt would be nominated, another case that he would be elected. It was war time. On behalf of Wood, I got Lyons Brown to deliver two cases of Old Forester to Henning Chambers.

I have fond memories of Derby weekends with Owsley Brown, Sr., and his son, Lyons, and Lyons' wife, Sally, at Ashbourne. Thirty-five years ago I collaborated with Sally on an article about the thoroughbred in Kentucky for the *Filson Club Quarterly*.

The offspring of Kentucky thoroughbreds will inherit the rate of speed of the sire and dam. Not all the get of superior horses also will inherit class or the will to win to go along with great speed, but there have been enough of them in each generation to keep Kentucky in the forefront. Human genetics involves more variables, but, like speed in horses, there is one constant. Children generally inherit the I.Q. of the parents. The offspring of superior parents generally inherit the high I.Q. of their parents, but all such siblings do not inherit the energy or motivation to succeed. The number of Louisville and Kentucky families who have produced leaders in each generation has always amazed me. Among such Louisville families are the Ballards, Haldermans, Browns, Clarks, Nortons, Joneses, Bullits, Speeds, Castlemans, Stolls, Wathens, Prices, Binghams, Thrustons, Farnsleys, Hennings, Hilliards, etc.

This is worth a genetic study.

Childhood Years and Medical Friends

If it is true, as Breaux Ballard remarked, that I know a lot about Louisville, it is because of my close and varied contacts with the city for 85 years. At the turn of the century I lived in Louisville four years while my father belatedly got his M.D. degree from the University of Louisville. We first lived in the vicinity of Dusty Rhodes' saloon and the National League baseball park near 28th

& Broadway, where, in 1903, as waterboy for the Louisville Colonels, I saw Honus Wagner, the most famous shortstop of all time, play his first game in his stocking feet. They couldn't find shoes big enough for him. Later, we lived three years at the s. w. corner of 8th & Broadway. The large McAuliffe family lived next door. One of them became a well-known Louisville pediatrician. Another playmate was Clifford Holburn, who lived at 8th & Chestnut. Cliff's frog eyes were unforgettable. I recognized him on an L & N train 40 years later. A paint drummer, he later sold us white creosote paint for our farm, barns, and plank fences. I had two memorable Jewish friends. One was Meyer Rabin, whose father owned a saloon on 9th near Broadway. Meyer became a famous musician. Muncie Goldstein's father ran a notions store at 10th & Broadway. Muncie went to Harvard and became a successful businessman in New York. I attended the Monserrat public school at 5th & York. The principal, a formidable woman, used a black strap to punish wrongdoers. A black school was located a few blocks west. We came home in groups, but I still have two scars on my head, souvenirs of the inevitable clashes with the blacks. Twice I went with Meyer and Muncie to the rabbinical school which they attended each day after our public school let out. The students recited out loud in unison. I can still remember the loud buzz. For about a year, I hustled newspapers for Big Jeff who had the concession at the L & N depot. I got 1 cent for each paper sold. For the next three years I was errand boy on a bakery wagon driven by one of the Scheppelman brothers, who owned a bakery near 2nd & Market. We served a west end region populated mostly by German immigrants. Schep had a beer every day at the same saloon, ordering a sarsaparilla for me. I received 25 cents a day for the short trips during the school year and $2.50 a week working full time in the summer. All spare time was devoted to baseball, which we played on the streets, vacant lots and the yard of the Medical College on Chestnut Street. There were no playgrounds short of Shawnee Park, miles away.

I was present when my father received his diploma in 1907, the year the medical practice act went into effect requiring each graduate to pass the state board examination before receiving a license to practice. The University of Louisville was better, but at that time there were six other medical schools in Louisville, diploma mills, grinding out hundreds of graduates each year. Only 15 percent, including my father, passed the new state board examination and received their license to practice. The rest melted into the general population as farmers, shoe salesmen, etc.

When I saw Dr. J. N. McCormack at my father's commencement, I didn't realize I was looking at the most powerful man in the history of organized medicine in the United States. He wrote Kentucky's first medical practice act and lobbied for its passage. For forty years he was the leader who built the A.M.A. into a constructive organization. Dr. McCormack's greatest contribution as head of the A.M.A. was to induce the Carnegie Foundation to appoint Abraham Flexner of Louisville to investigate all medical schools. Flexner's report in 1909 spelled the death knell of hundreds of proprietary medical schools, putting medical education under the auspices of universities where it belonged. His model medical practice act was copied and is still used by nearly all the states of the Union. In my book *Both Sides of the River,* I cover my connection with his son, Dr. Arthur McCormack, my association with Dr. Fred Rankin and later with Dr. John Bate, Rudolph Noer, Arnold Griswold, George Hendon and Frank Strickler in the formation of the American Association for the Surgery of Trauma. Two years ago, through Dr. Chris Shields, I was the speaker at the annual dinner of the Innominate Society founded by Drs. Spurling and Smith fifty years ago.

I saw Old Rosebud win the Derby in 1914 and I saw Mr. Bradley's horses finish one-two in 1921. Behave Yourself was first and Black Servant was second. Since the two horses ran as a betting unit, the order of finish made no difference to the public, but for Mr. Bradley the wrong horse won by a nose. The two horses were far out in front, but the jockeys rode furiously against one another to the finish. Mr. Bradley had a large bet in the winter book and would have won $50,000.00 if Black Servant had been the winner. Mr. Bradley didn't tell the jockeys before the race about his bet and, always the gentleman, didn't complain about the result. Thousands, like myself, who had no reserved seat, vied for a spot from which any part of the race could be seen. A black man was sitting on top of a stepladder. I offered him $2.00 for his perch. No response. Another man offered him $5.00. No response. Near post time when a man offered $10.00, the black didn't bother to climb down. He "jumped" at the offer.

The last Derby I saw before we had our permanent box in Section F was when Bubbling Over won. I was with Dr. George Knapp and Louis Werk, much older men. I stood on their shoulders and called the race.

My great friend Dr. Gordon McKim, famous Cincinnati urologist, operated on Mr. Bradley for his enlarged prostate gland. As a reward, Dr. McKim was awarded two seats in Bradley's second box. Each year Dr. McKim turned them over to me, giving us eight box seats. Our family used our box. Mary and I sat with the Olin Gentrys and Barry Shannons, Bradley's managers. Later and for several years we had a whole, second, free box owned by R. J. Reynolds obtained through his niece, Mrs. Ann Forsyth. Mr. Reynolds was staying out of the country to avoid litigation.

I bought some of my best early stock, yearling fillies, from Mr. Bradley through Olin Gentry and Tom Bohne, Bradley's secretary, a son of Barry Shannon's sister, upon whom I had operated in Cincinnati.

In previous books I mention Mr. Bradley's generosity to any former employee. About 1940 Dr. McKim referred to me a former exercise rider for Mr. Bradley. Later, working for another owner, this boy sustained a leg fracture. The case was closed with the Kentucky Industrial Commission. The rider, now broke, needed an osteotomy to correct his improperly set fracture. Dr. McKim said "Bradley isn't liable, but you call Barry Shannon. They will pay the bill." I did and they paid.

In 1946, the year Mr. Bradley died, we had our first Derby horse, Hampden, sold to Willie Dupont. Hampden finished third. A few years later we saw our Noureddin finish third and our Invalidate finish fifth, but our greatest thrill was watching Determine win the Derby in 1954. Our whole family was present, including my son, Dr. Taylor Asbury, then in training as an eye resident at the University of California. He and the members of his department had won a lot of money backing Determine in his preliminary races in California. They sent it all by Taylor to bet on Determine at 4 to 1 in the Derby. We carried $35,000.00 in cash until Monday before we could bank it and send checks to the winners.

We have won a number of maiden and allowance races at Churchill Downs, but our second greatest satisfaction was seeing Hail to Patsy win the Kentucky Oaks. Tommy Gentry bought this filly from us for a client in the Keeneland Summer Sale for $200,000. Brownian won the prestigious Falls City Handicap in our own colors.

My first speaking engagement in Louisville was at the pre-Derby dinner of the Kentucky Breeders' Association at the Brown Hotel in 1940. Pat Calhoun of Mississippi Barge Lines fame was the president, and I spent the night with him at his beautiful farm near the river east of Louisville. My subject was "Choosing Prospective Broodmares." Looking back at the principles I advocated, I wouldn't change them except that I wouldn't be as positive. Mr. Graham Brown, who bought yearlings from me, was present at the dinner. Later, Mr. Brown did me a great favor. A week before the Derby, Steve Wilson, president of Fram Corporation and our greatest farm customer, called and asked me to get him two rooms for the Derby weekend. I was desperate. This was impossible. As a last resort I called Mr. Brown, an old bachelor, who lived in his hotel. "All our rooms are sold" he said, "but I have three rooms of my own. You can have two of them."

Through Churchill Downs I met many Louisville people, including the Veenemans, Lusskys and Judge Church, who loaned me his box for Bob Taft and his friends in the Senate. All made it except Taft, whose wife had a stroke on Derby eve. I knew all the people connected with the track, among them Matt Winn, Stanley Hugenberg, Bill Corum, Russell Sweeney, Wathen Knebelcamp, Lynn Stone and Mr. Meeker, the present capable head. I started with Matt Winn and operated on two of his daughters who lived in northern Kentucky.

Writers

My exposure to Louisville was broadened by my son Dr. Taylor Asbury, who introduced me to his prominent Yale classmates and others, including Royden Peabody, Ed Middleton, Sam Miller, William Heyburn and Bob Rounsavall.

In addition to my Filson Club friends, I also cherish my friendship with many Louisville writers, past and present. The first was Tandy Ellis, who wrote a column called "The Tang of the South" for the *Courier-Journal*. His father, Dr. Percy Ellis, lived at Ghent, Kentucky, in my surgical territory and referred several members of the prestigious Tandy and Ellis family to me for operations, including Justine Tandy Campbell of Ghent, her sister at Aurora, Indiana, and Jeannette Tandy of Vevay, Indiana, author of *American Satire and Humor*. I know Mrs. Creason and never met the C-J writer Joe Creason, but I can recommend his book, *The Best of Creason*. Wade Hall, a professor at Bellarmine College and author of *The Smiling Phoenix*, has been a big help to me. I met Byron Crawford, columnist for the C.J., at Berea when both of us were performers in the Appalachian Humor Festival two years ago. In my book *Horse Sense and Humor in Kentucky,* I wrote extensively about Mike Barry, my friend for 30 years who is now on the broadcasting staff of the C. J. In my current book, *Both Sides of the River,* I recall other incidents and people with whom I was connected in the horse, medical and literary worlds of Louisville. I have a chapter in this book on Henry Watterson. Two of Watterson's products, Nixon Denton and Forrest Frank, were members of the Cincinnati Literary Club. Three other famous early members also came from Louisville: Charles Anderson, governor of Ohio, Larz Anderson, who married Nicholas Longworth's daughter and started a dynasty still prominent, and General John Pope, brother-in-law of the Anderson brothers. Dr. Frank Mayfield, famous Cincinnati neuro-surgeon, had his training in Louisville under Dr. Glen Spurling. Dr. Daniel Drake, of Mason County, Kentucky, founder of the Medical College of the University of Cincinnati, served 10 years on the faculty of the University of Louisville. Peter Stern, now the leading hand surgeon of Cincinnati, had his training in Louisville under Dr. Kleinert.

My last visit to Louisville was in 1985 to address the Rotary Club (through J. Ed. McConnell). Jim Bolus, writing the history of Keeneland, interviewed me after the talk. The standing ovation was a tribute to my age (90). I then went to see the restored Seelbach Hotel, especially the famous Rathskeller, whose walls, ceiling, floors and ornate columns are covered with Rookwood tiles made in Cincinnati.

FILSON CLUB

My most satisfying connection with Louisville has been through the Filson Club. The Derby we won lasted two minutes. My membership at the Filson Club has lasted 50 years. I was introduced to the club by Harry Brent Mackoy, eminent Kentucky lawyer of Covington and almost a founder member of the Filson Club. He was historian of the Cincinnati Literary Club, founded in 1849. I have held this position for the past 25 years. Mr. Mackoy and I often discussed the perpetual kinship of the Literary Club and the Filson Club, founded in 1884 by Col. Reuben Darrett. Two 19th century members of the Literary Club were close friends of Col. Durrett: William H. Venable, an educator and writer, and

Donn Piatt, born in Boone County, Kentucky, a judge and a writer in Cincinnati and later a magazine editor in Washington, D.C. Mr. Durrett was a guest of Mr. Venable at a meeting of the Literary Club in 1878. Mr. Venable caused Mr. Durrett to be elected an honorary member of the Philosophical and Historical Society, now the Cincinnati Historical Society. Mr. Venable often visited Durrett at his house in Louisville. Mr. Mackow said that Col. Durrett told him that out of his visit to the Literary Club and discussion with Venable came the idea to found a club in Louisville.

The purpose of the Literary Club was and is to meet each week for mutual instruction through essays, debates and discussions. The club, limited to 100 members, has heard over 7,000 papers and had many distinguished guests. Only one outsider has ever presented the paper of the evening.

This format did not suit the objectives of Col. Durrett. For many years he and his forebears had been collecting Americana, especially Kentuckiana. He visualized a club with unlimited membership which (1) would expand this library, and (2) meet once a month to hear presentations by contemporary historians who had done original research on Kentucky and related history. After discussions with Venable, John Mason Brown, Richard Collins and others, the Filson Club was born. Mr. Mackoy credited William Venable with suggesting the name of the new club. Venable was conscious that John Filson, the first Kentucky historian, was once a resident and co-proprietor of Cincinnati and was last seen on earth in Cincinnati.

In addition to John Mason Brown and Richard Collins, Col. Durrett enlisted co-founders Basil Duke, William Chenault, George Davie, Alex Humphrey, Thomas Speed and James Pirtle, leading citizens, ensuring the success of the club. As I point out elsewhere, these families, and others, have bred leaders in each generation. All have added prestige to the Filson Club, guaranteeing its continued prosperity.

The Filson Club was dominated by Col. Durrett until his death in 1913. All meetings of the club were held in the large library of his spacious mansion on Chestnut Street. Others, including writers, historians and Mrs. Dickey and her lady poets, often met there informally. The latch string was always out and cigars and wine were always available.

William Venable wrote a paper for the Literary Club in February, 1895, describing his experience during three days as a house guest of Durrett several years previously. He said the colonel looked like Longfellow and had the manners of Sir Roger de Coverly; that his library, containing books, letters and newspaper clippings assembled by three generations of Durretts, was the best collection of Kentuckiana in existence; that his home also was a museum, featuring portraits of Daniel Boone, General Wilkinson, John Filson, Indian fighter Bland Ballard and others, along with Boone's rifle and George Rogers Clark's compass. Venable was shaved by Rogers, a celebrated black 76-year-old barber who was known to have served the Clarks, John Breckinridge, and Henry Clay. At dinners and lunches Venable met Thomas Speed, the Rev. Broadus, Dr. Yandell, Henry Watterson, Madison Cawein and other leaders. The dinners featured mint juleps, cherry cobbler, and especially hoe-cake, which the Colonel served 365 days a year.

Sam Johnson was the czar of "The Club." Col. Durrett was the leader and soul of the Filson Club until his death in 1913. An unknown part of his library probably was the property of the club, but possession is nine points of the law. Durrett's heirs sold the entire collection to the University of Chicago. Otto Rothert, on a visit to my farm in 1937, bemoaned the loss but admitted that the Filson Club had owned only a small, unprovable part of the Durrett library. The club also failed to acquire the Lyman Draper collection, which contained the papers of George Rogers Clark and went to the University of Wisconsin.

After Col. Durrett's death in 1913, the club, under the successive leaderships of Bland Ballard, Otto Rothert, Judge Richard Hill, and the present regime of James Bentley and Nelson Dawson, has become one of the leading historical societies in the nation. It has grown to over 3,000 members, owns the Brennan house, its home on Breckinridge Street which houses a great library, and its new house on South Third Street.

The leading people of Louisville have always supported the Filson Club, both financially and spiritually, including the Ballards, the Owsley Brown family, the Brennans, the Farnsleys, Graham Brown, the Abells, the Speeds, the Bullitts and others.

I think so highly of the club that I bought life memberships for three of my family and recruited 16 other life members. One of them was Florence Booth Hollister, sister of an important Filsonian, Alex Booth. When I sent Florence's application, Judge Hill couldn't believe it. She had been away from Louisville for 40 years, married first to Richard Wigglesworth, a congressman from Boston, and after his death, to John Hollister, a congressman from Cincinnati. When I was president of the Literary Club in 1957, I invited Judge Hill to our anniversary dinner. He was the sole and honored guest of the evening.

I have had the privilege of writing three articles for the quarterly and the honor of addressing the Filson Club. Nelson Dawson edited my current book *Horse Sense and Humor in Kentucky*. The quarterly has carried reviews of my books, including my other current book *Both Sides of the River*. I credit this exposure for the sale of hundreds of my books. At the age of 91, I am preparing a final book, *Not Under Oath*. Part of the proceeds will go to the Filson Club. I hope it shows a profit.

CHAPTER 32

LEXINGTON

May 30, 1986

Lexington for 200 years has been the best known city of its size in the country. This was true even when the population was only 25,000. From the start Lexington was the Athens of the West. It has retained its supremacy, especially in the romantic phases of Kentucky culture.

The first settlers came in 1776, soon after the battle of Lexington — hence the name. They were invading the sacred hunting grounds of several tribes of Indians and found the most fertile land ever discovered on Earth. The salt licks, spring water, temperate climate and succulent cane also made it the best game producing region of all time. The reason for this unique phenomenon is geological. Lexington is near the center of an undulating plateau, roughly 50 miles in diameter, caused by a fault which long ago spewed up rock (elsewhere 500 feet under the surface) high in calcium, phosphate and all the trace minerals. On this rich mineral base rotted vegetation formed 8 feet of topsoil. Much of the vegetation came from cane, a biennual which dominated the area and prevented heavy forestation. In spots where the cane was tramped down by buffalo, exposing the soil to the sun, there were legumes and bluegrass, giving this region its name. The grass was green but it had a blue bloom in May.

That is why it is called bluegrass.

The first Kentucky settlers mostly were Scotch-Irish from Appalachia. Having been subsistence farmers and clan fighters for hundreds of years in the lowlands of Scotland and finally in America by way of Ireland, they were the only kind of people who could have fought the Indians and stood the hardships of the frontier. Tales of the new Garden of Eden were relayed back across the mountains. The Revolution was raging. In a few years the Scotch-Irish had the Indians under control. Kentucky became a county of Virginia. About 1780 many of the English Virginia gentry (or soon to be gentry), fearful of the Revolution and tired of their worn out land, brought their slaves, carriages, and thoroughbreds and, armed with lawyers, land grants, and a little money, took over the Lexington region.

Unlike the hordes of uneducated pioneers who settled most of Kentucky (80,000 between 1780-1790), the early settlers of the Bluegrass area included doctors, teachers, artists and architects who made Lexington an instant cultural center when Cincinnati was a cluster of cabins around Ft. Washington. They published newspapers. Within 10 years Transylvania University was established, developing the first medical college west of the mountains and a nationally ranked law college which boasted eminent graduates such as Jefferson Davis. They built fine houses, some still standing. The land was easily cleared and the fields near the residences were usually unplowed. Many fine oaks, ashes, and maple trees were not molested. All the farm products could be concentrated for easy export: the hemp was made into rope, corn was distilled to whiskey, and tobacco was refined for chewing and smoking. Purebred sheep, cattle, and horses were imported from England.

Racing and breeding became a way of life at Lexington beginning in 1783. Leading people were involved, including Henry Clay, who owned Magnolia, the best horse of his time. In all other states (except Maryland) enabling legislation had to be enacted before legal betting on horse racing was permitted. In Kentucky racing with betting has never been questioned. There has never been a vote on it, pro or con. Kentucky and Arkansas are still the only Bible Belt states which have legalized horse racing with betting.

In the War between the States, Kentucky did not secede from the Union, at least not until the war was over. This prevented the sure devastation of Lexington, but the sympathy of central Kentuckians was with the South. Most enlisted in the southern army before they could be drafted by the North.

After the war Lexington and the Bluegrass region resumed its agrarian prosperity. The only area in which the traditional way of life of the South survived, with little change for the next 80 years in the economy or size of the population, Lexington remained at around 25,000 until modern times. The families were small, the farms very large. Migration was unnecessary. Elsewhere in Kentucky the farms were small and the families were large. Lack of land and opportunity caused half of the natives to migrate to the industrial North, leaving the population of the state static even to the present time except in three centers (Lexington, Louisville, Newport-Covington). Also, except a minority in these centers, 95% of the people of Kentucky are descendents of the early settlers.

I have known Lexington for nearly half of its existence, before the arrival of the automobile and asphalt pikes. The main highways were toll roads, including the greatest of them all, the Maysville-Lexington Pike, now a designated part of the Pioneer National Monument, built in 1830 in the administration of Governor Thomas Metcalfe, who had previously (1814) built Forest Retreat (our farm home) on this road, then called the Limestone Trace.

Built by a private company (with the help of a $400,000.00 federal subsidy), using Irish immigrant expert labor, the Maysville-Lexington Pike was the first paved road west of the Alleghenies. It was a marvel of construction: wide and smooth but dusty. Some of the huge, dry, stone wall culverts are still in use today, one near my farm, so big that we used it to transfer cattle from one side of the road to the other side.

I traveled on this road as a child several years before it ceased to be a toll road in 1905. The toll was $1.50 for a horse and buggy at each toll station, about 5 miles apart, making a trip from Maysville to Lexington cost $12.00 (possibly $120.00 in today's dollars). Several families owe their early wealth to this road, an important link for most east-west and east-south traffic. My first trip to Lexington (1900) was on an interurban electric line which ran along this pike from Paris to Lexington. The dust from the traffic on the pike made the adjacent fields look as though they were covered with snow.

MEMORIES OF LEXINGTON

Memories are an old man's greatest treasures, more valuable than more money in the bank — if you already have a little. Moth and rust cannot corrupt them. Only Alzheimzer's disease could steal my early, still vivid memories of Lexington.

In 1914 and 1915, I played here with the University of Cincinnati against the University of Kentucky basketball team. At five feet nine, I was captain. U.K. had a great star named Zerfoss. We played in an armory with a floor too big for the basketball court. A woven wire fence was behind each basket. About two hundred spectators sat along the sidelines. They beat us. We stayed at the Phoenix Hotel, where the waiters, in their eighties, were ex-slaves, one having been a butler for Henry Clay. Another had been a waiter at the hotel when he was a slave. One night he was assigned to serve dinner in the room of an arrogant citizen. After he laid out the meal, the man said, "Now you can go." When the slave didn't budge, the man yelled "get out." The slave said, "Sir, I can't leave. The management holds me responsible for the silver."

Lexington has been pre-eminent in the horse, tobacco and basketball worlds. Few know that 50 to 60 years ago Lexington had the national championship auction and contract bridge team of four. I played on the Cincinnati team against them at the Lexington Club in 1930. They beat us and they beat everybody. They invented bidding conventions such as the "short club," known as the Lexington Club. They made history but didn't write. Goren incorporated their methods into his system. The Lexington team was composed of Pete Stoll, Dr. Robert Coleman, Tom and Bill Combs. My friend Rasty Wright, a sub, was the last survivor. He died a couple of months ago (1985).

I have memories of selling many tobacco crops at the Fourth Street Warehouse, owned by the Lebus brothers. My cousin, Hicel Asbury, was the manager. His father, Uncle Tom, had been a partner of the elder Lebus in three warehouses. Dixie McKinley and Doug Parrish later were partners of Clarence and Frazer Lebus. This warehouse was popular because the house would bid on your crop if it was going too cheap, and they gave favored customers an old ham at Christmas!

I have fond memories of speeches I made in Lexington: two to the Rotary Club 45 years apart; 3 to Thoroughbred Club of America; one to Farm Managers Club; one to the Medical Society; one at Idle Hour Club on behalf of Berea College.

Among my early writer friends, I am proudest of Joe Estes, Joe Palmer, Kent Hollingsworth and Haden Kirkpatrick, unequalled as turf writers. Johnny Clark wrote and dealt in horses. I bought a mare through him when he was 16 years old. Larry Thompson was a friend and guide for many years, as are Harry Caudill and Don Edwards. Judges Sam Wilson had his Cakes and Ale Club. Tom Clark and I are the only survivors. Admiral Gene Markey also had a one-man writer's club, the Versailles Pike Club, which met for lunch once a year at Calumet Farm. I am the sole survivor. Among the guests were William Townsend, Winston Coleman, Gayle Mohney and Jack Lansill.

I have fond memories of social events. In the thirties Clara Bell Walsh opened her house one day a year to stage the premier, pre-Derby lunch. After Clara Bell's death, Alice McIlvain took over for many years, followed by Katherine Raible. Virginia Payson's black-tie dinner now holds the pre-Derby social spotlight. For 40 years, until Bunker Hunt came along, Les Combs had an unopposed lunch on Sunday after the Derby. During this time, Forest Retreat has had a similar lunch for the less endowed, except that Happy Chandler, Charlie Hagyard, Bob Green and Bob Courtney have never failed us (Charlie Hagyard has been my golf partner at Idle Hour, of which I am a founder member), nor have my prestigious doctor friends failed us, including Ed Ray, Thornton Scott, Dick Crutcher and Jim Holloway. Long ago Dr. Marius Johnston, father of Dr. Coleman Johnston, planted 5 trees in our arboretum and Dr. John Scott gave us iris for the garden.

Most of my memories revolve around Keeneland. During the late twenties, I took Dr. Fred Rankin, Louie Beard and Price Headley to Reds baseball games. Later, when Keeneland was being promoted, I had just gotten my farm. Dr. Rankin and Beard enrolled me as a founder. I gave a dinner for Louie Beard in Cincinnati where he signed up six life members[1], closing this limited category. Keeneland was conceived to be a model track, a nonprofit operation run in the public interest because racing depends on a discriminatory privilege to permit legal gambling. Mrs. Payne Whitney furnished most of the money. The rest of us bought preferred stock in dibs and dabs, thinking it was a gift. With Price Headley and W. T. Bishop at the helm, the operation flourished. Within a short time our stock was bought back with interest. Later, under Louis Haggin and now and for many years under able Ted Bassett, Keeneland[2] has become a major racetrack and the premier thoroughbred sales center of the world. Keeneland has lived up to its purpose beyond the wildest dreams.

[1] R. R. Dupree, Charles Williams, Burton Closson, Julius Fleischman, O. DeGray Vanderbilt, Powel Crosley.

[2] We treasure the 40 gold and silver trophies our horses have won at Keeneland and the record-breaking prices of the yearlings we sold in the Keeneland Summer Sales, including a Kentucky Derby winner and a Kentucky Oaks winner.

Leading people such as Wm. T. Young and Alex Campbell are proud to be associated with it and with racing and breeding. Through Keeneland many important people have entered racing or bought central Kentucky breeding farms. Regardless of how famous a livestock breeder becomes, he may have to count the fringe benefits high in order to balance the books. One of the fringe products is manure; the manure you spread on the fields and the manure you spread on your friends. I have manured you with many statements about Lexington. None have been under oath. If anyone questions my veracity, I answer in the spirit of Adolph Rupp: How can I be wrong when I'm so sincere?

*Other Kentucky writer friends: Emily Asbury Wolfe (*Carlisle Mercury*), Warren Shonert (*Falmouth Outlook*), Mike Barry, Byron Crawford, Tandy Ellis (*Courier-Journal*), Wade Hall (Bellarmine College) and Nelson Dawson (Filson Club).

CHAPTER 33

JOSEPH ALVIE ESTES

The editors are pleased to present this tribute, written by a mutually respected and valued friend, Dr. Eslie Asbury of Cincinnati, Ohio. Dr. Asbury, a distinguished physician and surgeon, is a highly successful owner and breeder of thoroughbred horses, a member of the Jockey Club, and, as may be seen, an exceedingly literate author.[1]

Joe Estes was the most influential turf writer possibly of all time. No one has exceeded the integrity and realism he brought to racing and breeding. If I lost everything I ever put in racing and breeding, I would still be ahead because of my close friendship with Estes and others.[2] Memories of these friends are an old man's greatest treasures.

Joe Estes, son of William Estes and Mattie Jones, was born in Mayfield, Kentucky, in 1902, and died in Lexington in 1970. He came to Lexington in 1920, working his way at the University of Kentucky, variously as sports or city editor of the *Lexington Herald-Leader*, receiving an A.B. degree in 1927. He then went to New York, where he studied English at Columbia while serving as turf editor of the *Morning Telegraph* until 1930, when Tom Cromwell brought him back to Lexington to be editor of the *Blood-Horse*.

[1]Originally published in the *Thoroughbred Record* (1/9/71).

[2]Haden Kirkpatrick, the Hancocks, Col. Chinn, Hal Price Headley, Louis Beard, Louis Haggin, Ted Bassett, Olin Gentry, Charlie Asbury, W. T. Bishop, Mack Miller, Babe Wells, George Widener, Paul Mellon, Ivor Balding, Max and Buddy Hirsch, Abe Hewitt and Charlie Hagyard.

I came into the horse business soon after he was made editor of the *Blood-Horse* and one of the first people I met and, fortunately for them, one of the first people many newcomers met, was Joe. My other first advisor was Howard Oots who (along with his nephew, Howard "Babe" Wells) was among the greatest trainers of all time. These men, and all "hardboots," respected Joe, even though he surveyed the equine world from the heights of Olympus, while they, as practical horsemen, were absorbed in their everyday problems. This is not to imply that Joe was an "egghead." He had a more accurate long view of the horsemen's problems than they had. With no personal axes to grind, he forever called on breeders to appraise their stock realistically on the basis of performance, sales companies to print honest catalogues, and track management to card more filly, allowance, and distance races — forgetting immediate expediency.

For 30 years Joe and his charming wife Betsy, who complemented one another perfectly, were often either at my farm near Carlisle, Kentucky, or we were with them in Lexington. He helped me in buying yearlings and mares, and I helped him with some of his medical and surgical problems, of which he had more than his share and all of which he met without flinching. During these years I saw Joe develop and become known throughout the world of racing and breeding. In any country the *Blood-Horse* was always in evidence, and each copy passed avidly through many hands.

But the world of racing and breeding did not know him through his writing alone. Though never of robust health, somehow he found the energy to visit all the important stud farms of the U.S. and foreign countries. Joe felt it was a part of his job to be where the action was and his accounts of scenes, people, horses and classic races were not only the product of a master literary craftsman; they were the epitome of reportorial excellence.

Helper and Adviser Extraordinary

Through Joe we, and many others around Lexington, met the world. Most breeders from distant parts of the U.S. and foreign lands, planning a visit to the Kentucky horse country, made arrangements through Joe or looked him up on arrival. He gave much of his time in entertaining these visitors, and it was flattering and rewarding that through him many came to my own place, Forest Retreat. He also helped them with their problems. Until he became the official adviser to Bunker Hunt in the last two years of his life, he had been, throughout his career, the unpaid adviser to many important people. To him this was also a part of his job.

He guided Rex Ellsworth from the time Rex bought his first five mares in the fall sale at Lexington until years later when Rex took Joe abroad with him to buy bloodstock. The day before they left he brought Rex to Forest Retreat, where we spent ten hours checking the data on all the stallions that might be purchased in the $100,000 or less price range. Joe's first choice was Khaled and I agreed with him. The horse was a superbly bred, first-class two-year-old, and we felt that his wind trouble, whether climatic or genetic in origin, would not hurt his chances as a stallion in this country. The price for Khaled ($156,000) was higher than anticipated, but, with Joe's urging, Rex made the best investment of his life with loans from the Mormon Church.

Joe was involved in many horse transactions either as the adviser or as the go-between, and it would be belaboring the obvious to tell anyone that Joe was honest in all of them. He was honest even with himself and this chronicle for the record (no pun!) would be incomplete without mention of this unique, unworldly honesty. In nearly 40 years of dealing with diverse trainers, jockeys, farm manager and bloodstock agents, I found, almost without exception, that they follow an accepted code of conduct (in getting their "best holt") which if not always 1,000% honest by Diogenes's standard, keeps them practically or at least pragmatically honest. Joe went the final step. His material and intellectual honesty was so pure, to some it was at times painful and exasperating!

Blood-Horse Years

At the age of 30, thirty-eight years ago, when Joe became editor of the Blood-Horse, Tom Cromwell was the owner and publisher. Estes hired, first, Joe Palmer and then Brownie Leach to round out the staff. A few years later when the American Thoroughbred Breeders Association, under the leadership and financial backing of John Hay Whitney, bought the Blood-Horse and made it the official nonprofit organ of the A.T.B.A., Joe continued as editor. Mr. Whitney never lost interest, and with his backing and the help of his associate, Major Louis A. Beard, Estes was able to develop the most respected and statesmanlike turf publication in the world, without fear of or special favor to big advertisers and others in high places. He stood for truth in advertising and avoided publicity handouts but was quick to note real accomplishments of big or little men. If he showed any favoritism, it was to introduce and encourage any newcomer whom he thought to be a high-class addition to breeding and racing.

Joe, the antithesis of the popular picture of the executive type, never ruled his domain with an iron hand, but he had the love and respect of the capable personnel which he gathered around him and was an excellent executive. One of the reasons for his success was that he genuinely liked people, and in spite of the high standards he set for himself, he overlooked peccadillos in others if they had something to offer. He searched the world for special contributors and came up with men who were literary masters with knowledge, penetration, wit and sparkle. Among his favorites were Joe Palmer, George Ryall, Raleigh Burroughs, Mike Barry and Abram S. Hewitt.

Judging Yearlings

For many years, one of the features of the *Blood-Horse* was the inspection of all yearlings entered in the Saratoga Sales and later on, the Keeneland Summer Sale. He kept a private rating on all the yearlings he inspected and compared it with the later performance of each horse. As the years passed, his records, which I saw, proved him to be a fine judge of a yearling's "prospects," on a par with Sherrill Ward and Max Hirsch. His modesty and sense of his position prevented him from taking public credit for this work. In making reports on yearlings and in his editorial and journalistic stances involving all controversies of the thoroughbred world, he let the facts speak for themselves. He was quietly and humbly articulate, and many louder talkers went away with the false impression they had bested him in conversation or debate. If he was weak with the sword, he was an uncompromising tiger with the pen. A truly educated man with a superb command of the English language (and a reading knowledge of eight others), a distinctive style and a light touch, he easily knocked down such old false breeding formulae as the Bruce Lowe Family and Vuillier Dosage Systems, and the theory that old stallions lose their prepotence.

Average Earnings Index

Aided by his wife Betsy, he made a study of the science of statistics and their proper use, and it was in this medium that as a journalist and unprejudiced analyst he made his most important contributions to breeding and racing. If he had elected to study medicine he would have made a great name for himself in research, a field in which his son Worth, true to the genes inherited from both his father and mother, has already distinguished himself. His daughter Phoebe (Mrs. Alden Bryan) also is an intellectual.

His knowledge of genetics and his study of racing and breeding results very early convinced him that superior genes most often accompanied superior performance and that the best place to look for gold is where it previously had been found. From these studies, later made easier by the computer, finally evolved his greatest contribution, the simple, now universally used "Average Earnings Index."[3] He never claimed this index to be a cure-all that could be used blindfolded. To him and to smart breeders, it is an important guide on a rough, curving road along which many hazards must be anticipated. He was not a breeder and, as a journalist, did not want to get into factors that couldn't be handled by statistical studies. He realized that a stallion with few foals and one fine runner or a stallion that produced a lot of sound claimers or a stallion bred only to high-class mares would have a false rating. If pinned down, he would admit that a high-class stakes winning mare or stallion whose parents and grand-parents were undistinguished or unsound, carries a lot of inferior genes, and that a "Blue Hen's" well-formed daughter that, as Tesio said, "bloomed in training," may be a good broodmare prospect whether she runs well or not.

One commercial breeder accused Joe of hurting the yearling sales with his figures, and a less selfish argument by another went as follows: "If the ultimate formula could be found by which a great horse could be bred and trained, two or three of the richest men would own all the best horses. Who would want to dispel the fantasies of breeders and yearlings buyers or to kill the illusions of romance in human mating or to mate people by government decree, as the Nazis and Greeks proposed (Eugenics), even if we knew the result would be a superior race?" Joe's reply was that one of man's oldest and greatest efforts had been to pro-

[3]The Average Earnings Index, designed to compensate for year-to-year fluctuations in purse distribution, is the ratio between the earnings of an individual horse and the average earnings of all horses in a particular racing season. Thus, a horse which earned $2,221 in 1950 (the average per starter that year) is rated 1.00, equal to a horse which earned $3,678 in 1969.

duce the best horse and that no one, however rich and sound in his approach, had ever cornered the market.

Pre-Race Medication

In view of his usual realism, his editorials on prerace medication must have been partly tongue in cheek. In his zeal to expose ignorance, hypocrisy and semantics in the use of the terms "dope," stimulants and analgesics, he went a bit far when he said that medication had more effect on those who sat in judgment[4] than it did on the horses. Actually Joe seldom editorialized on this subject. Forty years ago, the governing bodies of racing began strict enforcement against the use of drugs, and prerace medication became a closed issue. The Butazolidin controversy started after he was no longer active as an editor.

Statistical Bureau and *Thoroughbred Record*

When the computer came along, Joe was the first to promote the use of the new electronic machines. To him this mechanism was the answer to true records of performance, in making up sales catalogs and in getting out stud books. For years he had tried to get the T.R.A., the leading owners and breeders organizations, and the sales companies to unite in backing this project with only limited success until 1963, when the Jockey Club agreed to set up a Statistical Bureau in Lexington with Estes as direc-

---

[4]Training wizardry and pure luck also create false "Average Earnings" figures for certain horses. In the old days, before rules against drugs were enforced, stimulants were another factor. The prerace medication may have stimulated the trainer and jockey more than they did the horse and it is true that nothing can make a horse run faster, yet properly used there are many agents that will insure that certain horses will run the best race of which they are capable and their worst race if medication is omitted. Smart experienced men knew that caffeine or benzadrine would help a sulky "Fair Play," that a shot of alcohol would make a timid filly or colt "run like a man," and that narcotics and more recently analgesics and anti-inflammatory agents such as Butazolidin would enable a bad-legged "Domino" to run at least one one good-legged race, all, of course, to the detriment of the individual horse. The man who was so "sentimental" about his colt that he trained him for his shortened brilliant career on Butazolidin, is like the old acrobat who so loved his acrophobic son that he forced him to train blindfolded on the high wire! I presume the son had a net in which to fall, but neither the horse nor the betting public had any such protection until prerace medication of any kind was prohibited.

tor. Three months earlier the Jockey Club had also purchased a majority interest in the *Thoroughbred Record*, and Joe, after spending 30 years in developing the *Blood-Horse*, became an editor (later Editor Emeritus) of the Record. In spite of worsening health, he continued as consultant to the *Record* and bureau until his death in 1970.

Other Publishing Activities

In addition to his executive duties, his editorials and feature articles, he somehow found time to contribute to foreign publications, to initiate the valuable Thoroughbred Sires and Dams-Thoroughbred Broodmare Records, and after John Hervey and Joe Palmer, wrote the annual volume, *American Race Horses*, for many years.

He played an important role in the organization of the Keeneland Race Course and, as one man wrote, "by molding dreams into words, Joe's prospectus for Keeneland helped raise the money." He was secretary of the first Keeneland board of directors, and after the initial gift was made, organized and supervised the Keeneland Library. Whether he was in New York, California or Europe, he was always on the lookout for more material for this library.

International Figure

His last important act as America's greatest Ambassador of Good Will for racing and breeding was his cooperation in a tour (1968) of the Central Kentucky horse country by the leading French owners, members of the French Jockey Club, dignitaries and trainers, culminating in a delightful dinner at the Idle Hour Club. The expressions of the highest esteem and respect for Joe that night were typical of those that could have been heard any place in the thoroughbred world, including, remarkably enough, his home town, Lexington, Kentucky, where the natives in 1962 conferred on him their greatest mark of distinction. They made him guest of honor at the annual dinner of the Thoroughbred Club of America. It is even more significant that respect for him grew the longer and closer one knew him.

The greatest tribute of all was in a recent letter to me by John Hay Whitney:

"Racing has had many heroes, but very few saints. In my view Joe was just that. His life was devoted to its improvement and his style was so gay that we seldom were aware that he was always raising our standards. The sport—racing and breeding—will miss him for his unique contributions."

So say we all.

CHAPTER 34

RANDOM THOUGHTS OF AN INCOMPETENT MAN

The Literary Club
May 30, 1955

After I read a recent paper, an outspoken member of the club, looking obliquely at me, remarked that all half-assed reactionaries fondly regarded themselves as high-principled conservatives. In this paper I said there was no antiintellectual movement in this country. The outspoken member disagreed. He said there was a fearsome antiintellectual atmosphere.

Others have voiced the same fear. The vociferations of the McCarthys and Peglers have made many writers, teachers and scientists share this belief. The writer flatly states that though a few intellectuals have incurred the ire of the country, there is no antiintellectual movement. In this opinion unprejudiced observers and the general public are in agreement. It is an historic fact that there has always been an anti-intellectual feeling in some quarters, sometimes deserved, sometimes not, and there are always extremists ready to stir up tempests in teapots. If there is no such widespread movement, why all the shouting? Because there is just enough truth in the idea to furnish plausible argument.

During the thirties young, inexperienced intellectuals, with un-concealed glee, foisted controls and bureaucracy on the country. They put over hurried and inept "must" legislation because they had the ear of a popular president. Many of these men, now matured, admit that they then believed in the inevitability of socialism or communism and wanted to be on the bandwagon. Their economic theories were failures except for the war, but the postwar intransigence and inept policies of the Kremlin let down the friends of socialism and communism and gave moderates and conservatives a chance to reorganize. The Cold War elected a Republican Congress in 1946 and the Russian backed Korean War elected a Republican president in 1952. It became unfashionable to sympathize with communism and, to the consternation of intellectuals, a few of their number were proven traitors. Our teachers, writers, etc., scared by the hue and cry of a few crackpots, seemed to think they were all indicted, and even the conservatives among them closed ranks, started group thinking, began to use a defensive vocabulary (McCarthyism), fought the harmless loyalty oath and the right of a university to discharge known working communists. The culmination came recently when a group of visiting lecturers scheduled to make a series of talks at the University of Washington all cancelled their dates when Oppenheimer was dropped from the list.

Our country as well as England has been fortunate in its leaders, most of whom have been broad intellectuals or, at least, not anti-intellectual. In fact, no great man in our history has been anti-intellectual, antireligion, antirace, or antibusiness. Washington, no intellectual himself, had their respect and was able to control the constitutional convention, which included such as Madison, Franklin, Adams and Hamilton. Adams, the brains of the Revolution, was a true conservative who disagreed with both Hamilton and Paine. Jefferson, Wilson, Senator Taft, Calhoun, and the self-educated Lincoln were all intellectuals. They were men of wide experience, mostly the products of broad educational disciplines, who could not have been swayed by group thinking and group vocabularies. They would have risen above our present educational system which, owing to the demands of technology, has tended to make highly efficient, narrow doctors, scientists and teachers at the expense of broad education. The public defies the scientist, wrongly regards him as an intellectual, but realizes that the naive Oppenheimer philosophy may not be as sound as that of a country storekeeper. Our doctors are subjected to the longest period of schooling, yet no one would call us intellectuals. Why then is it antiintellectualism to state the obvious, that as a group professors and scientists are not necessarily intellectuals? Many of our best thinkers and real intellectuals, such as A. Lincoln, had neither formal education nor training. At present, many of our best unlabelled intellectuals, for the first time in history, are in industry. A businessman must be able to read the *Harvard Business Review,* whose complex disquisitions require a broad knowledge of economics, sociology, philosophy and mathematics. We have many kinds of intellectuals, and too many people use the term *intellectual* when they really mean extreme professional liberal.

Unfortunately, our scholars, teachers and scientists are more underpaid proportionately than formerly, probably due to expensive buildings and the overall cost of forcing schooling on everyone whether they can take it or not. But part of the blame can be put at their own door. Instead of blind conformity to academic and political trends, instead of following the professional intellectual liberals, they should stand up for what they know is right in education and again lead the way in broad individualistic thinking and enlightment. Far sillier than an insignificant loyalty oath is that our teachers, etc., are tolerating a system which, in an age of abundance, in an age where the interchange of money is necessary to everyday life, is not providing them a just wage. Because of this system they are resigned to economic mediocrity, to avitaminosis and lack of incentive. Some teachers favor a planned economy and federal control of education, which is a greater threat to academic freedom than a hundred McCarthys and loyalty oaths.

Instead of worrying about such bugbears, our intellectual friends should plump for more individualism and demand greater financial rewards even if, as Sam Goldwyn quipped, they sometimes lose their jobs. Meanwhile, the doctors have done very well by themselves.

CHAPTER 35

IGNORANCE IS BLISS
The Literary Club 1972

The title was lifted from a poem called "On a Distant Prospect of Eton College," written by Thomas Gray in 1742. For purposes of this chapter the second part of the old quotation is irrelevant, if not downright false. The I.Q. of the public is low. Therefore, if ignorance is *not bliss*, how come there are so many "happy" people? The trouble is that this brand of happiness is an adscititious veneer.

The public demands happiness, politicians exude it, commercials are full of grinning people, obituaries carry smiling photographs of the deceased, your banker cultivates a foreclosure smile, and "Happy Days are Here Again" was the theme song of the paretic* speculators who rode the bull market to a crash in 1929.

Cocktail parties are further proof that ignorance is bliss. The hilarious noise they generate is attributed to martinis, but this is only partly true. The basic cause is stupidity. When stupidity is mixed with alcohol, the result is loud, meaningless chatter. Any intelligent person that regularly attends large cocktail parties should be convicted of happiness by association.

The compulsive search for happiness through martini lunches

*Paresis is a syphilitic disease of the brain accompanied by delusions of grandeur.

and after dinner drinks must also come from a defect of intelligence. Adult delinquents of this kind do not do the great work of the world. In defense of alcoholic lunches and certain other unhealthy practices, one man said it is easy for anyone to avoid things he knows will hurt him, that very little courage and willpower are required; that far more character is needed to deliberately follow harmful but pleasant practices. It does take character to commit suicide to provide insurance money for dependents, but slow suicide by excessive drinking has no such noble purpose. In fact, it may impoverish the family. The Victorian melodrama involving the drunken father is no longer enacted in a dirty saloon. It is in the plush cocktail lounges of the affluent society, where the little daughter can't enter to rescue her father. Hard drinkers with independent means who have never been under the pressure of business or a regular job may survive, but hard drinkers who have to work don't live long and half of the time when they are still technically alive they are not in the living world. They are under semianesthesia. The way-out alcoholics have their "anonymous," but the so-called moderate drinkers have no haven. Possibly a society for the promotion of unhappiness would be a solution.

The church of the Puritans was such a society. The Puritans equated unhappiness on earth with deferred happiness in the sky. They were educated and therefore unhappy people. Cotton Mather said he was always thankful for his early ill health which kept him away from the pleasures and temptations of youth. The Puritans even made happiness illegal. They burned deviationists and jailed Sabbath breakers. If all else failed to make sinners unhappy, they would educate "the hell out of them." They believed in education because it made people sad and sad people were good people. For proof they had Ecclesiastes 1:18. "He that increaseth knowledge, increaseth sorrow."[1]

[1] This quotation was taken out of context. The general conclusion conveyed by Ecclesiastes is that all is vanity except the pursuit of wisdom and piety.

We can joke about the Puritans, but they were the greatest of all educational forces in this country. They were the only large group of educated immigrants before the Revolution and, even if things didn't turn out as they planned, the educational systems and great schools they founded are still our best. After "culture conquering" the East, the Puritans moved their influence west with the frontier. The founders of Cincinnati, John Cleves Symmes, Israel Ludlow and John Filson, were Yankee schoolmasters, as were the founders of our public schools, most superintendents of schools, and nearly all the endowers and heads of private and public high schools and colleges. The names of McGuffy, Ray, Guilford*, Slack, Beecher, Sawyer, Ayres*, Taft*, Blackwell*, Craig*, Dyer*, Withrow*, Hughes, Woodward, Knight*, Stephenson*, Bliss*, Sykes*, etc., were typical.

If all were not Puritans, they were nearby Yankee cousins. Most were influential members of the Literary Club, where they stopped alcoholic revelry before the paper and smoking during the reading, but their greatest contribution to the club was opposition to *your* happy ideas. No one ever got truly educated who did not have sincere friends with different philosophies. These uncompromising people were the beloved but firm members who provided this kind of genial, blunt educational force in the club. They didn't hesitate to disagree with you. They would oppose your lousy ideas to your face, but they were genial about it and never boresome. They would have resented being called *nice* men. To our old-time members nice men were castrated[2] men, but this was a narrow view. Today anyone qualifies who doesn't beat his wife or interrupt your stories. To pin the tiresome label "nice guy" on a man is damning him with the faintest praise. The irreverent Durocher was nearer right. He said nice guys finish last. Nice happy guys may sell refrigerators and some achieve adscititious fame, but few become Harvey Cushings, Mark Twains,

*Members of the Literary Club (founded in 1849).
[2]Horses are gelded to make them "nicer" to train!

Geo. Bernard Shaws or Wm. Cooper Procters!

Many great men, like many great horses, were hard to get along with. It took five men to saddle Man o'War, Fair Play or Nasrullah, and get them to the post, but they were champion race horses and by more than coincidence they were our greatest sires. No one ever called them nice horses, a term reserved for moderate winners and happy mediocre people. If is fun but no great accomplishment to breed a nice horse and "nice" prospects for the Literary Club are a dime a dozen. The cult of agreeableness, of keeping everybody happy, promoted by Dale Carnegie and Madison Avenue, now pervades our whole society. It has even invaded academe. The chairman of a new studies department was interviewing a man for a teaching position. Keeping it on the level of exam questions for football players, he asked the prospective teacher whether the world was round or square. The wary applicant, hep to the prevailing academic conformity and realizing his whole future might depend on his answer, finally replied, "I don't know your policy on this; I can teach it either way!!"

But let us not give the wrong impression. Many faculty men are acceptably unhappy, and the happy ignorance of most regularly employed working people does neither them nor the country any harm. After the last Presidential election Democrats said working people need more education, but there is a possibility that the struggle with the common verities of life gives them more wisdom than is often shown by men in higher and happier places.

Admittedly, the smallest group in the population consists of the truly educated, with or without college degrees. They range from Big Charley, our black groom, or a rare country doctor up to a scattering of great men. These rare people, who are blissfully curious if not blissfully happy, prove that wisdom and at least satisfaction with life are not mutually exclusive. In any event, there are too few of them to refute the theme of this paper.

Recently, my theory that ignorance is bliss was bolstered by

Ed Merkel in one of the greatest of all club papers. He said that justice is not compatible with freedom. I think he also meant freedom is not compatible with happiness! He cited the Bible and other authorities who said that the rich man is an unhappy man. The Puritans, the Bible and Thomas Gray have shown, by the same reasoning, that knowledge brings discontent, but the unprejudiced pursuit of it produces the best state of mind of which man is capable.

More money and more knowledge may bring more worry, but in this world wealth and wisdom can sure put you in a helluva bargaining position.

If ignorance is bliss, I should rather be wise than be happy!

The Literary Club 2/26/73

CHAPTER 36

HAPPINESS OR SATISFACTION?

The Literary Club 1973

Animals are smarter than some people. They know they must compete or die. The female animal refuses sex except for procreation. Some people forget they also are animals, subject to the immutable laws of nature. A few years ago a small but conspicuous segment of youth, under the stress of the draft and wars they couldn't understand, adopted a "what's the use," "happy" attitude. Ignoring the wisdom of the centuries, the scriptures and the rules of nature, they said work, marriage, competition and decent dress were for the birds. To them, sex was for pleasure only; bathing and shaving were forgotten. Some academicians, forgetting history, anthropology and the laws of genetics, said youth had changed and that it would be disastrous to refuse the demands of the "new youth." These professors didn't remember that youthful fads have been recurrent throughout history and that a certain type is always looking for a pretext to cop out.

Even the better class of youth was a bit infected. Hard work and willingness to start at the bottom and work up became unfashionable. Harvard Business School graduates thought they had it made, that they should start at the top. They were looking for security, short hours, vacations, and generous retirement plans. They didn't go to be interviewed by a prospective employer; they went to interview the employer. Professional athletes, before they ever played a game, demanded 5-year, no-cut contracts; and rich men, who themselves had come up the work way and were looking for prestige through the ownership of popular sports franchises, were silly enough to accede to ruinous demands. George Steinbrenner forgot the experience of Tom Yawkey. Other rich notoriety seekers and social climbers humored themselves by paying unrealistic prices for yearling colts, thinking they could instantly buy their way to the top of the world of breeding and racing.

Some people in all generations have been guilty of such foibles, but I think my generation had fewer illusions. We admired the corny Horatio Alger hero who did not cry over rebuffs, discriminations and disasters but achieved success gradually by hard work and honorable behavior. Dr. W. J. Mayo built the Mayo Clinic, the Mecca of the surgical world, on a Minnesota prairie. His idea of a vacation was to visit an eminent surgeon or spend a week on his river boat, writing papers. Senator Robert Taft, Sr. never joined a social club. On his way to lunch, he arranged to think out a pressing problem. If he passed his own brother he was apt not to see him. Einstein, totally engrossed with mathematics, knew nothing about the world, nor did Henry Ford. Ford became the leading auto maker and Einstein a great scientist, but both were naive about public affairs.

A famous *New Yorker* cartoon depicted a paunchy businessman, clad in a bathing suit, sitting at a table under an umbrella, on the beach of a luxurious resort. On his right was a telephone and on his left a secretary with pencil poised, taking dictation. A friend passing by said, "John, don't you ever relax and enjoy yourself?" "No," was the reply. "If I relaxed, I wouldn't enjoy myself. If I relaxed, I couldn't afford to be here."

Clark Griffith, original owner of the Washington Senators baseball team, speaking of a great player, said, "In his early years he couldn't hit, he couldn't throw and he couldn't field, but he would find a way to beat you. By constant effort he finally became a super star."

A certain lawyer had a different approach. One of his law teachers, when asked about him, said, "He was a lazy student, but he wanted *badly* to be a lawyer."

"Did he succeed?"

"Yes, in his own way," replied the teacher. "He became a *bad* lawyer."

Another man, hearing someone speak fluent French, said, "I'd give $50.00 if I could speak like that."

The lawyer and the would-be linguist had the same trouble I had when I asked an agent to bid up to a limit sum on a mare. "I didn't get her," he said. "You didn't give me a long enough pole." The lawyer, the linguist and I, unlike Canova and Voltaire, did not use our longest pole. Canova lived in his studio and Voltaire lived in his study.

The achievement of greatness in anything, especially art and writing, is a full-time, full-time job. The muse consumes a man's life and makes it a lonely one. Great artists cannot be men about town. They can't socialize. To the world they are morose, self-centered, bad-mannered people. Distracting social life, mistresses and alcohol, have ruined many potential geniuses. One with talent who takes time to be charming may receive great applause for the moment but will not achieve immortality. Happy artists remain semiartists. The Declaration of Independence says everyone is entitled to the pursuit of happiness. For artists or writers this is wrong. An artist can pursue only *perfection*. People confuse happiness with satisfaction. The road to satisfaction in any field is the pursuit of perfection, which, in the end, may bring honor and riches, provided honor and riches are not the main goal. I am not saying that supreme success and fame are to be envied. Moderate success combined with avid avocations suits more people. I do say that, however many activities one undertakes serially or in tandem, he must give each one his best to realize any satisfaction from them, whether it is a vocation or avocation.

There are exceptional geniuses who broke the rules (drinkers, drug users, etc.) and still became immortal; and there are "Renaissance" men, Michelangelos, who successfully pursued and attained perfection in more than one field. Churchill was a great statesman, an artist, and a superb speaker who laboriously polished each word and intonation. His daughter in her biography said Churchill could not make an impromptu speech. He had to perfect each phrase beforehand. Anthony Trollope, the great novelist, subjected himself to a rigorous daily routine. Mark Twain's career suffered when he sidetracked himself into business ventures. Even the greatest humor is not spontaneous. It must be laboriously created.

The life of a genius is not the "summum bonum" of human existence. Geniuses have weaknesses. They are poor family men, unhappy men, and poor citizens. Most great authors, artists, and research scientists (Spock, Oppenheimer, Einstein, etc.) are naive. Outside their all-consuming fields, they are ignorant, inexperienced and uneducated. They are like academicians who know nothing of business and businessmen who have no intellectual curiosity. Neither Henry Ford nor Oppenheimer should be entrusted with worldly affairs.

Only a fool would elect to be a genius. He may make a great contribution; but, like a salmon, he spawns and dies, usually without savoring personal glory or a full life. Sensible people do best for the world and do best for themselves when they seek the highest proficiency as surgeons, farmers and writers and also engage in avocations that interest them. Broad education and experience makes them better everyday doctors, farmers, writers and voters.

They may not achieve immortal fame nor "happiness"; but they do achieve serenity, satisfactions, and the applause of their fellow men, the most sought, elusive objective of all.

CHAPTER 37

RESORTS AND RETIREMENT

Resorts are important in the lives of many people. I am no exception. This chapter is a commentary on my connections with vacation centers and areas where people go because of the climate. Cleveland Amory wrote a book about the fashionable resorts in New York, New England, and South Carolina as he saw them before World War I. In Amory's era the new rich went to resorts to mingle with the old rich, hoping to improve their social positions. Lavish parties were the main activity. Many people built magnificent houses at Newport and Aiken which they used only for short seasons. A few very rich people built winter homes in Palm Beach. In that era 80% of people remained at home both before and after retirement.

Until long after World War I most active business and professional people opted for summer rather than winter vacations. They sent their families to summer homes and hotels in Michigan, Canada and New England, where they joined them, off and on, during the hot months. After air conditioning became universal, most active, prosperous people with grown children have chosen to go south in the winter for their main vacations. Many summer resorts have suffered, though some, such as Lake Placid, make up for their loss of summer patronage by featuring winter sports.

More and more surgical meetings and conventions in general are now held in winter in southern centers. Golf and tennis resorts have sprung up wherever the weather is warm all year. Racial trouble in the islands has diverted much winter traffic back to Florida.

Retirement living is now the big story. An increasing percentage of the population is composed of retirees. In this era of prosperity people, especially doctors, are retiring at an earlier age. I worked 7 days a week for 40 years. At the age of 91 I can look back on 15 years of semiretirement and 10 years of retirement. Today, if I were 60 years old, I could not enjoy semiretirement. I would earn little more than the cost of modern malpractice insurance. That is why so many doctors now completely retire at a younger age. This is a general trend, though businessmen remain semiactive. Privileged people have pensions and savings. Working people have savings and Social Security. All classes are flooding into California, the Southwest, Florida and even the midsouth, where everyone can find housing to suit the pocketbook. People of lesser means use mobile (mostly immobile) home parks. Prosperous people have houses or luxurious condominiums. Those who can afford it retain their northern homes for summer living.

Thanks to modern surgery, antibiotics, a better diet and more exercise, retirees, both young and old, are healthier. Most adjust to the new life, some do not. I have observed that those who remain healthy and satisfied have good habits. They eat plenty of protein, salads and fruits, and, if necessary, take a teaspoon of metamucil a day to regulate a sluggish alimentary tract. They limit their liquor to 3 ounces a day. This amount of alcohol is beneficial to old people. It dissolves cholesterol. Sir William Osler said wine is the milk of the aged.

Whether a retiree remains at home or moves to a retirement center, he must have an objective in order to remain healthy. He needs a challenge. He needs fear and worry to activate the adrenalin glands which stimulate body functions. Starting with Adam, the Bible decreed that man must live by the sweat of his brow. This would be physiologically true without a biblical injunction. Some people can get their sweat from civic activities but it is not enough to contribute money. One must personally participate. Educated people can get their sweat from part-time teaching. Universities now realize they need the knowledge of educated people of the world to balance the naive liberalism of the regular faculty.

Some retirees go into a new venture. If money is important, the venture should be in a familiar field. Some wealthy old people struggle over their investments, forgetting that, however rich a man is, he can live only in one room at a time and eat three meals a day like everyone else. Those who can afford it do not have to live by bread and bonds alone. They can invest in projects which will give them great satisfaction, regardless of financial gains or losses.

An ordinary farm is a poor investment either for income or satisfaction. A gentleman farmer must have an objective, whether the object is to raise a better tomato, breed a better horse, or plant more trees. Racing suits many sports-minded old people. They can buy a yearling or two a year or go into partnerships. Waiting for young horses to develop slows time for them, just as waiting for Christmas slows time for youngsters. Time passes too fast for most old people.

People with previous experience can get their sweat from writing or making talks. Aside from golf, a dessert, and my farm, a main course, my chief activity has been writing 5 books and making about 200 talks to garden clubs, Rotary clubs, and various organizations, along with writing papers for the Literary Club. The profits of my books go to colleges. I write for pleasure and satisfaction. For retirees with literary experience, writing is a form of competition. It provides an objective, It fills idle time. Writing prevents boredom, the worst hazard of old age. That is why I write books.

During the past 25 years I have used many resorts. For several summers we went to the Lake Placid Club, a delightful waspy organization with all the amenities, including golf, horseback riding, and the Rochester Philharmonic Orchestra, subsidized by a foundation. The Nipperts, Dieterles and Daniels of Cincinnati have, for generations, been a part of the club, which has suffered by the change in vacation habits.

For 50 years I have spent a few days each year at Saratoga Springs, New York, where the leading people in racing gather during August for racing and the yearling sales. Before World War II, until the advent of the Keeneland sales, we sold yearlings at Saratoga. In 1942, when the bombs were dropping in London, we topped the sales, selling six (5 fillies and one colt) for an average of $1200.00. Tom Pratt averaged $200.00, not enough to cover the cost of shipping. Since 1943 we have sold our best yearlings at the Keeneland Summer Sales, receiving the highest average price in four different years.

However, I continued to go to Saratoga, never missing the annual Jockey Club dinner in forty years, staying at first in the ancient United States Hotel and later at the Reading Room, New England's peculiar version of a male club, situated adjacent to the race track, where eight members can sleep but also where the ladies can come for lunch and cocktails. In recent years my son, Dr. Taylor Asbury, has taken a house, temporarily vacated by the owner, providing accommodations for the family and friends.

For the past 15 years we have owned a summer home at Biddeford Pool in Maine, where the ocean is so cold (57 degrees) I never go swimming. The land area, a semipeninsula, limits the number of houses around a 9 hole golf course. I bought the last available lot. For the past 100 years Cincinnati families (Tafts, Benedicts, Kittredges, Duprees, Wilbys, Espys, Blakes, Andersons, and Blacks) have owned summer homes here. These people could afford lavishness but have opted for ostentatious simplicity in their summer way of life which I admire. This resort has not suffered.

In our semiretirement years during the winters we spent time at hotels in Hobe Sound, Delray Beach, Ft. Lauderdale and Miami Beach, all within easy reach of winter racing at Hialeah. At that time the traffic on the East Coast was bearable. For three winters we went to the Gasparella Inn at Boca Grande, owned and operated by Bayard Sharpe (a Dupont) with the best food and the best golf course we have ever used in the winter.

In 1965, on recommendation of my great friend Dr. Charles Haggard, we started to spend our winters in Scottsdale, Arizona, at first at the Camelback Inn, then in a condominium at the Scottsdale House. We had golf at the Mesa Country Club (basically Mormon); the air was dry, the days were warm and the nights were cool, good desert climate. Barry Goldwater, whom I had met in Cincinnati during his presidential campaign, introduced me to the Phoenix Club, where I had good bridge games, once playing with Bob Goldwater for 10 cents a point. Fortunately I came out a bit ahead. I didn't know how much we were playing for. After 5 years I sold our condominium. We were sensitive to the increasing smog, caused by 2 million trucks, autos, airplanes, and dust from irrigation farming.

For the past 10 years we have owned a condominium for winter use in Naples, Florida. Thanks to Addison Brown, Ned Putzell, Hamp Schroeder and the voter's league, this is the best regulated community in Florida. I write in the mornings and then enjoy golf at the Hole-in-the-Wall Club or have lunch, bridge, and persiflage at the Naples Athletic Club with Charles Duaray, Elster Copeland, Bob Benson, Jim Abernathy, Mark Arano, Truman Bidwell, John Cox, Eddie Anderson, Merton Durant, Norman Herren, Ed Elliott, Bill Keller, Fran Miller, Len Osterink, Don Lintz, Tex Colbert, Judge Smith, Steve Hartshorn, Al Wigglesworth, Cliff Harris, Bo Depuy, Ralph Guenther, and others previously mentioned.

Lunch is a great event for retirees. In Naples I often have lunch with the High Noon (Masonic) Club, where I enjoy the company of Dr. Sheldon Rogers, Jim Lusk, Cedric Vogel, and John Knox. As an "honorary" member, I lunch with the Maryland Club, where I see Hugh Rienhoff, Frank Mead, and John Leutekemier.

Families, prosperous for generations, usually own places at resorts where they go each season. Some people with a lot of money, earned or inherited, have little prestige or social recognition at home. They go abroad, where they become automatic big shots. They love the deference shown them by hotel managers and headwaiters.

As I get older I get less mobile. I hate the bother of travel. When you travel, you disturb your daily routine and you suffer from fatigue. To remain healthy old people must stay on a routine and avoid exposure to strange viruses to which they are not immune and which they are sure to encounter if they travel. The last three times I went abroad I returned with severe colds. Most people were forced to travel in their active years. To them, travel, without an objective, is a bore. Worst of all, long periods of travel interfere with the "work" of a serious retiree.

CHAPTER 38

THE CHALLENGE OF RETIREMENT

September 29, 1952

It has long been known that it is not necessary for a doctor to retire. All he needs to do is talk about quitting and his patients will retire him. Such talk starts the train of thought that the old Doc is getting old, that he is probably sick, and why not go to the young man who, it is proclaimed at afternoon bridge tables, has done such marvelous things with all the new methods. The author asks that this discussion not be held against him because he has no idea of voluntarily retiring.

In spite of the personal risk, I feel the Doctor should speak about the nonmaterialistic aspects of retirement whose significance seems underrated. A much greater percentage of our people are today facing the task of what to do with themselves after quitting their regular life's work. The working man has social security, the executive has his pension, and others have annuities, in addition to which most have savings and other resources in the world's richest and yet immature country. Teachers, government personnel, institutional and industrial executives, and working people are forced out at sixty-five or seventy; and many self-employed professional and businessmen with means, tiring of the modern battle, are prematurely retiring. Most of these people are healthy, robust, and far younger both physically and in their outlook than anyone of their years in the past. The average age expectancy is not only far greater but increasing, and the retirement age group is one of the main fctors in causing this increase, because most coronary cases have been expended before the age of sixty-five. Longevity has been promoted in the present generation by better nutrition, modern surgery, and protection from fatal and scarring infections through preventive medicine and antibiotics.

How shall we best use this lengthened span? How can we make retirement practical and satisfying? There is very little help in the literature, which seems to consist chiefly of statistical handouts from Washington bureaus and papers on the physical problems of the aged. My remarks shall apply only to serious people of either large or small means, who have made their mark in the world, leaving out writers, teachers, research people, etc., who, accustomed to living in a dream world, are odds on to make a success of retirement. Simple people, who have had little time for recreation, may be satisfied with loafing, fishing, and gardening. Such activity will not fill the needs of an energetic person of previous attainment nor will subsistence farming, which provides only food and exercise. If farming is to be the new effort (more and more people are looking in this direction for escape), fine livestock, improved plants and conservation should be the goals. To the retired and leisure classes of England during the past two hundred years we are indebted for nearly all the purebred livestock of the world. Incidentally, My Lord, because he took a personal interest in his animals and his people, because he was present at their funerals, parties, and community welfare meetings, still retains their respect after a social revolution. America is in a wonderful position to take over livestock development, but our new-rich city farmer will find that it is not enough to pay high wages and give to the local church and community fund. He must be there himself and participate in person. For older people who will accept the responsibilities, farming is satisfactory. No man with a fine mare in foal has ever been known to commit suicide, for he is confident she is carrying a Derby winner. The long wait for the foal and the longer wait for its development slows time in old age as effectively as the year-long anticipation of Christmas for old-fashioned children.

Lack of such a time-slowing factor is probably one of the reasons so many seemingly healthy men "go to pieces" on retirement, but, without having consulted a single geriatrician, the author concludes that accelerated degeneration in retired people is also caused by two other things: (1) lack of emotional stimuli, such as fear, on internal secretory glands, and (2) changing a lifelong physical routine to an irregular life. The single most essential emotion is fear, which will enable a man to jump a six-foot fence or study to pass an examination. Fear activates the adrenals and other glands of internal secretion which tone up body functions. If we haven't fear of hunger, we must have fear of either losing money or losing face to remain healthy.

Most of us, in our regular life's work, develop a physical routine. We eat, sleep, work, exercise, and have bowel movements at certain times. This makes it easy on the autonomic nervous system, makes for good health, and frees us to accomplish things. Whatever we do in retirement, we should keep on this old physical routine, though not on the same mental or work routine, since another cause of the complaint that time goes faster as we get older is due to fully routinizing our lives. A familiar road is short and a strange drive is long.

Properly pursued, retirement is not only an impetus to new achievement to the old, but youth is thus assured of its proper place. Therefore it is fitting that there be a set age at which the boss should clear out to allow normal succession. Professor MacEwen held the chair of surgery of Glasgow until he died at the age of ninety-four, damming back promotions for thirty years. Now all schools and many institutions have a mandatory retirement age because most people resent or fear retirement. Their instinct is correct since there is often a stigma attached to retired people. No longer in the thick of events, they have too much aimless time on their hands, they visit too often and too long, they live in the past and become bores both to themselves and their friends.

Then how can one retire and still keep health, zest for life, and friends? The answer is that when a man retires he must go to work. He must have one activity with the satisfying challenge of important achievement. Above all, aimlessness must be avoided. He must have planned a new serious career and practiced it enough to be sure of its deep interest for him. One must not be deluded that retirement is simple, that it consists merely in having income to quit work and enjoy life by such boresome pursuits as travel and golf. These things may have their place, but dessert must not be confused with the main course. When Seneca epitomized the whole thing in the sentence "First acquire a competence, then practice virtue," he was not expressing a witty cynicism. I think he meant that youth is the time of strife, of accomplishment, often associated with hard, rough behavior, and overworking gonads.

When this period has passed, when, as Plato put it, we are freed of that tyrannical monster (sex urge), we are in a position to enjoy life and help the community with our accumulated riches and wisdom. All smart men know that age sometimes brings wisdom but always the scars of experience which contract activity. Since youth is the time for controversy and battle, wisdom should, with brilliant exceptions, not try to lead the way, but should be content to point out the pitfalls along the way. To carry out the idea, Plato wanted councils of elders in his Republic.

President Hoover with his Boys' Clubs, university activities, and nonpartisan statesmanship is an example of successful retirement. Dr. Russell Wilder, retired head of internal medicine at the Mayo Clinic, worked for the government on problems of nutrition. Dr. Henry Helmholz, eminent pediatrician, was concerned with national child welfare programs. Bill Young is a leader in the civic affairs of Lexington, Ky. Happy Chandler is an elder statesman.

These men are hard at work. They are still in the thick of things and have set themselves a new dead line. Their glands are working sufficiently for good health but not hard enough to cause the acquisition of new or young wives. Actually, this disaster of age often results from mistaking prostatitis for real gonadal activity. This is not meant to decry normal sexual activity in older people; and actually the sex adjustment with a new wife is much easier than the radical change in personal routine and the annoyances incident to the constant politeness and studied consideration which, not demanded by the original, now must be lavished on the new partner. At best, the situation is rarely satisfactory, while, at worst, the new wife deliberately turns shrew and forces a payoff. A quiet, respectful, easily satisfied and mildly affectionate housekeeper would seem the best answer for the retired widower.

Concluding, I should say that those fortunate enough to acquire sense (and dollars) with age, become more and more concerned about the approval of the community and about the untaxable legacy of goodwill they can leave their families. They mellow and desire to placate their enemies and overcome their prejudices. But good works are not enough, for one's second career should be real work. After all, in the first race of all time, Adam set the pace.